RELUCTANT FEMINISTS
IN GERMAN SOCIAL DEMOCRACY

JEAN H. QUATAERT

RELUCTANT FEMINISTS
In German Social Democracy,
1885-1917

PRINCETON UNIVERSITY PRESS
PRINCETON, NEW JERSEY

Published by Princeton University Press, Princeton, New Jersey
In the United Kingdom: Princeton University Press,
Guildford, Surrey

Library of Congress Cataloging in Publication Data will be
found on the last printed page of this book

Publication of this book has been aided by a grant from
The Andrew W. Mellon Foundation

Clothbound editions of Princeton University Press books
are printed on acid-free paper, and binding materials are
chosen for strength and durability

Printed in the United States of America by Princeton
University Press, Princeton, New Jersey

Designed by Laury A. Egan

Womanbooks/18.50/ 1/22/80

TO MY PARENTS
LEO AND ANNE MARIE GREBLER

CONTENTS

LIST OF ILLUSTRATIONS

All illustrations are from the Archiv der sozialen Demokratie
(Friedrich-Ebert-Stiftung), Bonn.

LIST OF TABLES

PREFACE

The origin of this book closely parallels its subject. When I prepared my master's thesis on the so-called German Revolution of 1918-1919, I was mainly interested in the socio-economic antecedents of the episode and the role of Social Democracy in its outcome. In reviewing the literature, however, I was struck by the discovery that women's participation in the German socialist movement was treated lightly, if not cloaked in silence. Yet, when I thumbed through handbooks of parliamentarians in the early Weimar Republic, I noticed that nineteen female members of the German Social Democratic Party (SPD) and several Independent Social Democratic women (USPD) had been elected to the Reichstag in January 1919. These women obviously had been active in prewar Germany, and if not household names, they must have had public exposure. But in what capacity? My research interests at this point began to include feminism. I decided to study women involved in the socialist movement in Imperial Germany and wrote my dissertation on the topic.

While I was writing, the contemporary debates among and about feminists and the intensified research on the history of the female sex reinforced my diagnosis of German socialist women who were active in feminist causes as afflicted by an identity crisis. These socialists were reluctant feminists, facing persistent tensions between their loyalty to class and to sex. They were both feminists and socialists, but in their schema the cause of women bowed before the struggle for socialism when tough choices were required. True, female leaders advanced women's special interests in both Party and unions and managed even to maintain a degree of organizational autonomy in the Party while decrying separatism. Yet they were uneasy about privileges and accepted compromise when Party discipline required it. Paradoxically, these reluctant feminists also were often radical feminists who propounded a vision of a new life that promised women dignity and self-fulfillment in a radically transformed society. The apparent paradox of reluctant, yet radical feminism, forms a central theme of this book.

The work focuses on women associated with the Social Democratic women's movement from the 1880s to 1917. The period begins with the first coordinated organizing efforts by women and ends with the disintegration of German socialism just before the revolution. Under the anti-Socialist laws (1878-1890) working-class women began an alliance with the underground labor groups and founded unions and self-help organizations. Their capacity to offer a genuine alternative to bourgeois feminism was growing rapidly. After 1890, women openly joined the socialist movement and worked out their relationship to it on both the theoretical and political levels. In the decade before World War I increasing numbers of working-class women were attracted to the Party of the proletariat and to the unions. After German Social Democracy was torn apart, a group of new leaders inherited the women's movement, reformulated the prewar socialist analysis of the women's question, and redefined the roles of females in the Party and in public life. In 1918, when women achieved formal political equality in the Weimar Republic, their role in Social Democracy was altered radically.

In its various stages, this project has benefited from the support and interest of numerous persons in the United States and Europe. I am pleased to be able to offer my gratitude. Many thanks especially to Peter Loewenberg for encouraging and guiding me through the dissertation stage and for continued interest and aid in my work. Early on, Temma Kaplan supplied a much-needed feminist perspective, and Laura Oren has offered valuable comments, comparisons, criticisms, and materials throughout the period of revisions. Vernon Lidtke's careful reading of the whole manuscript—and twice at that—has proven invaluable. I profited, too, from my contact with Dr. Ernest Hamburger. He brought me in touch with Dr. John Caspari, friend of Marie Juchacz, who kindly related his experiences in the *Arbeiterwohlfahrt*. Similarly,

Professor Walter Friedlander spent considerable time and effort providing me with materials, information, and reminiscences, as well as the introductions to Drs. Karl Kautsky, Jr., and Carl Landauer, who offered personal perspectives on many of the figures in this book. My research was expedited by special courtesies extended by Götz Langkau in the Central European Department of the International Institute for Social History, Dr. Kuno Bludau, head of the archives at the Friedrich Ebert Stiftung, Dr. Luntowski, director of the Dortmund archives, as well as the cooperation I found in the archives of the German Federal Republic, the German Democratic Republic, and American libraries. For the financial support that made additional archival research possible beyond the Ph.D., I gratefully acknowledge the German Academic Exchange Service Study Visit grant for the summer 1975. I wish to thank Martha Ann Fitzpatrick for reading critically several chapters from a professional standpoint; lay perspectives were provided by Sharilyn Wood and Martha Dyckes. The professional, courteous, and expeditious manner with which the manuscript was handled is a tribute to the Press. My family deserves much credit as critics, willing listeners, and providers of the "supportive milieu" needed for the whole undertaking. There is no reluctance in offering my thanks to Donald, whose patience was, at times, tried but sure.

ABBREVIATIONS

BA   Bundesarchiv, Koblenz
FES   Friedrich Ebert Stiftung, Bonn-Bad Godesberg.
         Materials on German Social Democracy
HStAS   Hauptstaatsarchiv Stuttgart
HHStA   Hessische Hauptstaatsarchiv, Wiesbaden
IISH   International Institute for Social History,
         Amsterdam. Archive of the Second International,
         including the Archive of the German Social
         Democratic Party
Pr . . . Protocol of meetings, indicating place, date, and
         organization (Party, women's movement, union, or
         International)
StAH   Staatsarchiv Hamburg
StAL   Staatsarchiv Ludwigsburg
StAM   Staatsarchiv Münster
StAP   Staatsarchiv Potsdam
StAD   Stadtarchiv Dortmund
StAN   Stadtarchiv Nuremberg
ZStA   Zentrales Staatsarchiv, Potsdam. The following
         collections:
   RK   Reichskanzlei (Imperial Chancellery)
   RMdI   Reichsministerium des Innern
            (Imperial Ministry of Interior)
   RT   Reichstag (Parliament)

PART A
INTRODUCTION

CHAPTER I

FEMINIST AWAKENING

By the early twentieth century, friend and foe alike had come to recognize the success of German socialist women in creating a model women's movement in Social Democracy. Even the German police admitted their prominence in the socialist International, although in this case, without the pride in German excellence so common to the competitive era of *Weltpolitik*.[1] The assessment was quite accurate in light of decisions at the International conference in 1907 to designate Germany as the seat of the women's International and to declare the German paper *Gleichheit* (Equality) as the international organ. Efforts of other European socialist feminists paled by comparison. Despite the traditional sympathy of French socialism for women's emancipation, females comprised at best 3 percent of the members in the French Socialist Party prior to World War I. In 1914, 16.1 percent of the total membership of the German Social Democratic Party (*Sozialdemokratische Partei Deutschlands*, SPD) was female, numbering roughly 175,000, while the Free Trade Unions associated with the SPD recorded 223,000 women or 8.8 percent of the total.[2]

The German socialist women's movement was both socialist and feminist. German delegates affirmed this duality during the spirited debates at the 1907 International conference. As socialists in the Central European context, they decisively rejected collaboration with bourgeois feminism as well as suffrage tied to property qualifications, parting company with their English sisters. Yet, they threw up their feminist hackles at the decision of Austrian and Belgian socialists to forgo the demand for women's suffrage in the general compaign for democratization. The arguments advanced by the German representatives were adopted officially by the women's International.[3] The reputation and success of the German socialist women's movement in European left-wing circles rested on two elements: its close association with the German labor movement—the German Social Democratic Party was the pride and envy of the Second International—and its measured use of feminism in pursuing the proletarian liberation struggle.

THE HISTORIC CONNECTION OF CLASS
AND SEX IN GERMANY

Socialism had come to Germany at a time of intense economic and social change. The country was experiencing continuous industrial advance and the whole Imperial period was a time of transition to an industrial world at once challenging and strange. As late as 1914, many factory workers were newcomers to the job, still first or second generation, and they maintained close ties to the countryside. Some resided in outlying districts, preferring to commute to the inner cities for work, and cases of factory workers engaging in seasonal rural labor were not atypical.[4] Yet, an industrial labor class clearly had emerged in Imperial Germany; workers were adapting to the new wage-earning status, to the factory whistle as well as other manifestations of the disciplined life in cities. For many, socialism served as the ideal psychological and social support during a period of rapid industrial expansion. The strong and deep hold of socialism on a broad cross section of the German working class can be seen as a response to change as well as an effort to control and give meaning to the new character of life in industrial society.

The appeal of socialism was strengthened by the subordinated position of the working class. Under the Empire, workers were excluded from political decision making, denied social respect, and exploited in the labor market. Their efforts to promote their interests were viewed with great suspicion by the ruling groups—the courts, the landowning aristocracy, and the industrial bourgeoisie. Except for the twelve years of the anti-Socialist laws, the labor movement was legal, but its influence was quite restricted. Workers' unions were denied the legal right of collective bargaining until the Revolution of 1918, and the Social Democratic Party, which spoke for the workers, sat in a national parliament shorn of power and responsibility. Imperial Germany was an authoritarian political regime that sought to modernize the socioeconomic structure without political change—to stem the democratic tide by denying the lower classes entry into the system. Its character was shaped in part by the failure of the German liberal Revolution of 1848 and by the choice of national unity over parliamentary government made by large numbers of middle-class liberals in the 1860s and 1870s. As for organized workers in Imperial Germany, the combination of legality coupled with political and social ostracism[5] engendered two responses. Working-class leaders became preoccupied with the maintenance of legality to the point of resisting the revolutionary drive. Also, its isolation turned the labor movement inward; socialism became a subculture that greatly enhanced its attraction to workers. It offered psychic and material protection and compensation for the hardships of life, and it sought to instill new values through socialist newspapers, books, theaters, libraries, and educational courses.

Within the socialist subculture, the women's movement was a symbol of change and a challenge to traditional relationships between the sexes.[6] It gave graphic testimony to the fact that socialism was an alternative image of life, values, and human relations, not just a political movement. The subculture proffered a supportive milieu to women concerned with improving their lot as part of the proletarian struggle for human liberation.

Socialism had long-standing ties with causes for women's rights. Its commitment to sex equality went back to Fourier and Saint-Simon, the so-called French Utopian Socialists. These early reformers joined the fate of women and workers together. They observed that both were excluded from power and influence in the nineteenth-century liberal nation-state, and included the idea of women's emancipation in their schemes to restructure society and revamp social customs.

Several decades later in *The Communist Manifesto*, Marx and Engels linked women and workers as "instruments of labor," exploited by modern industry. Moreover, Engels would argue that only socialism offered both groups true liberation by abolishing private property, the root cause of social and sex inequality.

The acceptance of Marxism in the German working classes involved a series of stages in which the complex and dynamic ideas were converted into simplistic, popular notions. The tenor of the times insured stress on economic determinism—a belief in inevitable laws of development leading inexorably to socialism. In the 1870s and 1880s educated workers in Germany were enthralled with the fashionable natural sciences. A whole generation of Marxists came to historical materialism by way of Darwin and evolution.[7] With his *Anti-Dühring* in the mid-1870s, Engels won over future leaders of the German socialist movement such as August Bebel, Karl Kautsky, and Eduard Bernstein, convincing them of the superiority of the Marxist world view; the tract held out a "cast iron system of laws," which guaranteed the triumph of socialism.[8] Thus, in Germany socialism was a synthesis of simplified Marxist ideas and notions drawn from Darwinian evolution. If, as historians have indicated, the combination was deadly for the development of revolutionary tactics because the emphasis on determinism left the role of the working masses in the revolutionary struggle in question,[9] it furthered the socialist commitment to the women's cause. In 1873, for example, the socialist organ, *Der Volksstaat*, published an article claiming that Darwin stood for "the strictest equality between human beings," an ironic twist on the prevalent interpretation that justified social inequalities by appealing to the Darwinian idea of survival of the fittest.[10] More important, natural science lent its considerable prestige to the idea that woman, as any living creature, was a product of conditioning. Remove the artificial or harmful barriers to the blossoming of the species and it would evolve to the fullest capacity.

In the latter part of the nineteenth century, the socialist theme of improving the lot of the female sex was striking receptive chords in some women's minds. Works such as August Bebel's feminist tract *Women under Socialism* (1879) found a large audience. Several prominent members of the German socialist women's movement have reminisced about the book's impact. Their reflections give vivid testimony to the ways in which ideas can order inchoate feelings and restructure lives. Mathilde Wurm described the work's reception among middle-class women in the 1890s. She depicted vaguely dissatisfied wives, tired of waiting for the arrival of husbands to save them from "deadening boredom." They wanted more, but did not know where to turn, and their families greeted their desire to become educated or to work with mockery and ridicule. "If, by accident [Wurm wrote], one of these timorous creatures read Bebel's book, it was an eye-opener. She was not alone with her thoughts and feelings. Thousands felt as she did. . . . [She] recognized the rights of her personality and gathered . . . courage to follow her conscience."[11] Wurm added, to be sure, that only few bourgeois women went all the way to socialism on a "steep and long" path.

Wilhelmine Kähler, of working-class origin, also noted the liberating effect of realizing that her feelings of dissatisfaction were not unique. Yet she stressed how important it was for her to have acquired the tools to understand the origins of women's oppression as well as the influence of double morality and different standards on the lives of females. The assurance of liberation in the future socialist society was inspirational. She wrote, "Bebel's book encouraged me to awaken women by clarifying fully the whole process of enlightenment; it forged the most unshakable belief that tomorrow's dawn would also bring women deliverance." For those who took the path to socialism, Bebel's work often served as the springboard to other socialist literature.[12]

Ideas and material conditions stand in a subtle relationship. Ideas must relate to people's actual experience in order to have widespread impact. In the nineteenth century changes in the lives of working-class and middle-class women had been sufficiently drastic to cause many to adopt explicit formulations of present misery and to develop visions of future change. Industrialization played a key role in the process of transforming consciousness. It not only altered material life but furthered crucial albeit elusive ideas of "modernism" and "progress."

Industrial growth divorced two institutions regarded for centuries as inseparable—the family and the workshop—and profoundly transformed women's familial and economic roles. In the preindustrial world women had been an important if barely visible productive force. They spun, wove, supervised hired hands, assisted in business ventures, often for no remuneration, and performed their wifely and motherly tasks as well. The domestic industry system, centered on the home, had reconciled the need for female workers with the woman's biological function of childbearing and social role of childrearing. However, in the initial phases of industrial development, separation of the home and workshop introduced drastic changes. Generally, men left the home to seek employment outside and women assumed the main responsibility for domestic administration. A new norm of domestic life solidified when the home changed from a production to a consumption unit. The woman was idealized as a person who attended to maternal duties around the house and to her appearance. While economic necessity forced lower-class girls into factories, urban domestic service, and later the bureaus and offices, the married woman became an exception in the labor force.[13] The phenomenon of woman's work was hardly new, but in the nineteenth century the conditions of labor were being transformed and society was becoming conscious of increasing numbers of females entering the labor force as wage earners.

The functional and social changes associated with industrial society were reflected in new states of mind.[14] The process was slow, uneven, and often painful. For lower-class women work offered broader contacts, new experiences, and geographic mobility. The individualizing impact of monetary wages was retarded since they were pooled with the earnings of other family members to meet joint needs.[15] For middle-class women their roles as home managers encouraged independent thought as they came to make choices for a growing variety of goods and services. Increasing literacy and improving living standards offered them the opportunity to discard tradition in favor of individual preference as the guide for behavior. However imperfectly, women could begin to see themselves as persons with individual demands on life.

Nineteenth-century feminism was a product of these social and economic changes. As the *organized* expression of efforts to promote women's interests, it was new to the political stage; previous eras had recorded mainly lone voices for women's rights. Women's movements conformed to the "phenomenon of organization" that impresses observers of the nineteenth century.[16] As the state increasingly came to play a more active role in social and economic life, groups were forced to coalesce in order to influence decision making.

Socialist women were not alone in pressuring German society for feminist reforms, but only they saw reforms as a means to the end of human liberation in a radically transformed world. Beginning in the 1860s, middle-class women organized to champion their own interests. These women owed their intellectual support less to the liberal tradition of natural rights—since it was so weak in Germany—but rather to a "Germanic" balance between duties and rights. Feminism adapted itself to specific national traditions and to differing social and political contexts, although it showed marked similarities throughout Europe, reflecting, in part, the "universalism" of women's oppression.[17] The German middle-class women's movement adjusted to the authoritarian political traditions and structure in which it operated, and in marked contrast to the history of feminism in America and England, played down women's suffrage. It stressed, rather, women's important contributions to social life such as their efforts in social welfare reforms that justified their eventual claim on rights.[18] The middle-class movement, as elsewhere in Europe and America, fell into two basic categories: feminists proper and social feminists concerned with social reform.[19]

Bourgeois feminists in Germany struggled against the legal

and attitudinal barriers that restricted women's options in social and economic life, and they tried to insure a higher valuation of women's actual and potential contributions to society. Their movements were often run by females for females such as the National German Women's Association (*Allgemeiner Deutscher Frauenverein*) founded in 1865, but they were not necessarily sexually exclusive. The associations to train women for municipal work, the educational reform groups, as well as the professional organizations such as the teachers' associations or female white-collar unions that sought to remove disadvantages in industries or social institutions, were feminist.

Social feminists promoted causes that promised to ease women's lot by practical social reforms. The unique Central European and Scandinavian motherhood leagues advocating maternity care, midwife training, and rights for illegitimate children and unwed mothers fell in this category of feminism,[20] as did consumers' leagues and associations to banish state-sanctioned prostitution. If the term *social feminism* is to have meaning, it must be distinguished from charity and philanthropy, activities women have undertaken for centuries. A German survey in 1909 classified 78 percent of those women engaged in extradomestic activities (roughly 673,000 females) as performing purely charity and church-related work.[21] Social feminism moved beyond simply ameliorative measures in a charity mold to propounding a vision, however moderate, of structural change to improve social conditions. This distinction is partly subjective since it involves an assessment of motive and of women's perception of their role. Studies in America indicate, for example, that women could use church activity to exert influence and actually launch a challenge against men.[22]

The generalized class hostilities in Germany and the nature of the socialist subculture created a gulf between socialist women who spoke for working-class females and linked their cause to the general revolutionary struggle and bourgeois women who sought better educational and job opportunities as well as some structural reform. The German setting, however, only highlights clearly a general dilemma that feminism as a movement for social change has confronted everywhere: the crucial class, cultural, or even race differences that divide the female population and militate against the unity of all women. Although women share the experience of reproduction and of sexual discrimination, this kind of identity appeared quite fragile for the purposes of political mobilization. Thus, British feminists supported suffrage for middle-class women but not for lower-class women and men. American unionists who rejected the Equal Rights Amendment in the 1920s chose as their platform protective labor laws for female workers rather than women's legal equality, which was feared as an objective incompatible with special protection. Efforts in late nineteenth-century France to create a feminist association embracing middle-class and lower-class women collapsed over the issue of domestics: middle-class ladies were horrified at the idea of a day off for their maids.[23] And German socialist feminists were caught in the same dilemma as they sought to reconcile socialism, a class-based movement, with feminism, a set of ideals that transcends class.

Viewed from a feminist perspective, the German socialist women's movement might seem peculiar. The group scorned and rejected the label "feminist" (*Frauenrechtlerinnen*), yet it was decisively radical in feminist policies. Its resistance to the term was more than a verbal tactic to dissociate itself from bourgeois feminism. Socialist women saw themselves as part of a workers' party struggling together with men against their common enemy: capitalism. They did not conceive of themselves as a feminist movement. The trade union leader Gertrud Hanna crystallized their self-image when she said that "we are in the first place Party members, secondly unionists, and finally, if at all, feminists."[24] In practice, Hanna reversed the first and second priority, but the low status of feminism remains.

Yet socialist women active in the women's movement were more feminist than they liked to admit publicly. At a minimum, they were conscious of themselves as female. This distinguished them from women socialists such as the fiery radical Rosa Luxemburg who "regarded her sex as irrelevant."

Luxemburg held that women's oppression was an ephemeral capitalist misery that would disappear in the socialist society. All energies, she prescribed, had to be directed toward promoting the revolution, and she dismissed efforts on behalf of women as "old ladies' nonsense."[25] The leaders of the socialist women's movement, too, saw in socialism the only way to true emancipation of the female sex but deviated from Luxemburg over strategies *before* the revolution. They sought to mobilize working-class women as a special group and propounded a series of radical reforms designed to alleviate sex oppression under capitalism. Unlike Luxemburg, socialist feminists could not escape the twin pull of class and sex. On every level—theoretical, political, organizational, and tactical—they faced the crucial issue of how to reconcile loyalty to class and to sex.

Socialist women became reluctant, although paradoxically often radical, feminists in their effort to balance the alternating pulls on working-class women's identity. This paradox formed the central framework for women championing the interests of their sex in the German labor movement. It determined the extent of feminism within socialist theory and strategy as well as the women's organizational ties to both the SPD and the Free Trade Unions.

The leaders of socialist women sought to harmonize loyalty to class and to sex by defining feminism in class terms. This definition applied to strategies in the present capitalist state as well as to a vision of life in the future socialist society. In socialist strategy for the prerevolutionary period, feminism was a means to an end and directed specifically to the needs of working-class women. In socialist theory, the revolution was expected to solve the "women's question" by introducing a new era in human relations that would accord all men and women an equally dignified existence.

Socialists argued that work freed women from economic dependency on men, a prerequisite for their emancipation. At the same time, the female worker, unlike her upper- or middle-class counterpart, was oppressed by capitalist social relations. Thus, the situation of the lower-class woman differed not only from that of her more affluent sister but also from the

position of male members of her own class. She was both a
slave of her class and of her sex. Carrying Marx's analysis further, the socialists claimed that she needed liberation from sex
discrimination in order to join effectively with men in the fight
to improve the condition of the proletariat. Legal equality
with men in the capitalist state, in turn, would strengthen
women's class consciousness. To achieve this goal, the leaders
proposed radical feminist reforms that ranged from municipal
facilities such as day-care centers to more equal status for husband and wife in the family. They also sought to instill feminist
values of self-worth and propagandized expectations of a new
society that recognized women as full human beings. Their
radical feminism reflected, in part, their general opposition to
dominant ideas and norms in German capitalist society. Yet
German socialist women were reluctant feminists because
most of them regarded the feminist cause as a secondary concern, overshadowed by the larger task of the class struggle and
preparation for the new society. Their feminist plank incorporated only those demands compatible with the final end of proletarian revolution. Given the basic consensus among large
numbers of socialist feminists, those who sought to elevate
feminism from a means to an end had to do so cautiously. The
whole issue often became engulfed in ideological squabbles or
personal antagonisms.

If German socialist women put class before sex and judged
feminism by its contribution to the proletarian class struggle,
they adopted, however reluctantly, feminist tactics in developing their organization and preparing guidelines for
mobilization of the masses. In this endeavor, they faced a
major problem in working out their relationship to Social Democracy. What organizational structure and which specific
tactics promised greatest success in reaching working-class
women? The leaders' answer was a logical outgrowth of their
understanding of feminism. If the working-class woman was
sexually oppressed and countless social and psychological barriers restricted her options, would not formal equality in the
Party merely mask real inequalities? Would not the simple
adoption of tactics geared to mobilizing men prove inapplica-

ble for working-class women? In response to such questions, socialist women demanded special consideration, all the while loudly proclaiming they did not want a separate organization.

Since the women's movement (*Frauenbewegung*) was part of the political wing of German Social Democracy, the solution of the organizational problem was influenced by legal restrictions. Until 1908, laws in many German states prevented women from joining political organizations. Hence, the women's movement emerged in the 1890s as a semiautonomous group affiliated with the SPD but centered around local women representatives (*Vertrauenspersonen*). The legal prohibitions combined with the women's feminist preferences to insure considerable freedom of action within the Party. After 1908, when women officially joined the SPD, they sought to preserve their own sphere of activity.

Legal barriers against joining political organizations applied less rigorously to trade unions, and socialist women engaged in extensive unionization campaigns. The women's movement actually straddled the fence between political and union activity. Its close ties with both the Party and Free Trade Unions were a source of strength as well as a cause of strife. Female Party members faced a tactical dilemma of defining spheres of influence that corresponded to their feminist requirements. This dilemma became more acute by the turn of the century when German Social Democracy was plagued with ideological conflict and growing sensitivity of the trade unions to threats against their power and influence.

THE WOMEN'S MOVEMENT OF SOCIAL DEMOCRACY: HISTORIOGRAPHICAL ISSUES

The vast literature on German Social Democracy basically has bypassed the women's movement. This should come as no surprise because until recently, most areas of historical inquiry have reflected men's experiences and endeavors. The limited historiography has placed the movement solely in its socialist as opposed to its feminist context and left unanalyzed the contradictions arising from the need to harmonize loyalties to class and sex, even Party and union. Some historians have concerned themselves with the position of the women's movement in the ideological spectrum of German Social Democracy. Gerhard A. Ritter and Werner Thönnessen assert that it was "radical."[26] This simple characterization assumes an identity of views among socialist feminists that did not exist. Besides, it raises the thorny issue of defining political terms.

For the purposes of analyzing the German socialist *women's* movement the standard political definitions are not entirely relevant.[27] "Radical" should include a set of feminist criteria as well as positions on key issues that traditionally have defined political stances, such as the mass strike, noncollaboration with bourgeois parties, or refusal to approve the military budget. Radical feminist criteria would include, for example, restructuring of the household through communal kitchens and day-care centers or birth control. The radical socialist and the radical feminist positions often did not match. Thus, socialist feminists in favor of immediate reforms were more sympathetic to birth control than were radical socialists who feared the working class would be weakened by a reduction in numbers.

Classification of leaders in the women's movement is complicated also by a powerful wing around Clara Zetkin, a radical socialist. Zetkin defined in the mid-1890s the theory of women's liberation that was adopted by the Party, but she did not necessarily endorse a radical *feminist* stance on all issues. Furthermore, confirming the findings of the feminist writers Juliet Mitchell and Sheila Rowbotham who stress the unequal relationship of the historic alliance of socialism and feminism, Zetkin never modified her tactics for the women's struggle to fit the new age of imperialism, as she did with socialist tactics.[28] Feminism, as Mitchell points out, remained basically an adjunct of socialist theory, a set of ideals poorly integrated into socialist thought. This imparted a static quality to many of the debates that masked a slow process of social and attitudinal change in the women's movement.

In general, the commitment of men to the Party's official definition of the women's question varied proportionately with their adherence to radical socialist ideology. In view of great individual variations, however, it is difficult, if not impossible,

to establish a typology valid at any given time. Reform socialists such as Georg von Vollmar and Eduard David were quite
sympathetic to the German middle-class movement for wom-
en's rights and considerably less charitable with their own
women's movement that was hostile to bourgeois feminism.[29]
Even a feminist such as August Bebel showed a conflict between professed ideology and actual behavior. Furthermore,
as will be seen, socialist men showed little inclination in daily
practice to adhere to the official stance on the women's question.

In light of these ambiguities, it comes as no surprise to find
that the socialist world was sharply divided on both socialist
and feminist issues. The women's voting record at SPD congresses shows that their movement was as split as the Party as
a whole, with perhaps a higher proportion of leaders voting
"radical." This still leaves the attitudes of the rank and file unknown. In 1913, for example, when the political divisions had
crystallized, two important issues were debated: the mass
strike and the introduction of progressive taxation to finance
the military budget, a longstanding socialist demand. Thirty
women were among the 495 delegates who attended the 1913
Jena Congress; about 46 percent of these voted radical while
only 27 percent of the male delegates approved the radical position.[30] In sum, the women's movement as any other social
organization defies simple categorization.

Highlighting the interplay of the divergent views, this book
does not present a strictly chronological history nor a political
study nor a treatise on Marxist ideology on the women's question. Instead, it is working-class history "from above."[31] It
focuses on socialist feminists and their political and union
activities within the context of the German labor movement
rather than on the German working class as a whole. The great
mass of working-class females remained distant from, and
often hostile to, socialism. Why this was so can be ascertained
by attempting to determine who was politicized, how, and
what barriers to further mobilization existed both in the
socialist subculture and the society at large.

In its entirety, the work is an effort to reconstruct the world of socialist feminists in Imperial Germany, a world that, like Janus, showed two faces. One exhibited a sense of strength derived from belonging to the socialist movement with its larger revolutionary objectives and its promise of ultimate victory. In this respect, socialist feminists had an advantage over bourgeois feminists. They could act with the backing of German Social Democracy as a political and trade union organization and they could appeal to official canons of Marxism in furthering their cause. Also, the socialist subculture tended to shield them from the full force of societal disapproval since its professed values upheld the equal worth of men and women. In contrast, middle-class German feminists were isolated from party support; neither the Catholic Center Party nor the two liberal groups advanced, with any degree of consistency, women's rights.

The other face showed great tension. Socialist feminists experienced conflicts as socialists, the "antinational reds" in German society; as females involved politically in a community that regarded women's extradomestic activity as unnatural and dangerous; as members of the Party against Free Trade Unionists; as women struggling for recognition by male Party and union leaders; as socialist feminists against bourgeois feminists; and, most of all, they were in conflict among themselves about the priority of socialism over feminism in Party and union affairs.

CHAPTER II

"WORK HORSE, BABY MACHINE, CULTURAL DRUDGE"

The German Social Democratic Party was a party of workers in the industrial and craft sector. Peasants, urban lower-middle class, and intelligentsia, those whom Kuczynski calls their "natural" but "unreliable" allies, remained hostile to socialism.[1] The decision to limit recruitment to the working class had been deliberate. In a debate of 1895 on the revolutionary potential among peasants, and in the later revisionist assessment of a "new middle class"—employees in the burgeoning service sector—the SPD leadership succeeded in keeping mobilization efforts focused on the class that promised victory.

In Wilhelmine Germany the Party gained supporters steadily and attracted a core of skilled and semiskilled workers drawn, in good measure, from the newly emerging metal, machine, and chemical industries. Party mandates paralleled this growth in membership, increasing inexorably (or so it seemed) until the 1907 election disaster over Germany's imperial role reaffirmed socialist isolation in a country heady with nationalism. The commitment to parliamentarism, however, remained intact. The election of 1912 revealed the strength as well as the weakness of the strategy. The SPD emerged as the largest party in Germany with 110 deputies in parliament and a total of 4.2 million votes. Yet in the by-elections, the agreement between socialists and progressives floundered on middle-class refusal to vote "red." The political division in Germany clearly lay between worker on the one hand and the rest of society on the other. In its strongholds, in fact, the SPD had received 82.4 percent of the vote, nearly exhausting its potential. While the Party had won the mass of urban manual workers, as Bebel recognized that year, this was not enough to yield an absolute majority in parliament.[2]

While the Party represented the bulk of the working class, the socialist women's movement had failed to win over the large mass of urban working women. At the Berlin women's conference in 1913, Martha Arendsee charged that most industrial working women stood outside the women's movement. The rank and file, she felt, included many nonworking wives of SPD members. Police assigned to watch the women's movement corraborated the analysis. They went even further and indicated that the trade unions simply were not encouraging their female members to join the socialist women's movement.[3]

THE SOCIAL BASES OF THE WOMEN'S MOVEMENT

An analysis of the social composition of the women's movement reveals the cross sections of working-class females most receptive to socialist ideas. The movement's strength rested in those electoral districts with an overwhelming majority of working-class population. Its rank and file was working class. The leadership was drawn from all strata, although analyses indicate that by 1906 it, too, was shifting to working-class homogeneity.[4] The average age of the rank and file was above twenty-five, older than most working women in the German labor force. Wives of Party members formed the "large majority" of rank and file, a characteristic of the women's movement from its beginnings in the 1870s to the end of the Imperial period.[5] The socialist women's movement expressed largely familial political solidarity in the socialist subculture.

Further generalization becomes risky because of regional diversity. According to national reports around 1912, a large proportion of the low-level functionaries such as the local representatives, leaders of the educational sessions, and the women sent on tours, were proletarian housewives—women who had stopped working. Socially, they seemed to resemble their bourgeois counterparts although their sensitivity to labor, which reflected a work experience as young girls, produced a feminism fundamentally different from that emanating from the middle class. In Berlin, these functionaries were the wives of skilled workers, the better paid, upwardly mobile sections of the working class in, for example, the metal and construction industries.[6] According to Kuczynski, although no simple correlation exists between wage levels and political consciousness, the worst paid workers often were the most politically backward.[7] In contrast to the situation in most other areas, a majority of the thirty-five regional representatives in Bavaria were employed women. As police reports indicated, a low proportion of women's movement members were unionized, although once again Bavaria proved an exception. The close ties that existed between the unions and the SPD in Bavaria were reflected in the women's movement. Forty percent of Nuremberg Party women, comprising over one-half of female membership in predominantly Catholic Bavaria, were unionized as metalworkers and woodworkers, unskilled factory women, printers' aids, or domestics.[8] Not an insignificant number of the rank and file worked in the home industries.

A more detailed sociological profile can be gleaned from analyzing Berliners attending the women's movement reading sessions (*Leseabende*), although Bavarians were fond of pointing out that Berlin, i.e., Prussia, was not Germany. The Berlin women's movement made up the largest single contingent in the whole women's organization; in 1911, it had 16,947 female members. Roughly one-third of the membership attended the *Leseabende*. A four-and-one-half-year survey (between 1907 and 1911) encompassing 1,100 participants and a questionnaire to which 119 women responded comprise the sample.[9]

Half the participants at the sessions were between 26 and 35 years old. Only 3 women out of the 1,100 interviewees were social democrats against the "wishes and consent" of their husbands. Forty-two percent were working women; the remainder were nonemployed wives of workers. Of the gainfully employed, 68 percent worked outside the home in metal factories, in the garment industry as seamstresses, in needlework, as saleswomen, newspaper deliverers, hair dressers, cleaning women, and ironers.[10] One sees here a cross section of urban female labor: traditional "female" jobs as in the garment industry as well as domestic service; work in heavy industry and the commercial sector, both of which

began absorbing unskilled female hands by the turn of the
twentieth century; and 32 percent of those who worked for
wages did so in their homes. Only 26 percent of those working
were unionized, most in the Metalworkers Union, but also in
the Bookbinders and Printers' Aids Unions, as well as the Servants Union and Transport Workers Union. On the average,
women employed outside the home had 1.7 children, most of
school age between 6 and 14 years. The average number of
children per family for reading-session participants was
slightly higher, roughly 2.04. A study of family composition in
1885 indicated that only 15.2 percent of families in working-
class districts had 1 or 2 children, whereas 37.4 percent had
over 7 children. Later analyses note that the number of children was inversely related to labor skills and point to the
spread of family planning among skilled factory and craft
workers.[11] Clearly, a fair number of participants in the
women's movement practiced some form of birth control.

Husbands of reading-session members were predominantly
skilled workers. The largest single job category was metal-
worker and next came woodworker. But masons, shoemakers,
printers, brewers, and bakers were also represented as were
occupations that defy precise categorization by class: three
independent businessmen, one clerk, and four officials (presumably of the Party or unions) were included in the list. In
addition, 28 percent were designated as unskilled (occupations
unspecified). Religion comprises the final element in the portrait: police reports suggest that women rank and file had a
residual if not visceral attachment to the church. In radical
Berlin, on several occasions, discussion leaders' efforts to organize a mass exodus from the established church were foiled
by members who refused to make such an open and permanent break.[12]

The average woman in the SPD differed from the typical
working woman in the industrial and craft sector. Here the
female generally was younger, between sixteen and twenty-
one, unmarried, and an unskilled worker in consumer goods
industries such as textile, clothing, food processing, and wood
products. These industries began to record a relative decline

in growth in the Wilhelmine period as compared to heavy industry and commerce.[13] Arendsee's critique seemed to strike at the heart of the matter. If the movement won over the single working woman, chances would be good that she would remain in the fold after marriage.

The key variable in the politicization process, however, appears to be the family. If the family were active in the socialist movement, its women were most likely to join up. Next in importance was age and marital status. Yet it was clear that women were less receptive to organizational efforts than were men. Leaving aside for now the discrepancy between the numbers of men—fathers, brothers, or husbands—active in Social Democracy and the significantly smaller proportion of women (chapter VI), the root of the problem lay embedded in the social position of German women. Socialists were aware of the complexity of the question and the greater degree of interdependence of women's roles. It was harder, for example, to isolate the woman's role as worker from her other roles since her family position influenced her economic decisions; the work she sought, in turn, was conditioned by family considerations. Thus, the actual physical separation of work and home in industrial society was not reflected as distinctly in women's consciousness.

WOMEN'S POSITION IN THE SOCIETY
OF IMPERIAL GERMANY

One feature most clearly dominated the social world of German women: dependency. The reality of dependency rested on assumptions about women's social inferiority and served to reinforce low concepts of self-worth. Its presence was felt in all aspects of life—in the family, at work, and in the world outside. One discussed, analyzed, maligned, praised, and judged women's character, reached conclusions based more on tradition or generally accepted assumptions than rational thought, and consciously or unconsciously curtailed options and choices. The German attitude was summed up by a Progressive deputy in the Reichstag: women were seen as objects in social life and little was done to encourage independent thought or action.[14]

Although women were apparently on the offensive in the debates on the women's question, they faced a difficult challenge. They had to prove their worth, their brain size, their capabilities, talents, and contributions to the national community. Their opponents could sit back, quoting the church fathers or using and abusing history, psychology or physiology. Finally, antifeminists in Germany could point to the indisputable—men and women were different—and draw the disputable conclusion that "sex lay deeper than culture."[15] Not socialization but biology determined women's roles. Nature had created two distinct creatures and endowed each with immutable intellectual and emotional traits and corresponding "proper" spheres of activity. It was tempting God and destiny to challenge the division. It meant also courting political danger since the state rested on the family and the family could not absorb political strife.[16]

Germany was the land of the three K's, or four, since socialists mockingly added clothing (*Kleider*) to the triad of children, church, and kitchen (*Kinder, Kirche, Küche*). The natural boundary for woman was the family; to be wife and mother was her true profession. Women's emotionalism and their natural empathy were compatible with this sphere. She was to be educated to "gracious femininity" and the arts of domestic life.[17] Women could not stray over to other spheres because these were incompatible with their essential make-up. Nature had made them politically immature, presumably indefinitely. If appeals to nature failed to convince feminists, opponents had a perfect answer. Since women did not serve in the military, they could neither be interested in political life nor could they ever truly be equal.[18] (These conclusions were drawn time and again, too, by the police as they watched over the women's political activities.) In vain did socialists counter *Wehrpflicht* (military conscription) with *Wehpflicht* (women's labor at childbirth), and bourgeois feminists held up women's growing roles in social welfare as an equal contribution to the national community. But military values permeated German society and reinforced concepts of authority, hierarchies, and male dominance.

Laws in Germany mirrored these dominant attitudes although there were changes in the Wilhelmine period. Women ranked in legal status with children and idiots. They were disenfranchised for lawmaking bodies on the national and state level, but as property owners, possessed limited, indirect voting rights in the municipality, applicable often only if single. They could not vote or serve on trade courts that settled disputes arising from wage contracts and could not act as jurors.[19] Women could only vote directly for and join health insurance institutions that were mandatory for all wage or salary employees in factories. These bodies decided such questions as maternity insurance schemes. Yet, in 1908, only 30.2 percent of employed women in Germany belonged to the fund. In Hanau and Mainz, only .1 percent and .7 percent, respectively, voted in health insurance elections. In Berlin, with the largest female membership (52.3 percent), the numbers of women voting were minuscule (.006 percent).[20] The fact that working women did not make use of this right is a graphic expression of their state of dependency.

The laws that prevented women from joining political organizations applied, for example, to Prussia, Bavaria, Mecklenburg, and Braunschweig but not to Saxony, Württemberg, Baden, and Hamburg. Interested women found ways of circumventing the prohibitions by "putting on male coats and hats and disappearing into the crowd of people at the meeting,"[21] and by devising organizational schemes such as the socialist feminists' representative system (*Vertrauensperson*). The system allowed women socialists to engage in politics without forming clubs and associations. It lodged responsibility in the hands of one person since the laws of association did not apply to individuals.

Government policy began to change in 1902; the Prussian Secretary of State that year ruled that females could attend political meetings if they sat in defined sections and refrained from clapping or booing. For the next six years, the norm was "separate and silent." In April 1908, a revised national "law of assembly" granted women the right of association. The change was justified by the need for legal uniformity throughout the country and by the growing presence of women in public life.[22] Despite socialist hopes, this reform did not lead to women's suffrage during the Imperial period; it would be the socialists themselves who in the early days of the Revolution of 1918 passed the women's right-to-vote law.

Educational opportunities available to women also were severely restricted. Training for skilled jobs was pitifully inadequate for working-class women throughout the period. While the state of Baden had instituted obligatory continuing education, in Prussia, as late as 1911, it was impossible to require that female factory workers attend school; in Württemberg, by contrast, continuing educational institutions offering a two-year course were mandatory for males and optional for females. Instruction was given forty times per year in two one-hour sessions each week for girls and boys separately. (With some exceptions, notably the admittance of a small number of girls to boys' *Gymnasiums* in Baden, education was sexually segregated in Imperial Germamy.)[23] In 1908, several categories of female jobs—milliners, hairdressers, and seamstresses—were upgraded officially to craft (*Handwerk*) status, requiring a two-to-three-year apprenticeship. While female union leaders reacted favorably in this particular case, they rejected in principle indiscriminate extension of the apprenticeship system where none had existed before. They opposed the one-to-three-year state of dependency the young girl found herself in and feared a loss of job mobility as well as undue concentration on upgrading the older forms of production to the neglect of more modern types of work.[24]

For over twenty years, middle-class women, too, sought to restructure girls' schools, set up state-supported teachers' colleges, and gain women admittance to the *Abitur* (high school completion) exam and thus to the universities. Derision and hostility greeted these demands. Bourgeois feminists founded pressure groups (for example, the Women's Reform Association) and established their own high schools for girls.

Change came slowly. First, women won the right of auditing courses (*Hörerinnen*) at the universities with permission of the instructor. In 1901, the state of Baden admitted women to its universities; next Württemberg in 1903 reformed the system of education to offer women equivalent preparation for university study. Thus, the way was paved for the 1908 Prussian law that restructured the secondary girls' schools and sanctioned university study with the right of matriculation.[25]

The rights of German women in the private sphere and especially the family were greatly limited. Rationalizing prevailing laws in the several states, the first national revised civil code of 1900 defined women's status in marriage. It carefully anchored the principle of husband's legal guardianship (*eheherrliche Vormundsschaft*) within the family and legally discriminated against mothers with illegimate children.[26] The law limited women's parental control over their children; only widows or, if the husband forfeited his rights, divorcees had full legal guardianship over their offspring. Illegitimate children had no rights of inheritance even if the father recognized the child, and child support was geared to the mother's economic position in order to protect a wealthy father from financial abuse. The Prussian provision for divorce on grounds of irreconcilability or mutual desire was not incorporated into the new national code. Grounds for divorce were limited to guarantee the sanctity of marriage, and the law required a guilty party. Desertion, for example, had to occur against the will of the other person. The code respecified existing property rights throughout the Empire. According to the revision, a woman no longer needed her husband's permission to work and she controlled the income she earned during marriage, although he continued to administer property she brought to the union.

Safeguarding the family was an absorbing concern among lawmakers in the nineteenth century, and it often was done at the expense of women's individual rights. To believe contemporaries of all political persuasions, the family was in imminent danger of destruction. Most observers agreed on the cause: increasing numbers of women entering the labor force as wage earners. Growth in paid female labor was typical of industrializing countries, made possible by economic development, employment insecurity, and the low wages of men. In the early years of the twentieth century, women accounted for the following percentages of the gainfully employed: 44 percent in Austria; 34.8 percent in France; 30 percent in the German Empire; 24.9 percent in England and Ireland; and 14.3 percent in the United States. Because of the different census dates and definitions these numbers may not be strictly comparable, but they show at least the orders of magnitude and highlight the international extent of female labor that gave rise to the concern of the international labor movement with this phenomenon.[27] In Germany, only socialists reacted favorably to the presence of women in the industrial labor force. After all, their analysis held that work was the vehicle for women's emancipation as well as the cudgel to destroy the economic basis of the patriarchal family. In the sweep of history, the short-term dislocations in family life resulting from women's employment were more than offset by the promise of equitable familial and sexual relationships in the future society. Did women's labor in Germany fulfill these expectations? To what extent could it counter feelings of dependency? What potential existed in the working class for the mobilization of females?

ECONOMICS AND EMANCIPATION:
WOMEN IN THE GERMAN LABOR FORCE

Decades of economic and social change had prepared the way for sustained industrial growth in Germany by the mid-nineteenth century. In the name of economic liberalism, the Stein-Hardenberg reforms in Prussia, 1807-1819, had set the productive forces free, emancipating the serfs and abolishing the guilds. The Napoleonic Code, which destroyed the feudal social structure and loosened impediments to the development of capitalism, followed French victories in western and central Germany. Between 1816 and 1865, the population in Germany soared 59 percent. Modification of the three-field system of agrarian production increased agricultural productivity, and modern methods of transport met the needs of a growing market economy. The Prussian Customs Union of the 1830s stimulated foreign trade by abolishing internal customs duties among the affiliated states of Central Europe. Between 1800 and 1860, mechanization encroached on the home textile industry; products were increasingly commissioned by merchants who furnished the raw materials and obtained the finished goods at low margins. Later, factories sprang up and replaced traditional domestic work. An ever larger part of the output was earmarked for distant markets, and, as a result of these changes, large numbers of artisans lost their livelihood.[28]

The composition of the labor force shifted markedly during the first half of the nineteenth century. At the beginning of the 1800s, serfs, apprentices, journeymen, and master craftsmen comprised labor; there were fewer than 50,000 factory workers. By 1848, free wage labor—the factory work force—had emerged from emancipated serfs whose landholdings were insufficient to provide for subsistence, from unemployed apprentices and journeymen, and from craft masters unable to compete with large-scale production. Increasingly, women and children were drawn into factories, or they continued to work in crafts at home but under deteriorating conditions. Luise Zietz, a prominent socialist feminist, graphically described the personal meaning of these changes to her family in the early 1870s.

> To feed six hungry mouths is difficult for poor people at any time. In such families, hunger is often a constant guest. So it was in my parents' home where, through weaving and spinning, we had to earn enough to get by. . . . My father, utterly proud of his guild master status, fought a hopeless . . . struggle against the modern textile industry. Nearby my birthplace Bargtheheide, in Neümunster in Holstein, large mechanical spinning and weaving machines had been set up. Modern machinery, driven by steam, produced yarn and material cheaper

than my father could with his hand production. And, if periodically, he received contracts from the surrounding peasants, who were able to deliver raw materials from their own sheep and flax growing, thanks to competition he could only command a low price for his work. To provide just for necessities, mother and we kids had to help. We had to pluck apart and oil raw wool, press it . . . then it went to the carding machine. A couple of dogs, alternatively, drove the machine by a large tread-wheel and when one of the large dogs had died on us, we ourselves had to crawl onto the wheel.[29]

The processes of economic growth and mechanization received added stimulus with the unification of Germany in 1871. Heavy industry, located primarily in the Rhine-Ruhr areas and Silesia, began to outstrip the consumer industries, merchant trade boomed, and agrarian grain production successfully competed on the world market. A stock market crash in 1873, however, ended the economic surge and inaugurated a twenty-three-year price depression. The ensuing period of economic insecurity produced structural changes in the German economy with important political and social consequences.[30]

The depression caused a move to protectionism, advocated initially by south German textile manufacturers and large industrialists. A drop in grain prices in 1875 induced the large landowners in northeast Germany, the Junkers, to join the chorus. The protective tariff of 1879 was nothing short of a milestone: it not only underpinned the economic position of "iron and grain" but forged a political alliance between large landowners and heavy industrialists who most directly profited from the new status quo. With the commitment to tariffs the government, in effect, preserved the economic base of the preindustrial social and political agrarian elites while at the same time it won over the economically powerful representatives of heavy industry. Henceforth, agrarians and industrialists comprised the ruling group in Germany, although increasing industrialization threatened to undermine the precarious partnership. Government policy artfully safeguarded its ruling coalitions by various means: import restrictions and the unwillingness, until 1909, to reform the financial structure that favored indirect over income taxes as well as budgetary deficits, were powerful economic incentives to cooperation. In the loftier realm of emotion, clever manipulation of nationalist sentiment as well as a shared horror of socialism served to mask divergent interests.[31] Antisocialism had become one key component to the preservation of the Imperial German structure.

The series of economic crises beginning in the mid-1870s also undercut the smaller, less competitive business firms in favor of joint stock companies. Tariffs, too, furthered the trend toward large-scale production. Giant investment banks proliferated in the economy and extended credit to big business. In Germany, large banking firms allied with heavy industry in the promotion of cartels, monopolies, and syndicates. Unlike America, Germany not only tolerated but encouraged syndicates as guardians against overproduction crises. They were seen as modern forms of the former guild system of monopolies regulated in the "public interest."[32] These cartels, primarily in heavy industry, organized interest groups and fought to restrict the effectiveness of the emerging trade union movement.

The lower-income population in Germany bore the cost of the political and economic alliance. Indirect taxes were a real burden. Tariffs and limited domestic competition stimulated a rise in internal prices that was felt most critically following the turn of the century.[33] While real wages rose during the period from 1873 to 1896, thereafter they barely kept in line with the sharply increasing prices.[34] Consumption patterns reflect the price trends after 1900. Between 1870 and 1899, for example, annual per capita consumption of meat rose from 24.9 to 44.1 kilograms, whereupon it stagnated or declined slightly until World War I.[35] Kuczynski, analyzing meat consumption in different cities, indicates that it was lowest in areas where unskilled workers were concentrated, as in textile regions.[36] Tax returns from Prussia, which accounted for 60 percent of the total German population, can be used to measure income levels in the period between 1896 and 1912. There was a 5 percent decline in heads of *households* making less than 900 marks per year, while the households in higher-income groups rose between 94 percent and 167 percent. In the sixteen-year period, the population grew about 30 percent. There still were 16 million *persons* living on incomes below 900 marks (RM) per year in 1912, although their absolute numbers had declined by 24 percent between 1896 and 1912.[37]

Family expenditure provides an additional perspective on the standard of living of the German working class. Table 1 presents the expenditure side of a budget of low- and middle-income families in large- and middle-range cities for 1907-1908. The working-class population spent a high proportion of its income for such basic necessities as food and housing. These two items made up 71.2 percent of the expenditures of an unskilled worker's family. Socialists were quick to capitalize on rising prices, indirect taxes, tariffs, and nearly stagnating wages. By addressing the high cost of living issue, they struck a receptive chord among working-class women in their role as consumers.[38]

Growth and differentiation in the German labor force met the needs of industrial development. The growth trend of female employment accelerated after 1870. Legislation restricting hours of work for children and the prohibition in 1891

TABLE 1   Expenditures for Food and Housing
by Lower- and Middle-Income Families, 1907-1908

	FOOD	HOUSING	TOTAL
Skilled worker	51.1%	16.8%	68.3%
Unskilled worker	52.8	18.4	71.2
Private employee	40.9	18.7	59.6
Teacher	34.7	21.0	55.7
Middle-level official	37.9	18.0	55.0
Lower-level official	49.0	18.2	67.2

SOURCE: Gerd Hohorst, Jürgen Kocka, and Gerhard A. Ritter, *Sozialgeschichtliches Arbeitsbuch: Materialien zur Statistik des Kaiserreichs 1870-1914*, Munich, 1975, pp. 112-113.

of child labor (for children up to fourteen years of age) in factories encouraged the employment of women as the alternative source of cheap labor. The proportion of women employed to total working population rose from 31 to 36 percent between 1882 and 1907.[39]

Women's entrance into the labor market proved steady, and according to scattered data, even increased during recessions.[40] Table 2 shows the number and proportion of employed males and females and the percentage changes from 1882 to 1907 in agriculture, industry, and commerce. Particularly striking is the increase of jobs held by females in agriculture and commerce, whereas shifts in favor of women were

TABLE 2   Changes in Male and Female Employment
in Imperial Germany, 1882-1907

Year	Numbers engaged in the labor market Male	Female	Percent change between years Male	Female	Proportion of total Male	Female
AGRICULTURE						
1882	5,701,587	2,534,090			69.2	30.8
			−2.84	+ 8.61		
1895	5,539,538	2,753,154			66.8	33.2
			−4.61	+67.04		
1907	5,284,271	4,598,986			53.7	46.3
INDUSTRY						
1882	5,269,489	1,126,976			82.4	17.6
			+28.29	+34.97		
1895	6,760,102	1,521,118			81.6	18.4
			+35.39	+38.32		
1907	9,152,330	2,103,924			81.3	18.7
COMMERCE						
1882	1,272,208	298,110			81.0	19.0
			+38.96	+94.43		
1895	1,758,903	579,608			80.7	19.3
			+44.76	+60.69		
1907	2,546,253	931,373			73.2	26.8

SOURCE: Gertrud Hanna, "Die Frauenerwerbsarbeit im Deutschen Reiche nach den Ergebnissen der Berufszählungen von 1882-1907," *Statistische-Beilage des Correspondenzblatt*, 27 April 1912, p. 63.

relatively modest in industry. Nevertheless, the absolute number of female workers in industry nearly doubled within the twenty-five-year period.

Table 3 shows the changes in male and female employment in the working class in the same period.[41] Working-class female employment more than doubled in agriculture and commerce, while in industry it rose by 40 percent. In other words, compositional shifts in the German labor force as a whole were nearly parallel to the changes among the working class.

As a general rule, women in industry worked under men's supervision as unskilled assistants. Under the domestic industry system, the working woman had labored under her father's or husband's supervision. With industrialization, she still was subordinate to men, but these were generally nonrelatives.[42] Several trades stand out as exceptions. In metal foundries and brickmaking, for example, husbands brought their wives into the industry to help them.

Women very rarely performed the same work functions as men. The German textile industry offers a case in point. A report in 1902 showed clear sex differentiation of assignments. In cotton spinning, for example, women ran the bric-a-brac and drawing-frame machines as well as those handling the first and last stages of fabrication. In weaving, males were weavers and also linkers, dyers, finishers, and dressers. Although a small percentage of working women were weavers, too, the report indicated that most "rinsed, threaded . . . [that is] were unskilled assistants to the [male] weavers."[43]

TABLE 3   Changes in Male and Female Employment
in the Working Class, 1882-1907

Year	FEMALE WORKERS PER 100 MALE WORKERS		
	Agriculture	Industry	Commerce
1882	38.3	13.3	19.9
1895	42.4	16.7	29.6
1907	58.4	18.2	30.9

SOURCE: Hohorst, Kocka, and Ritter, *Sozialgeschichtliches Arbeitsbuch*, p. 67.

Women's standing in the economy paralleled their standing in the family. Subordinate in the latter, young girls grew up expecting nothing more than an unskilled job (*Hilfsarbeiterin*), held—if they were fortunate—only until marriage. The trade union leader, Paula Thiede, clearly saw the interrelationship. Large numbers of men, she said, believed that women could not "shed their subordinate position." Working-class homes simply had different expectations for boys and girls, with the result that girls were disadvantaged for life. Seen as worth less, she said, it is clear they will be unskilled workers (*Hilfskräfte*), just as it is self-evident that boys will not.[44] The wages of adolescent boys, often with their sisters' contributions, went for continuing education to learn a skill; no such attempt was made to help girls progress professionally. All too often, the response to women's desire for advancement was to let them contract "a good marriage." The unmarried working woman who lived at home turned over a good part of her wage to the family. Those who left the family acquired a peculiar freedom—the necessity to work.[45]

Female labor was heavily concentrated in so-called female jobs, often extensions of women's former household duties. The cleaning, garment and textile industries, inn- and barkeeping, and domestic service provided the principal female jobs outside of agriculture in 1907; 64.5 percent of all working women found employment in these five categories.[46] Their labor was cheap since it was seen as supplementary. In the late 1880s, women received roughly one-half to one-third less than the wages of unskilled male workers. This difference began to decline slightly after the turn of the century.[47] Women were modest, less demanding, and it was said, had less "material ambition," which made them attractive from the employers' standpoint. Socialists bitterly complained that entrepreneurs profited from sex discrimination, taking advantage of such conditioned traits as moderation, pliancy, and acceptance of male domination.[48]

Primitive technology with no requisite training characterized most of these female jobs. Inspectors' reports clearly indicated that two trends were at work: first, men were leaving unskilled jobs to seek better opportunities and higher wages elsewhere; second, as women replaced them, "long hours as well as poor pay" became the rule. Night shifts, for example, were introduced into the ready-made garment, textile, and artificial-flower industries in the 1880s. During the price depression, these industries faced competition and hoped to maximize profits with no new capital investment. Women who worked day shifts often were induced to extend their work into the night; in other cases, separate evening shifts were employed.[49]

Women's employment was also a product of technological advance, with specialized machines easing physical effort. In the early twentieth century, the changes began to open employment possibilities in areas such as the growing metal, machine, and chemical industries. In other cases, labor conflicts resulted in women's temporary employment, which, in turn, often became permanent, as described in the following report for Liegnitz: "During a strike over reducing the work day from eleven to ten hours, the sheet-metal workers in a lamp and metal factory laid down their work. Despite attempts to do so, the employer could not find replacements, so he hired a large number of girls who, since then, supervised by [male] sheet workers, are busy soldering light metal. . ..."[50]

Contemporaries observing the labor force noted a shift from male to heavily female labor in three sectors: agriculture, domestic service, and the home industries. The *Gesinde-ordnung*, which regulated rural and service labor relations, placed workers under special laws and forbade collective bargaining. These laws were held responsible, in part, for men leaving the rural areas or domestic service to seek more favorable conditions in cities and industry. Observers remarked on the general trend of country-city migration among males who often remained in cities after performing their military service, a decision facilitated by greater freedom from their families than that enjoyed by females.[51]

Increasing employment of women in the home industries was also carefully noted, although the sector was in decline. Yet it played a more significant role in economic life than previously recognized when seen from the perspective of female labor.[52] Roughly five times as many working women as men were estimated in domestic industry in 1907, although the exact numbers are difficult to determine. For tax and status reasons, workers hesitated to admit their employment. In these industries, predominantly fabrics, lumber products, food, and apparel, labor worked at home on products destined for an entrepreneur, not directly for the consumer. Workers were paid low wages, often piece rates. The workers, themselves, had to bear the cost of heat, light, rent, machines, and raw materials. They worked long hours, up to sixteen per day, were isolated from fellow workers, and remained outside the protective labor laws that governed conditions in factories.

Despite the abuses, the home industries were seen as a solution to the twin problems of economic need and motherly duties. The case of Ernestine Lutze, one of nineteen majority socialist women elected to the National Assembly in 1919, is typical of a whole generation of working women who moved from factory employment to domestic industry once the tension between motherhood and employment seemed irreconcilable. Lutze was a child of the proletariat. Her father died when she was nine years old and, from that time on, she was forced to help support her mother and brother. First, she did char work and when she was twelve years old, she worked afternoons in a factory for the production of artificial flowers. When she married, poverty required she continue her job. Every morning at six o'clock, she went to the factory, her two children were cared for during the day, and she returned at seven or eight in the evening, often bringing work home. After the birth of her third child, the cost of child care was prohibitive and she worked solely at home.[53]

The blending of factory and domestic industry was typical of female labor. In certain trades, not only the artificial-flower but also the dress and underclothing (*Kleider und Wäsche*) industries, women would take work home at night after putting in a full day. This extended their work day by four or five hours. Employers used this practice to get around the law requiring an eleven-hour maximum workday for women in factories passed in 1891. Women often solicited work from different employers than those for whom they worked during the day, or, in the hope of making a decent wage, they worked evenings as waitresses in beer halls and restaurants.[54]

A rapid expansion of female labor was taking place in commerce and trade, particularly after the turn of the century. Bourgeois girls and daughters of skilled workers began to fill employee positions in banking and insurance, and in commercial enterprises. In industry, female employees increased from 2.3 percent of all employees to 9.3 percent between 1882 and 1907; in trade and commerce, the proportion soared from 2.2 percent to 15.8 percent, rising absolutely from 3,000 to 80,000. Also, just as industrial divisions of labor had created categories of low-paid, unskilled jobs, a similar pattern emerged in commerce with the appearance of the typist-stenographer and the salesgirl.[55] Their work required minimal training; it was monotonous, dull, and boring, a product of specialization of function and standardization of goods and prices.

The presence of married women in the labor force and particularly in factories evoked the most frequent comment and controversy. This testifies to the tremendous change that industrialization had introduced into women's life experiences. By the last third of the nineteenth century, gainful labor had become essentially a transitional stage before marriage in a working-class girl's life cycle. The new norm of domestic life that glorified a woman's wifely and motherly roles to the neglect of her productive functions had become generalized in German society. Gainful labor was seen as basically incompatible with marriage and motherhood. Yet by inspectors' accounts, the numbers of married women in industry were rising steadily throughout the Imperial period, "strikingly" as was said in 1907. The years between 1895 and 1907 saw an absolute rise in married women's employment from 140,804 to 278,387, a jump from 9 percent to 12.8 percent of the total number of working women. In 1899, married women comprised 28.7 percent of the female industrial working population over eighteen years of age.[56] They had their own employment cycles that followed closely the business cycles.

These employment trends prompted a governmental inquiry in 1899 on the extent as well as the impact of married women in the factories. The reports were nearly unanimous throughout the country on the cause that drove wives into factories: need (*die Not*). As for social background, it was overwhelmingly the wives of unskilled workers who sought employment in the factories. (Roughly 20 percent of employed married women, however, were widows and divorcees.)[57] Skilled workers were said to be proud to keep their wives at home. Only if a wife earned a good wage were skilled workers inclined to let her go into the factory.[58] Table 4 presents a 1907-1908 budget for sources of income. The wives of unskilled workers contributed 7.7 percent to their husband's income as compared to only 3.5 percent for skilled workers' families and considerably less for the lower middle classes. Furthermore, 4.8 percent of the unskilled workers' income came from subletting, the highest proportion for the occupational groups included in the statistics. Behind the numbers were misery and overcrowding in already inadequate, small, dark living quarters.

Since necessity rather than choice dictated employment, the married women, happy to get any work, tended to accept the most unpleasant chores—the physically demanding, hard,

TABLE 4   Supplemental Income of Lower and
Middle-Class Families, 1907-1908

	INCOME OF WIFE	SUBLETTING	TOTAL
Skilled worker	3.5%	2.8%	6.3%
Unskilled worker	7.7	4.8	12.5
Private employee	3.3	1.0	4.3
Teacher	0.2	0.2	0.4
Middle-level official	0.4	1.2	1.6
Lower-level official	1.2	2.1	3.3

SOURCE: Hohorst, Kocka, and Ritter, *Sozialgeschichtliches Arbeitsbuch*, pp. 112-113.

and dirty jobs. Her wages were generally low. She worked in the quarries, at brickmaking and dyeing, in chemical and sugar factories, in textiles and cigarette making as well as in food processing. In Germany as a whole, the largest percentage was employed in textiles.[59]

Whether married or single, woman's work did not stop with the factory whistle. She was burdened with home duties as well. Working women, and in particular married women, were very conscious of their additional workload. When asked, for example, on the length of her workday, a woman stated bluntly that she worked nine hours in the factory, beginning at five o'clock in the morning, and she was never able to rest before eleven at night; another woman added that on wash days, her workday ended at one or two in the morning. It was estimated that about 70 percent of the employed married women cared for their homes alone with no help from relatives or paid domestics.[60]

Through official and unofficial surveys, inquiries, and studies, the German government as well as the political parties kept close tabs on the growth in the female labor force. Different motives prompted the inquiries, and varying perspectives and conclusions introduced sharp controversy into the political debates.

Socialists were motivated by two complementary considerations. The first was the desire to win over the working woman for the class struggle and the need to devise mobilization tactics geared to women's place in the labor force. Second, socialists were appalled at the abuses caused by women's work under capitalism. While ideally, they said, female labor should reduce hours of work and spread prosperity more evenly throughout society, in reality, under the capitalist system, women were transformed into "dirty competitors of men." Still another objection was that they were torn from their families and their children.[61] Beginning in 1893, socialists advocated special protective labor legislation for female workers. Protection was necessary, they had come to believe, because capitalism exploited women with no regard to their other roles as mother and wife.[62] This position marked a crucial shift in socialist thinking on the women's question and the first step in an effort to flesh out the socialist feminist conception.

At the founding congress of the Second International in 1889, Clara Zetkin, future leader of the German socialist women's movement, had objected to special laws for working women. "We demand no other protection than that which work in general proposes against capital."[63] This stance was compatible with the assumption of Marx and Engels in the *Manifesto* that industrialization destroyed age and sex as "distinctive" social variables for the working class. Yet observation taught a different lesson. Women suffered doubly in the labor market as females and workers. Sex was an important variable and special legislation would help equalize the social position of the female and male worker. Furthermore, advocacy of special laws had the advantage of distinguishing socialist from bourgeois feminist. With the exception of its left wing around the turn of the century, German middle-class feminism rejected special protection in the name of formal equality.

Labor laws became a cardinal plank in socialist feminism. Beyond the eight-hour workday for all labor, socialists proposed the prohibition of work in jobs detrimental to women's health and future childbearing role, an absolute end to night employment, free Saturday afternoons, health and sanitary regulations in the work place, and the extension of these controls to categories of working women outside of industry. They called for female factory inspectors, for women's voting rights for the trade courts, and, finally, for an extensive maternity insurance program designed to reduce the conflict between biology and productivity in the marketplace. Beginning at the turn of the century, the insurance program assumed more importance concomitant with the growth of female labor. Socialists, armed with statistics, documented cases of infant mortality and diseases among working-class children, of women with abdominal problems, of death at childbirth or the lack of adequately trained midwives. They wanted the health insurance program to be broadened to offer maternity support during the last two months of pregnancy and the first two months after birth. Women were to receive free doctor and midwife care. All working women and those living in low-income families would be obliged to belong to the fund.[64]

The Catholic Center Party, Z (Zentrum), at times the linchpin in the legislative coalitions, shared socialists' disgust with the abuse of women's employment. Catholics, too, advocated protective laws for working women such as no night work and a reduced workday, but from diametrically opposite assumptions. They held up an idealized concept of motherhood and sought protection as an interim solution to the eventual abolition of female labor, at least in the factories.

Central to Catholic ideology was a traditional vision of role divisions that placed men outside and women inside the home. Women's true, natural, God-given role was to be a mother and care for children. Nothing provoked Catholic ire more than the statistics documenting the growth in married women's employment. The married woman, they said time and again in the Reichstag, should be in the home performing her natural tasks. If a family needed assistance, the wife could become a domestic in someone else's home. Employment, it appears, was appropriate as long as it was confined within the four walls of a family's home. Ideally, even the young girl and certainly the young wife should not work because the family too easily would become accustomed to additional income. Beginning in the 1890s, the Center party fought a lone and unsuccessful campaign to banish married women from the labor force. Their views, however, had an impact. In the Catholic Rhineland, for example, the proportion of married women employed at the turn of the century was considerably lower than in the eastern German provinces.[65] Catholics kept their pressure up until World War I, bluntly asking which was being valued, the profit of the employer or the health and sanctity of the family?

With pious sentiments and considerable rhetoric, the government, the conservatives, and the two liberal parties answered, "both." They argued that a distinction between married and single women was impractical, would disrupt German industry, and would cause untold hardships in working-class homes. They sought to balance the needs of German industry with, they said, the needs of the individual family: neither could do without female labor. Conservatives feared that too thorough control of women's employment in industry would affect their interests. The regulations might be extended to agriculture that depended on women's "delicate, gentle hands."[66] Conservatives agreed that ideally women should be finding their work at home. In their scheme, domestic industry had great potential because it permitted females to perform their motherly tasks while bringing in added income. They went so far as to advocate that the factory inspectors work to promote a shift to the home industries.[67] National liberals were concerned with the impact of protective laws on workers' productivity.[68]

In the 1880s, during the era of Bismarck's social policies, the Reichstag was won over to some protection for working women. Two related motives combined to insure this step. First, the ruling groups feared that socialists would reap political advantage from unregulated female labor. A conservative deputy in the Reichstag openly expressed this concern. He stated that socialists came to villages in which industry used women for night shifts and "people no longer vote[d] conservative." Indeed, "the seat of extensive female labor is the Social Democratic stronghold: Vogtland, Wupperthal, Breslau, Leipzig, Magdeburg, Nuremberg."[69] The second motive reflected German paternalism; lawmakers felt that certain jobs and certain conditions simply were not compatible with "womanhood." This attitude had its obverse side in the desire to minimize disruptions in the working-class family by placating the male worker so he would be less inclined to criticize existing conditions. The protective laws applied to working women in industry; generally, they left domestic industry and rural or service employment unregulated. They were carefully designed so as not to inhibit German competitiveness in the world market.

In 1891, an Imperial Industrial Code was promulgated that included provisions for factory working women. The maximum workday was set at eleven hours, women were not permitted to work beyond five-thirty on Saturdays and before holidays; they received a one-hour mandatory noon break, and an extra half-hour for married women "on request" (subsequent reports claimed that married women were too timid to make use of the provision). A four-week rest period after birth was made compulsory; this was extended to six weeks in 1903. An amendment of 1911 granted women two weeks paid leave in the last stages of pregnancy. Germany stood at the forefront in Europe for protection of working mothers.[70]

Throughout the Wilhelmine period, additional protective legislation applicable to specific industries was passed. For example, laws regulated conditions in brickmaking, sandblasting, and glassmaking; they forbade night labor in the ready-made garment industry in 1897, and set a maximum workday in food processing during the season.[71] In 1910, night work was prohibited in industry and the maximum workday was set at ten hours. (By then, workers' unions had won an average workday of nine and a half hours in industry.) Five years earlier, the Bern International Congresss for Workers' Protection, to which Germany subscribed, had advocated the end of women's employment at night. Prior to the promulgation of the law, the German government conducted a detailed survey to determine what impact the prohibition and reduction of the workday would have on the German textile industry in relation to its competitors in Italy, Belgium, Austria-Hungary, and Switzerland. A positive conclusion secured a green light for the law.[72]

The protective laws were not well received in the working class. They implied short-term hardship, reduction of wages, changing work patterns, and in some cases, even loss of job and search for employment elsewhere, perhaps under less favorable conditions in domestic industry. Accounts from the Rhineland after 1891, for example, indicated that workers accepted the prohibition of child labor in factories (later reports showed that children went into unregulated domestic industry), but raised numerous complaints at the shorter workday for grown women. Overall, the daily wage was reduced except in weaving. In the latter occupation, "zealous and punctual" work (more intensive labor) secured for women the same pay.[73] Marie Juchacz, a prominent socialist feminist, described the confused response of working women in the garment industry to the restriction of night labor. After an illness incapacitated her father, Juchacz had gone into the factory. "First, I spun, then worked on a machine that sealed finished nets. . . . We worked day and night. I still remember with horror, the misery of this night work. . . . The factory employed only women. . . . Suddenly, a few young boys were employed to be trained by the most skillful women. The women inquired why the boys were hired and were told that from a certain date, all night work would be taken over by them. The women became excited . . . and were angry that such a law, detrimental to [their interests], was being passed."[74]

A final verdict on special labor laws for women has yet to be reached. Many contemporary feminists find them inherently suspect, "protecting" women from prime jobs and overtime pay as well as being unduly patronizing. These assertions usually give scant attention to the extent of enforcement or the impact of the laws on women's work.[75] A good case can be made for both the validity and the justice of the socialist position, even though it had its critics among the working masses. The working woman was extremely vulnerable in the late nineteenth and early twentieth centuries, prey both to the mechanisms of the market and to a socialization that inhibited collective action. Whether single or married, she had responsibilities at home as well as in the labor market. German socialist feminism drew a conclusion not too different from the motives put forth for affirmative action in the United States in the 1970s: given social inequalities and age-old discriminatory patterns, women very well might need special privileges to insure their struggle for equal rights.

The laws in Germany neither led to the removal of women from the industrial labor force, as some feared, nor to a change in the character of women's work. Women continued to work for low wages in unskilled, nonchallenging jobs. Work did not alter women's feelings of dependency and inferiority because its basic character was dependent and inferior. The working classes had absorbed notions of role divisions, manifest in skilled workers' pride in keeping their wives at home and in the different occupational expectations for boys and girls in working-class families. As late as 1932, a commentator could remark that women's participation in work had made no dent in the distinction between boys and girls when career objectives were considered.[76]

If women's participation in gainful employment failed to meet socialist expectations, work coupled with motherhood and wifely duties offered ripe potentials for mobilization. The young, single woman was difficult to reach for a labor movement since she viewed work as a transitional stage before marriage. Marriage plus work experience seemed to provide cause for reflection—the stimulus needed for the female to ponder her "stake in the marketplace," role in society, and functions in the family.[77] Yet socialists, too, capitalized on rising prices and reached the woman shopping in the market if not working in the marketplace. They did so via socialist feminism, a dynamic fusion of socialist ideas with the life experience of working-class women in Imperial Germany. The discriminatory laws and negative attitudes toward women's work and worth provided the concrete targets for change. But German socialist feminism was equally a product of the interaction of individual leaders who spearheaded the effort to win over the lower social strata for the class struggle. In the process, the original socialist conception was broadened and deepened to embrace the needs of woman not only as worker but also as wife and mother. The net result was an important milestone in feminist thinking, in the ongoing effort to tie the improvement in the status of women to general social progress.

PART B

SOCIALIST FEMINISM
IN GERMAN SOCIAL DEMOCRACY:
PERSONALITIES AND PERSPECTIVES

FIGURE 1 Emma Ihrer

FIGURE 2 Ottilie Baader

FIGURE 3 SPD Women in Parliament, 1920, with Helene Grünberg
(fourth from left)

FIGURE 4 Gertrud Hanna

FIGURE 5 Clara Zetkin (Set against a Mass Political Rally in Russia)

FIGURE 6 Luise Zietz

FIGURE 7 Lily Braun

FIGURE 8 Marie Juchacz

Socialist feminism was a vision of life for women inherently different from that prescribed by German society. Despite the diversity in tactics and theory in the socialist subculture, it shared certain assumptions. The socialist world view posited that the revolutionary economic changes of industrialization created the preconditions for women to step onto the stage of history as fully active participants. These transformations were expected to offer females broad options and provide the basis for new consciousness and unstereotyped roles. The woman in the labor force automatically broadened her perspective beyond the home, but even the housewife and mother, given rising prices and taxes, tariff wars, and international tensions, could not neglect the external world that profoundly influenced personal life. Thus, within the overriding goals of creating proletarian consciousness and promoting the class struggle, socialist feminists sought to mold a new working-class woman who would be fully aware of her rights and willing to assume responsibilities in public life.

Eight women leaders did the most to shape the socialist feminist alliance in Imperial Germany: Ottilie Baader (1847-1925), Lily (von Gizycki) Braun (1865-1916), Helene Grünberg (1874-1928), Gertrud Hanna (1876-1944), Emma Ihrer (1857-1911), Marie Juchacz (1879-1956), Clara Zetkin (1857-1933), and Luise Zietz (1865-1922). They symbolize alternative strategies on the women's question in Social Democracy. All were feminists in that they sought to advance women's status, but some stressed the path of reform, others revolutionary action, and still others unionization.

Part B explores the nature of the feminist component in socialist thought through the personal histories and interaction of the eight leaders; the same women then figure prominently in the effort to devise feminist tactics explored in part C. Inclusion of biographical materials is prompted by this writer's preference for history with names and faces rather than more abstract and impersonal discussion. By supplementing the leaders' writings with personal data, one can obtain insights into their expectations and hopes for the female sex that are more penetrating than an analysis of the written word alone. These socialist women were prolific writers and expressed themselves in a highly personal style that facilitates the accumulation of biographical material. They sought to mobilize working-class women "by sharing experiences,"[1] and were eager to discuss their own lives as young girls and women at home or in the factories to help relieve isolation and point up the larger social context of their personal development. The biographical approach has the additional advantage of permitting generational differentiation and casting in a personal mold the main themes debated by socialist feminists. What alternative strategies existed among socialist feminists in their common effort to advance the position of women? How far did the feminist vision go? What limits did socialist ideology itself place on the feminist ideals? These questions form the specific themes of part B.

CHAPTER III

EIGHT SOCIALIST FEMINISTS:
DIVERSITY WITHIN UNITY

Socialist feminists shared important characteristics that set them off as a distinct pressure group within German Social Democracy. They were rebels in a double sense, challenging in word and deed traditional concepts of women's place and rejecting the capitalist system as exploitative and dehumanizing. Capitalism, they believed, not only perpetuated but thrived on women's second-class status. Their decision to ally socialism and feminism required that they choose the most effective roles women could play in the struggle for the new society. The leaders shared the need to determine how the cause of women could best be related to the larger political and economic issues. In brief, they were faced with problems of priorities never confronted by male socialists or even by female socialists such as Rosa Luxemburg or Julie Bebel who stood outside the socialist feminist movement.

The careers of the eight women leaders chosen as representatives of socialist feminism reveal considerable diversity in the ways each settled priorities. German Social Democracy allowed wide latitude for women to fight the double battle of socialism and feminism. Just as the movement as a whole divided broadly into two wings—the Party and the Free Trade Unions—so socialist women approached feminist questions as unionists or Party members.

Female unionists such as Emma Ihrer, Helene Grünberg, and Gertrud Hanna were concerned with developing ways and means to organize working women in the existing Free Trade Union structure. They saw female labor as a special category with its own unique requirements. As hard-nosed social analysts, they studied women's place in the labor market so they could gear mobilization tactics to the specific concerns of working women. They were pragmatists intent on achieving immediate gains for working women and thereby improving the conditions of the working class generally. Although they could hold positions within the SPD, as Ihrer and Grünberg did, they were unwilling to subordinate the union movement to the Party.

Women who identified primarily with the Party were determined to stand relatively aloof of the organizational structure. They saw quasi-independence for women as a condition for winning females over to socialism. The women's movement of the Party with its semiautonomous bureaucracy, independent educational institutions, and separate biannual conferences symbolized this position. Party women, with help from female unionists, put together a legislative packet of progressive feminist reforms. They aided unionization and sought to attract the nonemployed working-class female to the socialist cause. After the turn of the century ideological controversies introduced diversity among Party women. Radical socialists such as Clara Zetkin and Ottilie Baader as well as the less militant Luise Zietz were opposed by revisionists such as Lily Braun or reformists such as Marie Juchacz. Each ideological stance carried with it a specific response to the marriage of socialism and feminism as well as assumptions about Party and union ties.

This chapter traces the careers of these eight leaders from the early stirrings of the proletarian women's associations in the 1880s to the ideological antagonisms in the first decades of the twentieth century. As will be seen, the choices of priorities made by the individuals in their common battle to improve the lives of working-class females differed a great deal. At the same time, some of them acted in tandem.

TENTATIVE BEGINNINGS AND DIVERGENT PATHS:
EMMA IHRER AND OTTILIE BAADER,
AND THE YOUNGER TRADE UNIONISTS,
HELENE GRÜNBERG AND GERTRUD HANNA

German socialist women traced their origins back to the trade union movement in the Saxon textile industries. In the 1860s the trades allowed women into unions with men, gave them equal rights and duties in the organization, and upheld the principle of equal pay for equal labor.[1] In the early 1870s, educational and trade associations for working women were founded in cities such as Munich and Frankfurt am Main to promote the intellectual and material interests and rights of their members. The clubs discussed such issues as the nature of women's emancipation and equality, the pressing need to organize employed females, and the competition the capitalist mode of production engendered between male and female workers. Such topics were too sensitive for officials, and the women's close ties with the Social Democratic trade cooperatives also made the police uneasy. Each association was shut down shortly after its foundation as a threat to the "moral and social bases of the [German] nation."[2]

During the period of the anti-Socialist laws, activity shifted largely to Berlin. In the early years of the laws middle-class groups began to organize self-help clubs for working women because the repressive legislation undercut socialist efforts to found their own organizations.[3] Thus, the reemergence of proletarian women's organizations independent of middle-class reformists was an expression of growing dissatisfaction with bourgeois feminism. Emma Ihrer's career in the 1880s typifies efforts of women to step out from under bourgeois influence, while Ottilie Baader's political maturation, largely independent of middle-class feminists, shows the growing impact of socialist ideas on working-class women.

Emma Ihrer came to Berlin from Glatz, Schleswig, in 1881, as part of a wave of urban migration during the price depression of 1873-1896. One observer estimated in the mid-1880s that 950 women per month were pouring into the capital lured by job opportunities.[4] These women resurrected the dying domestic industry system and transformed it into an urban component of the capitalist economy. With the influx of cheap labor, conditions deteriorated, housing proved inadequate, and there was much public discussion of the plight of working women.

Ihrer's father had been a shoemaker, proud of his craft traditions, and she sought work in the ready-made garment industry (*Konfektion*) among the "elite" of working women to support herself and her mother. A sensitive yet determined individual, she was appalled by working and living conditions, and soon joined the ranks of middle-class reformers. She entered the executive committee of an Association for Female Manual Workers, which supported an employment service and set up communal reading and eating rooms. The club refused to take in factory working women but admitted middle-class men and ladies. The effort to reach across class lines proved to be its downfall. Differences in approaching the working women's question were too great to bridge but, as Ihrer later admitted, a lesson had been learned: one could rely only on the self-help of working women to end the exploitation of female labor.[5]

An opportunity to form a purely proletarian women's organization arose from the English crusade against prostitution. Josephine Butler's campaign against state-sanctioned vice in the 1870s had spawned its counterpart in Germany, the Cultural Society, headed by Gertrud Guillaume-Schack. At a public meeting in Berlin that Guillaume-Schack called in 1883 on the morality of working women, females in the audience stressed that wages not morality lay at the root of the question. Ihrer criticized the speaker for offering palliatives not cures, and she found sympathy for her view that morality reflected economic conditions and living standards. The attack should be launched on the character of labor and the "hunger wages" paid by the capitalists. After the meeting, Ihrer met those women who thought as she did, and in 1885 they founded the Association for Working Women, which attracted initially 325 working-class members in the garment industry. Affiliates sprang up throughout the country. Within several months, as the police wryly noted, the association had given money to SPD leaders.[6] The women's organization sought to foster the intellectual and material interests of its members and granted monetary support during wage disputes. It set up commissions to study various branches of industry headed by women who worked in the trades. The members gathered data on conditions of employment, spoke at branch meetings, and sought to spread their views among their work colleagues.

The first major activity of the association consisted of calling meetings to protest a yarn tax. Since workers in domestic industry paid for the raw materials they received from their employers, the tax added an additional burden borne by the hard-pressed workers. Public outcry led to its removal. When Ottilie Baader, a domestic industry seamstress, attended her first public meeting, the issue was the rising price of yarn. She came into contact with Ihrer and soon stood in the center of the proletarian women's movement.[7]

Baader, born in Rackow in Schleswig, had come to Berlin in 1861 when she was thirteen years old with her father and three siblings. Forced to work, she wrote in terms applicable to her working-class sisters that "it was unnecessary to hold a big family council to select the right occupation because at that time there was not much of a choice for girls."[8] Baader became a seamstress, a typical job for young working-class women. She sewed shirts and, to earn extra money, she worked on sleeves and cuffs at night. Ill health caused her to bring the factory into the home. She bought a sewing machine and experienced that fate of home industry workers. "From mornings at six until twelve o'clock evenings, with one hour for lunch, I peddled continuously. I arose, however, at four in the morning to put the house in order and prepare meals. While working, I used a small clock to make sure that one dozen collars took as long as the next to make. . . . That lasted five years. And the years went by without one noticing one's youth or getting anything from life."[9]

During the early 1870s Baader belonged to Lina Morgenstern's Working Women's Club dedicated to raising the intellectual level of its members. She took mathematics, composition, and German, but "not all teachers came on time so we often lost precious Sunday morning hours."[10] Under the anti-Socialist laws, she and her father, a radical democrat who had participated in the Revolution of 1848, observed discrimination against ordinary workers and read up on socialism. "My father read and we discussed the works while I sewed."[11] Acquiring Bebel's book *Women under Socialism* transformed her life. She experienced an almost "religious rebirth," and describes the book's impact as follows:

Life's bitter needs, overwork, and bourgeois family morality had destroyed all joy in me. I lived resigned and without hope. . . . News came of a wonderful book that . . . Bebel . . . had written. Although I was not a Social Democrat, I had friends who belonged to the Party. Through them, I got the precious work. I read it nights through. It was my own fate and that of thousands of my sisters. Neither in the family, nor in public life, had I ever heard of all the pain the woman must endure. One ignored her life. Bebel's book courageously broke with the old secretiveness. . . . I read the book not once, but ten times. Because everything was so new, it took considerable effort to come to terms with Bebel's views. I had to break with so many things that I previously regarded as correct.[12]

The book, she recalled, brought hope and joy to live and fight.

Baader's first official activity was at a trade union meeting of spats workers (*Schäftearbeiter*) where she participated in the discussion. It was so unusual for a woman to speak that she was elected to a committee. With like-minded women, she soon organized the women's section of the union.

The early proletarian women's movement had a trade union rather than political focus, a consequence, in part, of the limitations placed by the anti-Socialist laws and those of assembly. Its concerns were better wages, work conditions, and a maximum workday. While based on a notion of women's "right to work" and, as Ihrer put it in 1886, pride in being working women's (*Arbeiterinnen*) rather than ladies' (*Frauen*) associations,[13] the movement advocated, at the most, equality with male workers but left unanswered under what conditions and by what means. After the end of the discriminatory laws, two broad alternatives for change opened in the socialist labor movement: union or Party activity, and the careers of Ihrer and Baader diverged.

Ihrer came to feel that unions were indispensable for women not only because of the law that hindered political activity (until 1908) but also because women could not wait for favorable legislation in the future. Low wages and long work hours in the present sapped physical and intellectual energy. In the early 1890s she mounted a successful effort to change Free Trade Union statutes to admit and recruit female membership. At the same time she sought to orient the women's movement toward unionization. In contrast, Baader stressed the overarching importance of the political struggle. She emphasized the need to subordinate union activity to the final revolutionary goal or, at least, infuse it with the political spirit of Social Democracy. Only if women became involved in politics could they defend their interests adequately.[14] The two women differed not so much in action, since both worked hard to recruit for the unions, but they placed varying degrees of importance on unionization and had distinctive perceptions of their role. In Ihrer's case, the conflict between loyalties to union and Party remained dormant and she was called on often to mediate between the two camps. Her heirs later found it more difficult to reconcile loyalties. Younger women such as Helene Grünberg accepted leadership positions in both the union and the women's political movements and found their roles in conflict. Still others, such as Gertrud Hanna, sought to resolve the dilemma by devoting themselves exclusively to trade union activity. Both Grünberg and Hanna, too, symbolized a more general phenomenon in German Social Democracy of "organizational fetishism,"[15] a position opposed to any tactic that might threaten organizational integrity at either the Party or union level. Thus, they came to resist the drive toward revolution as inimical to stability.

Information on Helene Grünberg's background is scarce.[16] Of working-class origin, she was a seamstress for a Berlin apparel firm, Gerson's, and worked on women's suits, including original models. She joined the Tailors Union in 1896. The union was progressive on women's questions and had early recognized the need to unionize working women in part because female labor made up such a large component of the garment industry. In 1890, it had passed the first in a series of resolutions calling on the recruitment committees to actively organize women. Grünberg's move into the union coincided with the largest strike by working women in the garment trade prior to World War I. Unlike many of her colleagues who joined temporarily, she soon played an important role in the Berlin local. Elected in 1898 as auditor, she coupled that function with the more "feminine" task of preparing the union's parties and festivities.[17]

In 1905, Grünberg applied for a job in Nuremberg as working woman's secretary in the workers' secretariat. The job carried a salary and offered a challenge. The structure of the Nuremberg industries, mainly light manufacture calling for a great deal of seasonal work, favored the employment of women. The numbers of female employees had nearly doubled in the years between 1895 and 1907; yet, in 1904, only 3 percent of working women had been unionized.[18] The Nuremberg workers' secretariat unanimously chose Grünberg to oversee efforts to reach the employed women. She was the first female to hold a position in any of these local union organizations in Germany. Shortly after her appointment, she helped found a women's movement branch and was elected political representative (Vertrauensperson).

Grünberg was sensitive to the union chain of command often at the expense of her role in the women's movement. "Strong unions are the field on which we can securely build our future," she said, expressing her basic philosophy.[19] She was disturbed by the continuous expansion of unskilled female labor that, she felt, was prey to the mechanisms of the market. In her scheme, unionization was the only effective answer to the exploitation of working women. Union life offered them concrete, immediate advantages—better wages and work conditions—as well as educational opportunities for needed labor skills. She stressed time and again the importance of the organization for helping women give meaning to their lives.

The Bavarian milieu influenced Grünberg's approach to political questions. Bavaria was the seat of reformism in the SPD. Less industrialized than Prussia and characterized by fewer class antagonisms, Bavaria seemed to offer the SPD a unique opportunity to effect change through alliances with other parties. Although collaboration was condemned by national SPD congresses, the Bavarian Social Democratic Party won minimum reforms by allying itself with the Catholic Center Party against the liberal oligarchy and later by joining the liberals in an effort to oust the Catholics.[20] The Bavarian setting permitted Grünberg to follow her moderate and cautious inclinations in political matters. Her job as union secretary limited her purview to daily, practical questions and she brought both her pragmatism and circumspection to her role as women's movement leader. Grünberg became the most outspoken, though provincial, reform socialist in the women's organization.

In 1909, Gertrud Hanna was appointed working women's secretary in the Free Trade Union executive, the general commission. She epitomized the organizational woman more concerned with immediate results than future goals—Robert Michels's technocrat whose whole education and training was in the union hierarchy.[21] Her career as a unionist who never held a political post points up growing specialization among socialist women prior to World War I. Yet, she attended the second International socialist women's conference in Copenhagen in 1910 to discuss the activity of the union secretary. Her presence symbolized one side of the dual effort to mobilize working-class women.

Hanna was a printer's aid in Berlin from the age of fourteen. She came up through the Printers' Aids Union to assume her new position in the general commission. She had acquired considerable skill in union administration as a member of the executive committee. Self-taught, hard-working, and endowed with a mind for concrete social and economic analysis, she was both typical and atypical of her proletarian sisters. On the one hand, she shared with many working-class women an impoverished background, minimum schooling, and an unskilled job subordinate to skilled male workers. On the other, her membership in the union had opened up opportunities for advancement, both intellectually and materially, which she cherished and utilized to the fullest.

The union in which Hanna had acquired her expertise was "an elite organization,"[22] and an active training ground for several other prominent women in the trade union movement: Paula Thiede, its president, Gertrud Lodahl, the secretary, Clara Bien, and Frau Teske. The central Printers' Aids Union stood at the forefront of organizational experimentation and was hailed as a model for other unions with large numbers of women members. Contrary to Free Trade Union practice, its dues were scaled to wages regardless of sex. Officials recognized that in many large cities such as Berlin, working women received higher pay than did men in the same job in small towns and villages. They realized that the traditional view echoed by most Free Trade Unions—working women had "fewer needs" and therefore, uniformly received less pay— was not born out by the facts. The union offered unemployment insurance, and after 1908, a special maternity insurance. The job referral bureau coupled with carefully planned pressure tactics accounted for the nine-hour workday the union won in 1896 and for a continuous increase in pay for its members and regulated overtime. Year after year when business flourished, the union presented its demands to the printing firms, which had to meet contracts, and alternately engaged in small one- or two-day strikes. Employers found it difficult to engage strike breakers since some skill was required of printers' aids. In 1909, the central Printers' Aids Union had 8,348 female and 6,377 male members. According to the 1907 census, about 26,000 women were employed in the book and allied printing industry. The union had recruited an impressive 30 to 32 percent of the women in the period 1906-1909.[23]

Hanna joined the first Berlin local of Printers' Aids in 1893 after working three years oblivious to its existence. The woman at the job referral agency chided her for disregarding the plight of her fellow workers in the industry. As Hanna later recounted, this gave her quite a shock and penetrated her consciousness.[24] Against the wishes of her parents, who failed to see the importance of unionization for their daughter, she soon became active in union life.

For eighteen years, Hanna's local was female in both membership and leadership, an anomaly among the sexually integrated Free Trade Unions. In 1890, it had rejected merger with its male counterpart and worked under the banner "march divided and fight united."[25] It was a dynamic branch, one of the first to develop a shop-steward system, and it jealously sought to preserve sexual exclusiveness. The local provided an extremely supportive milieu in which women learned leadership, administrative, and mobilization skills. It offered members continuous education in special courses and the rank and file were regarded as among the most capable and self-assured within the whole trade union hierarchy.[26] These female unionists were vigilant guardians of union autonomy, champions of gradualist reform tactics, and often outspoken critics of Party women and particularly of the radical socialists who formed a leadership wing in the women's movement.

RADICAL FORMULATIONS:
CLARA ZETKIN AND LUISE ZIETZ

Radical socialists coalesced around Clara Eissner Zetkin who became the leading theoretician and schoolmistress of the socialist women's movement. Self-proclaimed "inveterate Marxist,"[27] she was born in Saxony into a progressive middle-class home that was surrounded by the insecurity of domestic industry weavers facing industrial competition. Her early introduction to poverty made her sensitive to the human side of economic growth as did her later schooling in Leipzig, which, in the 1870s, was in the throes of industrialization. Clara Eissner showed a strong independent character, in de Beauvoir's scheme, escaping from "female servitude" by reading and by sibling rivalry with her brother.[28] Her parents channeled her talents toward the typical middle-class profession of teaching. Other occupations were closed to women of her social class. In 1872, the family moved to Leipzig, in part, to enhance the educational and career opportunities of the children. Through her mother's contacts with the bourgeois feminist movement, Clara was admitted to Auguste Schmidt's teachers' seminar. In 1865, Schmidt, a prominent champion of women's rights, had helped found the National German Women's Association. Although Clara looked back with warmth on her early contact with bourgeois feminism, the seminar failed to still her preoccupation with the root causes of social inequalities.[29]

In the 1870s Leipzig was the seat of the nascent socialist movement. Socialist ideas seemed to answer some of her questions, but not until contacting a group of Russian emigrés and students did Clara Eissner commit herself to Social Democracy. The decision was aided by one student, Ossip Zetkin from Odessa, who helped place her new commitment in a sound theoretical framework. He loaned her books by Marx and Engels, clarified aspects of scientific socialism, and encouraged her to live with workers to bridge the gap in social classes.[30] During the period of the anti-Socialist laws, the new convert collected money for the victims and supported herself by teaching. The decision to embrace socialism carried with it personal and financial sacrifice, a break with family, relatives or friends, and a semi-outlaw status in society. The sacrifices were greatest for those of the upper or middle classes, and Clara found herself isolated from her former bourgeois world. Yet even working-class members and women in particular were not immune to hostility and opposition similar to that encountered by Hanna when she announced her decision to join a union.

In 1881, with the declaration of martial law in Leipzig, Ossip Zetkin was exiled. Persuading Clara to follow him, he went to Paris, the home of the Commune, and joined socialist emigré circles there. Clara left Leipzig the next year, detoured through Austria, Italy, and Switzerland, and in late 1882, joined Ossip in Paris where they lived together in common-law marriage and had two sons. Her letters to Karl Kautsky, chief theoretician of Orthodox Marxism in the SPD, and to Eduard Bernstein, whom she had met in Switzerland, reveal the tension she experienced with her dual roles as worker and mother. Clara complained of poverty and the miserable Bohemian life: "I am the court's tailor, cook, cleaning lady . . . in short, 'girl friday.' To that, add two sons who leave me not a minute's peace."[31]

To support themselves the Zetkins free-lanced, Clara tutored, and they were, at the same time, active in political life. With Marx's daughter, Laura Lafargue, Clara began to recruit Parisian working women for socialism. Both Zetkins fell ill from overwork, Ossip mortally, "a reaction of nature against the years-long irregular emigrant life."[32] Clara's mother, learning of her bad health, offered reconciliation and a trip to Leipzig to recuperate. The journey proved decisive. She contacted her old comrades and met Wilhelm Liebknecht, who with August Bebel had founded the German Social Democratic Party in 1869. She spoke at secret meetings, and wrote enthusiastically about illegal party activity and particularly about women's growing role in the movement: "The German workers, speaking of the Leipzig comrades, are splendid fellows; as I got to know their life and work so intimately, for the first time in my life, I was proud to be German. What gave me the most joy was that women are being drawn more and more into the movement. I met quite a large number of women . . . distributing brochures, flyers, and election appeals. Most comrades see participation and activity of women no longer as a nice convenience, but as practical necessity. Quite a transformation in attitudes since I left Germany."[33] Returning to Paris, she assumed the whole burden of providing for the household, nursed Ossip until his death in 1889, and helped prepare for the founding congress of the Second International.

Zetkin had been elected *in absentia* by German proletarian women to represent them at the Paris congress along with Emma Ihrer. Her writings from France in the late 1880s had been read and debated in the women's education and trade associations in Germany. The SPD leadership had even promoted her reputation by dispensing her work throughout the country. The leaders were worried that their nascent working women's organizations were not "sufficiently socialist," i.e., too oriented toward bread-and-butter issues. They had hoped that Zetkin's articles would provide the necessary clarity and focus for a "true" understanding of women's emancipation.[34] At the congress, both she and Ihrer established the union of socialism and feminism—Zetkin dealt with the women's question analytically and Ihrer translated theory into organizational strategy—and they called on their male colleagues to adopt wholeheartedly the cause of women's equality. International socialism was being directed toward the goal of women's liberation.

Zetkin's active participation at the International congress enhanced her reputation and when she returned to Germany after the lapse of the anti-Socialist laws, her mission seemed clear. She would put at the service of socialism the often "unrecognized" and "untapped" energies of women, clarify and deepen their socialist commitment, and weld them to the class struggle.[35] From her base in Stuttgart, she began to establish contact with socialist women who were surfacing throughout the country after 1890.

Despite her talents, reputation, and political experience, Zetkin's sex consigned her at first to the fringe of socialist activity as a free-lance writer for the socialist press.[36] Not until late 1891, when she was asked to become editor of *Die Arbeiterin* (Working Woman), an early proletarian woman's paper founded and personally financed by Ihrer, did she embark on a challenging role. Zetkin transformed the paper into *Gleichheit* and, for twenty-five years, used her editorial position to secure power and influence. In line with her first love, the paper's major task became the political awakening of readers and their schooling in socialist theory. The semimonthly publication untiringly differentiated between socialist and bourgeois feminists, socialist and bourgeois goals and tactics, and it related socialist theory to tactics and the movement's reform proposals to theory. The socialist world view and the class struggle were its lodestars and the ultimate gauge on which all events and actions were judged. As she would explain to Wilhelm Dittmann, her friend and supporter, she was concerned with the larger theoretical questions and the interrelationship of theory and the social fabric; she was less attracted to immediate reform proposals.[37]

To provide the theoretical framework for propaganda and mobilization, Zetkin drew up a socialist theory of women's liberation in 1896. The SPD Gotha Congress that year adopted her formulation of socialist feminism. The theory synthesized ideas that she had been working on since publication of an 1889 essay on *Die Arbeiterinnen- und Frauenfrage der Gegenwart* (Working Women's and the [General] Women's Question in the Present).[38] Her analysis was based on Engels (*Origin of the Family, Private Property and the State* [1884]); on Bachoven and Morgan, who provided the basis for Engels's work; on her readings of Marx, which included *Capital*, *Communist Manifesto*, and *Holy Family*; and to a certain extent, on Bebel's *Women under Socialism*. Yet, as late as 1897, Zetkin expressed dissatisfaction with Bebel's "Frau" (as *Women under Socialism* was called affectionately by German workers), claiming it contained ideas not carried to their logical conclusion.[39] The book was, in part, too feminist for Zetkin, who was seeking to lodge her group comfortably in the socialist mansion. It contained divisive ideas for a movement joining working-class males and females together in one united struggle. Bebel's failure, for example, to dramatize class differences among women, his willingness to tolerate working-class and middle-class collaboration on issues affecting females, and his statement (from Zetkin's perspective heretical indeed) that "in fighting for their rights, women should expect as little help from the men as working men do from the capitalist class" could make the Zetkin wing, seeking to build a class-based feminist organization, uneasy. For tactical as well as ideological reasons, radical socialists sought to minimize conflicts within working-class homes. To be sure, socialist feminism was infused with historical materialism but its ideas and strategies were a product, too, of hard experience of the 1880s and tactical considerations after the lapse of the anti-Socialist laws. Moreover, as subsequent chapters will demonstrate, it went beyond its ideological fathers in the understanding of women, their potentials, and their contribution to the class struggle.

According to Zetkin, women's oppression was not a modern phenomenon. Following in Engels's footsteps, she traced its origins back to the emergence of private property. Male egoism and strength and female dependency during pregnancy assured that patriarchy and its corollary, monogamy, would triumph over matriarchy once revolutionary economic transformations (the emergence of surplus in the ancient world) gave economic impetus to male domination. Matriarchy was equated with primitive communism, and socialist feminism expressed a circular view of history. It envisioned a return to communism that would give back to women their rights, although the new society would be based on greater control over nature and more prosperity than its primitive variety. This relationship between matriarchy and communism served to instill pride in female socialists, as evidenced in Bebel's work.[40]

If women's oppression had a long history, the women's question was modern and involved the convulsion of the very foundation of women's existence: the family. Until the modern age, Zetkin said, the stages of economic development had harmonized with women's functions at home. Industrialization, however, was revolutionizing women's world, and dialectically, generating the forces that would solve the problem of sex oppression. In socialist analysis, women's oppression was a function of prevailing property relations. It was assumed, naively with hindsight, that by socializing the means of production and thereby creating new consciousness, sex discrimination shorn of its material root would automatically cease.[41]

Zetkin stressed the point that the impact of economic change varied with the women's class status. Females in each social strata (upper, middle, and lower) had specific and distinct needs that precluded a common struggle based on sex. She argued as follows: the emancipation movement among upper- and middle-class women pitted them against men. Upper-class wives sought the right to control property, while bourgeois women, tired of being "dolls in a doll house," demanded entrance into the so-called free professions. Zetkin expressed sympathy with these demands, particularly in light of the weak liberal tradition in Germany. In fact, she said, German liberals feared all reforms because the proletariat might be the main beneficiary. Thus, Social Democracy had to step in to champion women's rights. Yet she was quick to point out that sympathy was a far cry from collaboration with

bourgeois women. Socialists had one main task: to demonstrate that conflicting interests existed between capitalists
on the one hand and workers of both sexes on the other, not
between working-class men and women. She then called on
socialists to organize working-class men and women together
in unions, and, where legal, in the Party.[42]

When Zetkin presented this formulation to the Gotha Congress, it was the first and last time that the women's question
came up before the SPD congresses as a theoretical issue. In
subsequent years, women's suffrage was stressed at one point,
maternity insurance at another; the call for day care or communal laundry service was then added to the list of socialist
feminist demands; occasionally male colleagues challenged
basic tenets that resulted in a flurry of activity underscoring
the theoretical validity of a belief. Gotha, however, had
created an official interpretation of the women's question that
became one hallmark of radical Party members in their
ideological battles against reformists and revisionists.

A second hallmark of the radical socialist position in the
women's movement was a definition of the relationship between Party and Free Trade Unions. From the socialist perspective, it harnessed both organizations in the service of the
revolution, rejecting unionization as a goal in itself. From the
feminist, it harnessed persons from both groups into a joint
mobilization of their common female constituency. By 1895,
Zetkin in *Gleichheit* had reconciled, in theory at least, the efforts of both wings, but not before several years of an extremely tense relationship.

After the end of the anti-Socialist laws, Party women had
raised two specific questions concerning unionization. First,
what promise did unions hold for the proletarian class struggle
in general? Second, what did they offer the employed woman?
In the early 1890s, Clara Zetkin answered the first negatively
and the second much more positively. Reflecting dominant
Party sentiment, she interpreted the class struggle in political
terms. Only a party committed to the principle of class struggle insured the destruction of capitalism.[43] Unions could not
break the chains that held the working class down. Nonethe-

less, the trade union movement performed several important functions. It offered workers "more bread, more time, more freedom," and awakened feelings of solidarity and class consciousness. Within socialist strategy, the economic struggle had crucial political byproducts. In Zetkin's view, the unions were to concentrate on winning over the indifferent masses, and above all, the woman wage earner. Unorganized women, competitors of men and potential strike breakers, threatened proletarian efforts to improve work conditions. Women, unenlightened, exploited, overburdened, were helped by unionization.[44] The dual nature of Zetkin's appeal was typical of the women's efforts to obtain a greater practical commitment from Social Democracy: they stressed both socialist self-interest and the inherent justice of easing women's existence.

Although attitudes toward the unions were ambivalent in the early 1890s, they became more favorable by the middle of the decade. The shift among Party women, in part, mirrored their preoccupation with the plight of working-class women who were hampered politically in joining forces because of the laws of association. Usually sharp and biting toward opponents, Zetkin had adopted a surprisingly moderate tone in the debate over the role of the unions in the struggle for socialism. In mid-decade *Gleichheit* noted that the proletariat waged its struggle not only in the political, but also the economic spheres. Shortly thereafter, the journal carried a clear statement that foreshadowed theoretical reconciliation of both political and union tactics: "The working-class movement is one and indivisible even if . . . it confronts us in two streams; the proletarian class struggle is undivided, even if it is conducted by the Party in the political sphere and by the unions in the economic sphere."[45] Radical socialist women had come to see the political and union battle as twin means to promote the revolutionary class struggle. As will be seen, these leaders steadfastly adhered to the harmony between both wings and an identity of views on goals despite mounting evidence to the contrary.

The women who maintained adherence to the 1896 theory of women's liberation, and to the definition of union and Party relationship worked out by the mid-decade, comprised an effective leadership group for over ten years under the suzerainty of Clara Zetkin. Given the unanimity a movement tries to present to the outside world, it is difficult to identify Zetkin's supporters. Primarily, they were women active in Berlin. Sources refer to "the Berlin comrades" as if they formed a well-defined group. Time and again, *Gleichheit* credited both Zetkin and "the Berliners" with various decisions, new proposals, and plans affecting the women's movement into the early twentieth century. Berlin women and Zetkin were at the forefront of all major policy formulations throughout the period. For example, in 1894, they had successfully promoted adoption of the representative system (*Vertrauensperson*) because the police had been disbanding their propaganda committees time and again for pursuing political aims. In addition, Berliners obtained a dominant position in the bureaucratic structure that was created at the first national conference of the women's movement held in Mainz in 1900.[46] Not all socialist activists in the capital, however, belonged to the small inner circle. Most Berlin female unionists remained outside, whereas Luise Zietz, based in Hamburg until 1908, Marie Wackwitz in Dresden, Marie Greifenberg in Bavaria, and Käthe Duncker in Stuttgart, supported their ideological sisters in Berlin. A minimum list of Zetkin followers includes the following Berliners: Ottilie Baader, Margaret Wengels, Klara Haase Weyl, Mathilde Wurm, Frida Wulff, and Agnes Fahrenwald.

Baader, "by nature, soft and acquiescent," looked to Zetkin for moral support, used Zetkin's name to add authority to her proposals, and carefully orchestrated the speakers' lists at the women's biannual conferences to insure a radical orientation.[47] She was women's representative in the fourth Berlin district in the mid-1890s, Berlin central representative in 1899, and national central representative of German Social Democratic women during the eight years prior to their incorporation into the SPD. Margaret Wengels, active in the Berlin propaganda committee in the early 1890s, became Berlin central representative in 1897 and 1898 and head of Berlin women after Baader took up the national post.[48] Klara Haase Weyl was prominent in the sixth Berlin district, founded women's clubs, and participated in various Berlin committees and provincial SPD meetings. Mathilde Wurm, from the second Berlin district, and Frida Wulff and Agnes Fahrenwald, both active in the fourth district, were elected at times to official posts in the Berlin women's movement.[49] To speak, as a recent scholar does, of a team of agitators that emerged between 1890 and 1895, and continued after 1900, gives an exaggerated impression of cohesion.[50] In reality, there was a coalescence of various power groups, some relatively stable reflecting a basic ideological consensus, and others more ephemeral, joining with the inner circle over a particular issue.

The inner group formed a "united front" and collaborated in relative harmony until around 1908. At that time, a split became evident. Typifying a less militant radical position on socialist and feminist issues was Luise Zietz, who sat on the national executive committee after women entered the Party in 1908. Zietz's position of "responsibility" in the Party leadership seemed to act as a moderating force that tamed her radical bent. After 1908, she was more and more hesitant to act independently and against executive wishes. In 1911, for example, she publicly supported the executive committee in the Moroccan controversy, and in 1913, on the two key issues of financing the military budget and supporting a call for the mass strike, she did not vote "radical." She was also increasingly unwilling to collide with male leaders over the feminist demand for quasi-autonomous status within the Party. Zetkin recognized her cooptation when she chided Zietz during World War I saying, "The famous German discipline has two sides, one of which can become very questionable."[51]

Contemporaries observed that Luise Zietz's most outstanding characteristic was her vitality. She was totally animated by hatred of the established capitalist system. Daughter of a handicraft weaver in Schleswig threatened with mechanization, she had helped her father, as was seen in chapter two, with his pathetic battle against mechanical looms. Her childhood was one of poverty and despair and "remained a shadow over the rest of her life, but also the spur that drove her forward."[52] In 1879, at fourteen years of age, she had moved to Hamburg and worked as a maid. Resenting the lack of free time, she became a factory worker and chose cigarette production, attracted to the industry because of the flexible hours. There, she had time, at least, for her major preoccupation: reading. Consumed by a desire for learning, she entered the Fröbel school for kindergarten teachers. In 1885, Luise married a dockworker, Karl Zietz, and, through him, contacted members of the SPD. Her personal experience with deprivation had predisposed her to study social problems, and among the socialists she found sympathy for her ideas. According to Robert Michels, when Karl recognized the oratorical and organizational talents of his wife, they held a conference and he stated that she, as the more gifted, ought to devote full time to the Party while he would continue to work.[53]

Zietz rose to national prominence during a harbor strike that wracked Hamburg in 1896-1897. Together with Helma Steinbach, she mobilized the wives and daughters of dock workers to support the strike and became convinced of the importance of women in the fight for socialism and of the need to create political solidarity in working-class homes. She successfully demonstrated her agitational talents and effectiveness as a speaker during the trying months. From then on, Zietz was recruited to speak before meetings by Party and union groups throughout Germany. Her long-time friend, Wilhelm Dittmann, described their first encounter. As district head for East Holstein, he invited Zietz to address a gathering. "The meeting was attended by many people from the city and nearby villages. It was a sensation that a woman spoke in public. Zietz spoke with such fire and conviction. . . . [P]roletarian pride . . . radiated from her. . . ."[54] She became women's representative in Hamburg in 1900, a position she held until 1906 when the local executive committee incorporated the semiautonomous post into the Hamburg Party against the women's wishes.

Zietz's experience in Hamburg illustrates the problem of

translating the socialist principle of women's equality into practice. In Hamburg, females could join political organizations. They chose, however, to preserve their freedom of action in the representative system that operated largely outside the jurisdiction of the Party. Time and again, Zietz encountered the outspoken hostility of her male colleagues. She complained that leading men had accused her of accepting the women's post simply to get a guaranteed mandate to the SPD congresses. She said that when she was sent to the Stuttgart Congress in 1898, for example, male colleagues declared it was a scandal that a woman represented the first electoral district (of Hamburg).[55] Many other women, too, could document cases in which the official commitment of Social Democracy to women's equality remained a dead letter.

POLITICAL CHALLENGES:
LILY BRAUN AND MARIE JUCHACZ

Between 1896 and 1914, radical socialist women prevented groups with different visions from mounting a successful opposition, but several changes served to bring the radical formulation into question. First, a number of socialist feminists saw progressive currents emerging in the middle-class feminist camp as opportunities for cooperation. The development of an ideologically fortified right-wing in German Social Democracy reinforced this line of thinking. Second, as the organized working class turned toward advocating social reform in general, it entered a realm populated by bourgeois reformers, and limited collaboration on specific issues appeared desirable. Third, the day-to-day activity in the Party and unions coupled with an expanding bureaucratic apparatus undercut the delicate ends-means relationship that radicals sought to preserve. People in official positions acted with limited reference to the end goal of socialist revolution. As the divisions in 1917 show, in the broadest terms Social Democrats became split between those seeking revolution and those advocating reform as the most effective way to bring about the new society and with it meaningful roles for women.[56]

The radical leadership wing in the women's movement faced a number of challenges. One proved highly disruptive though only temporarily. Between 1897 and 1903, Lily Braun waged an unsuccessful campaign to encourage cooperation with middle-class feminists as well as to promote reforms geared specifically toward improving women's social position. She was a lone voice and, in defeating Braun, radicals banished the most outspoken advocate of tactical change in the prewar women's movement. The second threat was less visible although ultimately more damaging to radical principles. It came from a broad-based group of younger pragmatic women who had grown up in the movement. An examination of the career of Marie Juchacz, typical of the second-generation leadership, reveals a subtle change in consciousness that undermined the theory and practice of women's emancipation as formulated by Clara Zetkin.

Lily Braun was a most unlikely candidate for Social Democracy. She was a nobleman's daughter and granddaughter of Baroness Jenny von Gustedt, a friend of Goethe and a member of a literary circle in Weimar. Braun wrote in her memoirs that her first childhood experiences were of Sanssouci Park where she played with the children of Crown Prince Frederick. The formative influence on her early development came from her grandmother, a humanist with a strong social conscience, and activist who impressed her granddaughter with the importance of doing something meaningful in life.[57] In her recollections, Braun described herself as a rather lonely, restless child who never quite fit into aristocratic circles. The distance from her social class was sealed in 1890 when Kaiser Wilhelm II refused to promote her father, Hans von Kretschman, to commanding general, apparently retaliating for a series of slights during mock army maneuvers. Von Kretschman resigned his command immediately, and the sudden shift in fortune and social standing affected Lily greatly. Her family, she said, suffered "tremendous embarrassment."[58] The humiliation must have contributed to Lily's sense of alienation from her class. The family moved to Berlin where von Kretschman went into politics, writing for a conservative journal that opposed the Kaiser's "new course." Lily was forced to work, first as a seamstress, but she soon succumbed to the lure of the pen and wrote on Goethe's circle for the yearbook of the Goethe Society. In her own words, however, "I wasn't suited to be an historian."[59] The need to make not just write history proved more compelling.

Meeting Georg von Gizycki, a philosophy professor in Berlin, changed the course of her life. Von Gizycki, a nonconformist in academic circles, leaned toward socialism but based his view on ethical foundations rather than economic determinism. He never accepted the concept class struggle and sought a more equitable social order founded on universal ethical principles. In the early 1890s, he helped establish the German branch of the Ethical Culture Society. Von Gizycki edited the club's weekly newspaper, *Ethische Kultur*, and after his friendship with Lily deepened, brought her onto the editorial board. This position gave her economic independence and security. Over the objections of her family to the crippled man, Lily married von Gizycki in 1893 and experienced a highly fruitful though short-lived relationship terminated in 1895 by his death. In a letter, she assessed his importance to her: "You have opened up a new world for me. . . . You are the first living person I encountered who treated me as a human being and not as an illiterate woman. . . ."[60]

Von Gizycki introduced Lily to socialist publications and gave her special instruction on contemporary politics and modern literature. Together, as she described it in her memoirs, they read and discussed Marx's *Capital* and concentrated on questions of wages, work conditions, and prices. He took a progressive stand on the women's question and encouraged Lily to learn about feminism, giving her the works of Mill, Condorcet, and Bebel. Through his support, she became active in the Berlin radical bourgeois feminist club *Frauenwohl* (Women's Welfare). Contact with socialists and Marxist literature, however, convinced her that bourgeois women engaged in Sisyphean labor. At a public meeting in 1896, she declared that middle-class goals profited only a small number of women while they left the "mass of suffering women untouched."[61] She also warned that bourgeois antipathy toward Social Democracy "had led to stagnation in our bourgeois women's movement,"[62] and criticized middle-class leaders' hesitancy to adopt radical reforms for fear of being identified in the public mind with socialists. In a telling debate with a former colleague, Wilhelm Foerster, president of the German Ethical Culture Society, Braun explained her decision to embrace socialism. She wrote that had she compassion only, she would have remained a reformer. Deliberate study and personal experience, however, had convinced her that middle-class reformers, no matter how radical, failed to attack the roots of the problem and offered mere palliatives, "bandaids for festering wounds." She proclaimed, "My position is that each of my former class comrades . . . who is serious about freeing humanity from economic and moral oppression must become a Social Democrat."[63]

A socialist from basically humanitarian concerns, Braun rejected the class biases of the socialist world view. Historical materialism, with its claim to scientific objectivity, likewise was alien to her. She eagerly embraced Eduard Bernstein's *Evolutionary Socialism*, first published in 1898, and became an ethical revisionist, closer on the ideological spectrum to reformers than to radicals. She wrote that the "cool, clarity of [his] arguments had a crushing effect" and henceforth, it became "a matter of intellectual integrity" to examine Marxist principles critically.[64] With her second husband, Heinrich Braun, a socialist writer and publicist, she stressed the importance of social reform based on careful investigation of existing social relations and conditions. Concrete historical research of the roots and evolution of social life coupled with clear understanding of socialist ideals were required for political action.[65]

Lily Braun shared with reform socialists the belief that practical, immediate reforms of the present society provided preconditions for the emergence of socialism, which would banish misery and inequity from the world. She diverged subtly from them, however, in her unrelenting critique of sex discrimination and offered novel solutions to the problem of women's oppression. Her feminism leaned toward sex not class identity and included willingness to work with middle-class feminists for common goals, a strategy that was anathema to radical socialists. In general, reform women, too, were more inclined to collaborate with bourgeois feminists. Bereft of ideological tools, however, these pragmatists generally adopted more modest interpretations of women's roles and potentials in the Party and in public life, although on specific issues they could be radically feminist. In prewar Germany, the reform cohort chafed under Zetkin's revolutionary and international stance, but after the SPD disintegrated in 1917, its leaders redirected women's activities mainly into social work at the municipal level. This did not correspond to Braun's position. Braun had warned time and again that "social welfare of all types had nothing to do with the women's question."[66] Braun's reading in scientific socialism deepened her perspective on the women's question even though she rejected basic tenets of historical materialism. In her own case, feminist consciousness matured as class consciousness waned. Her distance from the mainstream of various camps provided a unique opportunity to question governing assumptions. Although clearly atypical within the socialist women's movement, Braun's ideas serve well to highlight basic values and priorities and uncover latent tensions in the alliance of socialism and feminism.

Marie Juchacz, a leader of the reform women who later replaced Zietz in the SPD's executive committee, was born the second of three children in a family of poor farmers and carpenters in Landsberg an der Warthe one year after promulgation of the anti-Socialist laws. Juchacz wrote that despite their poverty, her father did not see himself as a member of the proletariat. He had come from the country to the city to settle down as an artisan and construction craftsman.[67] She looked back with warmth to her early years, although the limited educational opportunities in a small village school and lack of institutions to train women remained a source of dissatisfaction.

During the decade prior to 1900, Landsberg experienced the dislocations wrought by industrial change: the city's population doubled, foreign workers were imported to meet the need for labor, and trade union and SPD locals were founded.

After having served in the army, Marie's brother returned a convinced Social Democrat and introduced his sister to socialist literature. Among other things, they read the Party's Erfurt Program of 1891, but she wrote that even after his explanation, she failed to understand the theoretical section. They discussed "often and earnestly" the second section that presented the immediate reforms the Party advocated. The "empty juxtaposition of final aim and present tactics" could contribute to the formation of pragmatically oriented socialists.[68] Juchacz began to attend socialist meetings, read their provincial paper, and exchange ideas with socialist friends of her brother; generally shy, she was willing to voice her opinions in such circles. Several events in 1903 completed the politicization process. That year's election campaign in Landsberg as well as the Crimmitschau weaver strike involved her in public meetings and taught her more about women's employment and the conflict between labor and capital. The pending dissolution of her marriage to the tailor Juchacz around 1903 left a void that socialist ideas and participation in Party life seemed to fill. This is how she explains her turn to socialism at a time of personal crisis. "It was a very decisive time for me. . . . [E]ntering the socialist world of ideas helped me bear my fate. . . ."[69] She joined the movement not from identification with the proletariat as a class, but out of humanitarian concern with its living conditions as well as the expectation that the Party could enable her to develop more fully as a human being.

Feeling the intellectual constraints of provincial existence, Marie and her sister, Elizabeth, moved to Berlin in early 1906. They solved the dilemma posed by the pull of motherhood, professional life, and later Party activity by sharing the burdens and caring for each other's children. In Berlin, they had hoped to work for the Party directly, but legal prohibitions on women's political activity channeled them into the women's movement. "Looking back [she would later explain], I see clearly how we women inevitably moved from general political interests . . . to a particular concern with the women's question. . . . To be more than just 'fellow travelers' . . . we had to make the detour to the socialist women's movement."[70]

Both joined the Women's and Girls' Educational Club in Schöneberg and began to devote their talents to the cause of women's equality. The second-class status of the female sex assumed greater importance as they found themselves irritated when they could not get a cup of coffee after meetings because women were not allowed in cafes without escorts, or, as Juchacz wrote, when "male comrades had a quiet smirk for our activities."[71] In 1912, when Cologne comrades were looking for a woman to coordinate propaganda among the female working class, they chose Marie Juchacz. Her rise within the Party bureaucracy did not depend on selection by the membership, as was customary for leadership roles in the early years of the movement. In all cases, Juchacz was nominated by the executives; in 1917, too, Friedrich Ebert asked her to come to Berlin to represent Social Democratic women in the national executive committee.[72]

In Cologne, Juchacz turned to municipal welfare activity following a 1911 directive encouraging socialist women to enter this new territory. She set up vacation excursions for school children and soon *Gleichheit* reported numerous cities following her lead. She held meetings to interest women in municipal affairs, but the war cut short her efforts to win working-class women for socialism through "municipal politics." She had come to believe that women showed considerable aptitude for practical work in city administration and that this sphere was not only tailor-made for them, but offered wide possibilities for recruitment.[73] As was demonstrated during the debates at the SPD Würzberg Congress in 1917, large numbers of socialist women had reached similar conclusions.

An examination of the careers of eight women leaders has revealed the presence of a pressure group united in its concern for working-class women. Although strategies varied, each sought to integrate women into the labor movement and orient the larger organizations to the specific social world of the potential female constituency. And each had to balance the needs of women with the requirements of the general struggle.

Several events in the 1880s had encouraged a lasting association with the labor movement. The gainfully employed female fell victim to economic insecurities accompanying the price depression. While middle-class liberals failed to advance an effective program of reform, future socialists such as Emma Ihrer formed their own unions and associations for working women geared to immediate issues of wages and work conditions. The underground socialist movement, itself victim of the anti-Socialist laws, had inherited a commitment to women's rights and sought to infuse the women's movement with socialist ideas. It clearly capitalized on heightened class antagonisms as a result of the discriminatory legislation.

While organizational legality in 1890 favored more open recruitment, it also permitted the emergence in the subculture of alternative solutions to the women's question. The leadership wing around Clara Zetkin advanced an official interpretation, a materialist analysis of the root cause of women's oppression that stressed class divisions and the importance of revolution. Between 1896 and 1908 it monopolized key positions of power in the women's movement and sought to instruct union activities. But unionists adopted their own methods and means; others quietly learned new skills in municipal welfare work and turned to piecemeal reforms; and, after 1908, power slipped to a less militant protector of women's rights, Luise Zietz.

Yet the very diversity of careers, emphases, and views gave a unique richness to the socialist feminist vision. Its wide purview came from the integration of both the political and the economic focuses. Still, there was enough agreement on women's issues to comprise a shared body of notions that can be labeled "socialist feminism," although, of course, less consensus existed on the tactics to achieve the end goals. The next chapter presents the major ideas of German socialist feminism as reflected not only in the literature but in the eight leaders' own life histories. Much can be gleaned of the feminist component by examing the specific reasons why women became socialists and the meaning of the socialist movement to them.

CHAPTER IV

THE NEW WOMAN:
A SOCIALIST VISION

The socialist subculture offered rich alternatives to the prevailing negative judgment of women's worth and work. The options comprised a vision of a more meaningful and rewarding work and home life that served to inspire mobilization efforts among the female constituency. The careers of the women leaders themselves showed the working-class female an enormous range of possibilities once the dominant social norms were challenged.

The vision at times was ambiguous and inconsistent. In part, socialist leaders failed to pose specific questions relating to the ways in which women could find fulfillment. Rather, they offered implicit answers in articles and speeches on a host of diverse topics. Some even questioned the intrinsic importance of drawing the portrait of "a new woman," for example. In 1896, Zetkin cynically stated that middle-class feminists in Germany might sketch the woman of the future, but Social Democrats alone would struggle for her political equality.[1] Nevertheless, a substantial feminist element was embedded in the writings of socialist women. These individuals were, after all, pioneers in the struggle for women's equality, pathfinders in analyzing the reasons for and offering solutions to women's inferior status. Among the first to challenge age-old assumptions, they proposed radical reforms; at the same time, they unconsciously internalized certain traditional attitudes.

This chapter employs two complementary techniques in presenting German socialists' feminist vision. One involves the traditional historical method of dissecting the women's writings and speeches. The other, less customary approach, derives from biographical analyses of the politicization process primarily of the eight representative figures. Their expectations for the female sex both in the capitalist and future socialist societies represented a determination to banish the humiliations and frustrations they had experienced firsthand.

POLITICAL MOBILIZATION AS
AN EXPRESSION OF FEMINIST CONCERNS

While biographical information is available for each of the eight leaders of this volume, the depth and range of data varies greatly. Only Lily Braun and Ottilie Baader wrote their memoirs; both autobiographies reflect growing hostility toward parental expectations for girls and toward the roles assigned to women generally. Zetkin's letters from Paris graphically described the tension she felt in her dual capacity of "girl friday" at home and of chief breadwinner outside the home. The reaction of others to Bebel's *Women under Socialism* attests to acute feelings of dissatisfaction. Zietz claimed after reading his book that she "was able, as so many of the proletariat were, to remove the blinders before [her] eyes." She had felt her position in society as "humiliating" and "disgraceful," and Bebel's book helped her understand why. Grünberg, too, explained that Bebel showed why "we [women] were burdened under capitalism."[2]

Despite biographical gaps and the necessity for conjecture, certain generalizations can be offered on reasons why activists became socialists and on the meaning of the socialist movement specifically to women. From biographical materials, it is clear that an important motive in sustaining female membership was the perception of the SPD as the most forceful advocate of women's equality in Imperial Germany. Socialist feminists were intent on improving the position of the female sex and especially of the working-class woman. There were motivational differences between men and women in the socialist subculture that accounted for tensions between them, despite the common class allegiance. It is fair to assume, for example, that women's political and economic liberation stood low on a man's list of reasons for membership in the SPD, but at or near the top on the list of women. Female leaders were determined to make other women share their priorities. One of the best means to this end was to help working-class females become conscious of various alternatives in life.

Although the subjects shared a similar purpose, no "typical" pattern emerged in the politicization process. Lily Braun and Emma Ihrer moved from the middle-class feminist to the socialist camp once they became convinced that the bourgeois world offered no effective solutions to the women's question. Their hope of a better world for women triggered concern with the social question. Clara Zetkin had close contact with bourgeois feminism but never actively joined the middle-class women's movement. Rather, like Marie Juchacz, her political activity expressed the intellectual attraction of socialist ideas. The conflict between her roles as mother and worker helped channel Zetkin's political awakening to the specific needs of working-class women. Juchacz, too, turned to the women's question once she joined the socialist movement and was made aware of sex discrimination. Luise Zietz and Ottilie Baader became politically active when they perceived their second-class status as both woman and working-class member, while Helene Grünberg and Gertrud Hanna experienced oppression as female workers. The two unionists seethed under social limitations that assigned women unskilled jobs in the labor market. The trade union movement offered them a chance to improve their economic position and satisfied these two women's material and emotional needs. All the eight figures expressed great emotional satisfaction at the feeling of belonging to the movement and collaborating with like-minded individuals.

Several examples document the fact that membership fulfilled personal needs, an important requirement for organizational vitality that social scientists have recognized.[3] Baader failed to marry, and only when she turned to the socialist world view and found another content to life did she accept spinsterhood. The case of Juchacz whose move to socialism filled a void created by the dissolution of her marriage has already been described. Braun's move to socialism only months after the death of her first husband can be seen as an affirmation of his life's work against his former colleagues. Participation offered her as well the chance to satisfy one overwhelming desire: to be active. Hanna was inclined toward melancholy and seclusion, according to Juchacz. "Her work brought her into contact with many persons and prevented her from sinking into isolation."[4]

The women's movement had an added meaning for females. It can be viewed as an alternative route to social integration for those who rejected the paths to fulfillment offered by the dominant society. Zietz found comradery and a milieu in which she could follow her ideals.[5] In short, participation gave women not only the chance to dream about alternatives for women's existence, but the opportunity to act out their vision in the present.

The memoirs of Baader and Braun indicate some other reasons why women became socialists. Both works record a growing sense of frustration at societal and familial constraints on their ability to develop freely—a frustration widely shared by women activists. Consciousness of a dependent status, the low valuation of females as "only women," and opposition to parental expectations catalyzed their political awakening.

Baader portrayed her father as a worker and radical democrat who, nevertheless, held traditional ideas on women's place in the family. He taught her reading and writing and, when she was ten years old, sent her to a Catholic institution (*Mittelschule*) considered "a good school." That meant, Baader explained, that "girls were trained there mostly in 'good manners.' To be soft, tender, and gentle was the woman's ideal of this time."[6] Her decision to embrace socialism came a good ten years after she had left the Catholic church. Baader herself is silent on the reasons for the break with Catholicism. According to a friend and confidant, she had been deeply religious as a child, but became increasingly "repelled" by the structure and practices of the church. After an Easter service, she vowed never to return again.[7] Through her friends in a Unitarian congregation, she came into contact with socialists. Since she never married, she ended up supporting herself and her father for twenty years, a situation that proved the major source of frustration. Baader described her feelings of resentment. "I experienced myself the great dependency of women, even working women, on the male members of the family. . . . Even though I had been for a long time the sole supporter of our small household, I remained for my father 'the daughter' who does not need to have an opinion of her own and who has to adjust to him without question."[8]

Baader's penetration into the socialist world view at the late age of forty transformed her whole life. By understanding for the first time reasons for her subordinate position as a member of the female sex and the working class, she felt rejuvenated and willing to face the present and work for a better future. A similar transformation occurred in Braun who at twenty-seven wrote her cousin about her new political commitments. "I have the future for myself . . . and I feel the strength in me to make each year one of progress. . . ."[9] Less explicit, but similar expressions of courage, hope, and faith in progress accompanied the political awakening of such figures as Juchacz, Zietz, Zetkin, Grünberg, and Hanna.

For Baader, the step to socialism meant final independence from her father, which she said "was not so easy." He had helped her understand the socialist world view and, as they read the literature, she learned to form her own opinions. He prevented her from going to meetings alone until she put her foot down and challenged him. She later wrote, "This burst of energy must have taken my father by surprise. He remained completely silent and did not object any more to my going out alone."[10] Men typically exerted considerable influence on the politicization of socialist women. Husbands, brothers, or male friends aided the political maturation of females—a reflection of the broader educational and political opportunities available to men.[11]

Lily Braun's case was unique. As a member of the upper class, she received explicit instruction and training for her deportment and future role in life. Familial designs were clear: she would grow up to be a lady and marry an aristocrat. In her memoirs, Braun depicts continuous pressure to mold her into an acceptable member of the upper class. References to norms such as "the female's task [is] to please" or "we women simply do not belong to ourselves" filled her childhood and early adolescence. When she was sixteen, her parents sent her to Augsburg to visit an old aunt who reinforced the socialization process by speaking constantly of her future husband and home. By then, she wrote, she had become truly a "young lady" and internalized the values of her family.[12]

Several experiences shattered the mold. Conflicts arose over her relations with the opposite sex and her growing desire to do something meaningful in life. She wrote angrily on one occasion to her cousin after her parents forbade her to talk to a young man in a lower social class because he might get "ideas." "Can't you see how disgusting this is: what a grave offense against our sex? Female dogs are not judged differently from us."[13] She began to feel being bred for mating was a disgrace and that women had more to live for than just catching a man. A determination to work stirred as she perceived the empty, superficial, and boring existence in high society. In a revealing statement, she crystallized her resentments. "I am twenty-three years old, healthy in mind and body, perhaps more able to achieve than many others and not only do I not work, I don't even live, rather my life is being arranged."[14] The passive voice at the end of the sentence symbolized her feelings of being an object in life unable to control her destiny. Life was passing her by, her fate had been decided at birth because society dictated that gender defined a person's expectations and opportunities.

Braun could satisfy her needs only by rejecting the views of her family and social class. Her memoirs describe the family's attitude that she now found to be intolerable. Explaining to her father her desire to work, she heard him argue: "If you had been a man, I would certainly have guided you to paths which would guarantee a meaningful content to life—but as things are—you are just a girl, destined for one job only—all others would be nothing but sad stopgaps."[15]

From the working classes echoed a similar feeling of resentment of being an object in life. Grünberg described women in the labor force as "playthings," bantered about by forces beyond their control. Reflecting a common grievance, she complained that society inadequately trained them for employment since their true profession was seen anchored in the home. Women were unprepared for work and had no possibility of making life easier and meaningful through labor.[16] Both Braun and Grünberg felt that women should be free to define their own course in ways that would allow them to develop and mature. The trade union movement offered Grünberg the chance to control her own life and improve the options of other women as well.

RESTRUCTURING WOMEN'S LIVES:
THE SOCIALIST FEMINIST PLATFORM

Socialist feminists did not deny their womanhood. They believed that women were capable of performing what society defined as men's tasks without apeing men. A clear indication of their redefinition of femininity to subsume traditional male roles is found both in the obituaries and in the short characterizations of one another they wrote on birthdays or other occasions. Pride in their "womanly nature" or "motherly way" complemented praise for public activity. Zetkin's obituary in 1911 for Ihrer typifies their ideal. "The implacable foe of all prejudice . . . was an utterly good woman, a womanly nature through and through. Life truly did not spare Emma Ihrer bitterness, but it did not wither her . . . sensitivity. . . . Enthusiastic studies broadened and secured her . . . socialist knowledge, yet her service remained always a matter of the heart. So in our memory, she is perfect proof that the woman . . . can be a true fighter without giving up being a woman. . . . [17]

In the mid-1890s, in response to an ongoing discussion in the bourgeois feminist camp and to contemporary novels depicting an emancipated woman, Braun and Zetkin sketched their ideal woman. The attributes further attest to these socialists' pride in being female. Both Zetkin and Braun felt that the models held up by feminists and contained in literature were incomplete. Braun criticized authors such as Ibsen for failing to portray a whole woman. She felt his Nora in *A Doll's House*, whom most saw representing a woman yearning for freedom and a chance to develop her personality, in fact, symbolized egoism and lacked "heart and femininity."[18] According to Braun, women's one-sided struggle against men in England and Scandinavia produced truncated literary figures—"abnormal women," and she pointed to Gerhart Hauptmann's heroine Anna in *Einsame Menschen* as an ideal, a true woman "healthy and strong in spirit and body and delicate and soft as well."[19] The new woman would be free to develop her individuality, maturing in an occupation that corresponded to her abilities. From youth on, she would be able to socialize with men as innocently as with women, from friendship love would grow, and the emancipated woman would stand at the side of a man as a true comrade.

Zetkin sought to harmonize the traditional view of women that saw them as sexual beings only (*Nur-Geschlechtswesen*) with the feminists' portrayal that depicted them as humans to the neglect of their sexuality. She felt that a woman was neither just a person (*Nur-Mensch*) nor totally female (*Nur-Weib*) but a full human of the female sex (*Weiblicher Vollmensch*), with corresponding duties in the family and public life. Both sides of women's nature required cultivation. To neglect her humanity would cripple a woman's growth as a female and restrict her influence at home. Conversely, satisfying her needs as a woman saved her from becoming "a superficial copy of man," a mere working *Mannweib*.[20] The capitalist society, however, forced women to choose work or family; only socialism would nurture women's dual nature.

The visions of Zetkin and Braun were daring and bold, yet contained sentiments that are distracting to a modern feminist reader. Succinctly stated, neither succeeded in freeing herself from a male-centered standard. Braun described the new woman as man's comrade, partner, and fellowfighter, but unaware of the potential contradiction, stated also, "she will belong to the man of her choice."[21] For Zetkin, the fact that men did not bear children did not make them half-human (*Halb-*

menschen); rather, women were true human beings when they worked as hard and well as men did while succoring and mothering. She conjured up a modified bourgeois ideal. "Rooted and active in the world at large and in the family, she can make the man in the home once again comfortable. From her own rich, expansive sphere of activity, grows clear understanding for his strivings, struggles, creations. She doesn't stand next to him as an obedient maid . . . but as a companion in his struggle, as a comrade in his trouble . . . supportive and receptive."[22] For both, the emancipated woman was still, in part, man's creature, even if she freely chose the man.

Socialist ideology saw customs, morality, and values mirroring stages of economic development. Most socialist feminists felt that women's role in life as well as characteristics attributed to them had been socially conditioned. They scornfully rejected assumptions about women's mild, pliant, or weak nature and they fought stereotyping at every turn. Zetkin held that centuries of subordination in the patriarchal, monogamous family, codified in religious and legal doctrine, had produced the "weak, blindly accepting" female. She granted only that mothers were the natural succors of infants and rejected all other roles assigned to women because of their presumed nature.[23] Ihrer judged that women's double burdens at home and work had made them "mild" and she challenged the pseudo-scientists who "proved" woman's inferiority by the size of her brain: if one hears that only the largest brains are suitable for intellectual capabilities, one could then send whales to the university, she mocked at a meeting in 1890. Ihrer concluded that women had been "intellectually crippled" by the schools and the kind of education they received as well as by their dependency in the home, factory, and workshop.[24]

The *bêtes noires* for socialist women were the prevailing stereotypes that "women belong in the home" and "men provide for the family." Grünberg represented the sentiments of her colleagues when she disdainfully rejected both platitudes "since . . . million[s of] working women are torn from their homes and families and work for the capitalist state." The same employers using female labor "scream bloody murder" when women begin to concern themselves with public life, she added. And Braun, in a similar vein, censured as philistines those who cried "how unfeminine" when proletarian women, driven into work, engaged in strikes for higher wages.[25]

Socialist women sought to instill new values in harmony with the revolutionary economic transformations. They wanted women to live their lives as "free, independent personalities."[26] To further the rights of the personality even within the capitalist state, the leaders advocated a series of reforms that were decidedly advanced for the time. They expected growing self-awareness to encourage class awareness.

Women's suffrage was a key demand. Unlike the bourgeois feminist argument that regarded suffrage as one of the inalienable rights of individuals, socialists championed the vote as a social right. With women's increased participation in public life, it had become necessary for them to defend their interests; the foundation for women's suffrage lay in social necessity and represented recognition of their useful functions in society.[27] Bourgeois women, socialists contended, wanted political reform to preserve their society; proletarian women needed the vote not only as a defense against exploitation and for the sake of social justice, but as a weapon to fight the bourgeois class. Unlike the contemporary British and American feminists, German socialist feminists never overestimated the importance of the vote in and of itself. They were all too aware of the ways in which the effect of universal male suffrage in Germany was diluted by constitutional manipulations and chicanery. However, since radical socialists conceived of the class struggle as a political struggle, women needed political rights to participate fully in the liberation movement.

In the context of socialist feminism in Europe, the German record is exemplary. The SPD could trace its commitment to women's political rights back to its formative years. The Gotha program of 1875 had implicitly called for female suffrage when it advocated "universal, equal, direct suffrage . . . for all citizens," and the 1891 Erfurt program explicitly excluded "distinction of sex" in the call for democratization. Thereafter, on propaganda tours, lecturers broadcast the principle of women's vote. The Party took pride in being the sole advocate of female suffrage in the German political arena prior to the formation of middle-class suffrage leagues beginning in 1902 and even thereafter, it was the only political party to champion, in word and deed, women's suffrage.[28] In the stormy days of November 1918, the socialists made good their long-standing commitment in promulgating votes for women.

Suffrage was a divisive issue elsewhere for socialists. While women's political equality was incorporated into the Italian Minimum Program in the late 1890s and was part of the platform of several French factions (the radical Hervé who shunned parliamentarianism in general was an exception), no serious effort was made to press for the reform in these two countries. When the issue became acute as during the suffrage debate in Italy around 1910 or as a result of pressure from the French bourgeois suffragettes, Anna Kulischoff, the Italian socialist, found herself a lone spokeswoman for the idea and the French party split badly: suffragettes, it was maintained by many socialist men in France, "set women in a state of disloyal competition with men, and against their own interests."[29]

European socialist feminists were themselves divided over the practice of dropping the call for women's suffrage during the campaigns for democratization, as occurred in Belgium in 1901 and later in Sweden and Austria. The French Feminist Socialist Group, the closest parallel to the German women's movement, actually commended the Belgian action "in the superior interest of universal male suffrage."[30] No such bow toward expediency, or as Zetkin caustically labeled it, "opportunism," occurred in the mainstream of German socialist feminist thought (although some dissent was voiced mutely). In 1907, the women's International socialist conference debated the issue and Zetkin was quick to expose her opponents' errors. The Belgian hope to barter removal of women's vote for liberal support of universal male suffrage had proved illusory, she pointedly noted. "What decided the outcome [was] power not content." She questioned why her Austrian sisters eliminated the demand for women's vote at the start of the campaign. In her view, this negated the first rule of propaganda: to keep revolutionary demands before the eyes of the masses in order to instill higher consciousness. To the fear (correct, as it turned out) that women might vote conservatively, Zetkin countered that the vote did not signify political maturity but "was a means to assemble the masses, to organize and educate them."[31] The Zetkin wing consistently upheld the feminist goal because it served class interests well. Austrian women later came to regret their willingness to demonstrate solely for male suffrage in 1906. The bargain had not paid off: in the citadel of power—parliament—male socialists had failed to press for women's vote.[32]

Women's political rights were but one part of the socialist feminist platform that included as well the goal of familial equality. In concrete terms, German socialists opposed the reformed Civil Code of 1900 because, in Zetkin's words, it translated the biblical saying "he should be your master" into law.[33] Socialists felt that the code failed to recognize the ongoing revolution in social relations that was destroying the "chains of economic dependency" tying women to men and to the family. They believed this revolution was irreversible and ultimately destructive of men's domination in the family and society. They called, too, for easing the grounds for divorce. "A marriage whose moral prerequisite—reciprocal love—has disappeared is a moral absurdity." Without divorce, cohabitation could become "friendless, miserable, and morally destructive."[34] Also, most socialists believed that women should have the right to limit the size of their families, although the degree of commitment to this radical feminist position varied. At the same time, they affirmed the view that motherhood satisfied an important part of women's needs. Zetkin, for example, held that abortions and contraceptives were morally justified, but could be used hypocritically to hide extramarital affairs and egotistically to shed the care for children. She judged that a rich woman rejecting motherhood destroyed her last remaining personal dignity and worth.[35]

Braun's whole philosophy on love, marriage, and the family was centered around the need for motherhood to help women realize their true nature. As a young woman, angry at the limitations to her development, Braun had dreamt of having a son, "never mind from whom, a living part of myself . . . who would fulfill my dreams and become what I had hoped but failed to be."[36] The world lay at men's feet and she had envisioned living her ideals vicariously through a male child. Although Braun later broke the barriers hampering her personal development, the yearning for a child remained. The birth of her son in 1897 was the most important emotional event in her life, and she translated these feelings into a cardinal principle: motherhood is the apex of womanhood. "Love and motherhood . . . are the key forces in women's lives."[37] Her deepseated commitment to motherhood made Braun critical of women advocating a childless existence, possible with the then fairly effective contraceptive methods, but she approved of limiting births especially in the case of working women.[38]

In the years before World War I, birth control became an extremely emotional and divisive issue. On the one hand, the German government unsuccessfully sought to improve the falling birth rate by preventing the sale and use of contraceptives. On the other, a minority within the socialist camp advocated viewing birth control as a "revolutionary weapon" in the class struggle, more important, some said, than even the parliamentary tactic.[39] The ensuing debate displayed a collision of socialist priorities with feminist goals.

Government efforts to encourage births were prompted by a slight decline in the birth rate beginning in 1902 and the tendency in the age of nationalism to equate power with population.[40] The government's proposal concerning contraceptives met with general derision in the socialist camp. Zietz denounced the law as a "monstrosity" and an "act of stupidity" while Juchacz and Grünberg opposed it because it destroyed women's rights of self-determination as mothers and females.[41] Others went even further. Alma Wartenberg was tried (and acquitted) for lecturing to sexually integrated working-class audiences on such matters as sexual relations and diseases as well as birth control. Her talk included a slide show, which greatly upset burger sensibilities. On one occasion, she proposed that "the woman must be mistress of her own body. I grant her the right to protect herself from pregnancy even against her husband's wishes."[42]

The question of birth control placed the SPD leadership in an uncomfortable position. According to its official response, limitation of births was a private matter to be discussed in a couple's bedchamber or with a doctor. Yet the public call for using the practice as a political weapon forced an open debate. Emotions ran high for over a year; on one occasion, Zetkin was personally threatened while Zietz was reduced to tears when critics in the reform socialist camp claimed she had lost all understanding and empathy for working women. The strong emotions on the issue reflected, probably, the spread of birth-control practice among the rank and file of the women's movement in urban areas. As seen in chapter 2, Berliners (and much of the stormy debate on the issue took place in the Protestant capital) generally had smaller families than did the working class as a whole, and studies done at the time established a direct correlation between skill in the marketplace and family planning. Many of the women's movements' adherents came from the upwardly mobile, skilled section of the working class.[43] The arguments advanced by the advocates of family planning struck a receptive chord among this group of rank and file.

Proponents of the birth strike saw reduction of births as a means of mitigating the present misery in working-class homes. They hoped to ease the burdens on working-class families, improve welfare and the educational opportunities of each working-class child, and assure more freedom for the individual woman. This was a progressive feminist position. As a byproduct, the potential for political mobilization among women with less children would be greater. Birth control would also deprive the German military of future soldiers.[44]

The debate has a contemporary ring. The arguments resemble those hurled between the industrialized West and the Third World over population and poverty in the 1970s. The opponents of the birth-control strike in the socialist camp, most vigorously, Kautsky, Zetkin, Wurm, and Luxemburg—center-to-left socialists—rejected the neo-Malthusian analysis that population was responsible for poverty. The culprit was rather the unequal distribution of goods and services, i.e., capitalist society itself. They feared that concentration on the population issue would divert the masses from the main goal of overthrowing capitalism or, secondarily, of winning from capitalism child care and other municipal services. As Zetkin put it at a public meeting called by the Party, a restructuring of the family might reconcile the individual to existing social conditions. "For the working class, it is not a question of making the individual more comfortable in the bourgeois class system by restructuring his relationships, but for the proletariat, it is a question of disentangling the individual from the class system and leading him to the class struggle."[45] Drawing on her reading of history, Zetkin implied that "numbers not quality" guaranteed victory in social struggles. Furthermore, if one struck against the military, the number of soldiers for the revolution would be reduced as well. Quite simply, although birth control might help the individual, it hurt the class. Zetkin also questioned the claim that large numbers of children kept women away from the movement. The relevant criteria were not numbers, but the health and intellectual alertness of women. She admitted that children added problems, but so did husbands who expected to be catered to by their wives, a statement that produced enthusiastic response from the generally cool audience.[46]

The socialist leadership squashed the issue in October 1914 shortly after the outbreak of the war. The executive committee, adhering to Zetkin's views, met with the two leading proponents of a birth strike, Drs. Bernstein and Moses, and insisted that they cease and desist. It also reprimanded female Party members who continued agitation for birth control. Party leaders—male and female—decided that individual or family needs in this case were immaterial for the working class as a whole. Birth control might be liberating for individuals, but its inclusion in the Party's program would be inimical to the collective interests of labor. Thus, Party opposition stood in the way of achieving a feminist goal.[47]

Because their ideology equated work and emancipation, socialist feminists rejected traditional role divisions between men and women. The position of some leaders on the issue of domestic duties, however, was not devoid of ambiguities and compromises. The writings of Zietz, for example, clearly reflect a mixture of traditional and radical ideas. In her view, reforms advocated by socialists, ranging from the eight-hour workday to maternity insurance to protective legislation, would allow women to perform their domestic tasks more effectively. Zietz explicitly stated that women needed protection because "employment did not free [them] from housework," implying that housework was, after all, women's domain.[48]

To achieve a better balance between work and domestic functions, proposals were made to socialize some of the latter. Institutions were needed to help lower-class working women save time, energy, and money in the performance of domestic duties. Suggestions for municipal programs to be initiated in the capitalist state included communal eating and laundry services, day-care centers, playgrounds, obstetrical wards, and maid service for pregnant women. Socialists called on the city to set up guidelines and programs for installing central heat and light in apartment buildings as well as maintaining hygienic standards. As Zetkin explained it, "[this] social reconstruction that substitutes the municipality for the single family home in many areas is the foundation on which gradually a harmonic coexistence of women's professional and family life can be realized."[49] Nevertheless, the writings expressed a certain nostalgia for an idyllic home life beyond the grasp of working-class women. Socialist women could hail education of children and administration of the home as "holy duties" and, at the same time, demand that society help perform these functions since a woman could no longer be the "capable Hausfrau" of yesteryear.[50]

As a corollary to the working-class woman's growing self-awareness, socialists envisioned an improved status for women in the labor market. Their ultimate ideal for the working woman in the capitalist state centered on transforming her from a dirty competitor into a comrade-in-arms and cooperator-in-work.[51] They also opposed society's automatic relegation of working women to unskilled "coolie labor." Drawing on personal experience, Hanna extolled the virtues of unionization. By joining trade unions, she said, women will step into jobs commensurate with their intelligence, talents, and physical capabilities. She predicted that this would destroy the practice of assigning women unskilled work with no regard to their abilities. She believed that women's efforts to improve their position would produce a change in the attitudes of men who generally saw female workers as wage depressors and resisted their attempts to rise professionally.[52]

Socialist women demanded reform of education to provide training and broaden women's employment opportunities. In contrast to bourgeois feminists, they criticized the tiered educational system that perpetuated class divisions through differential schooling costs and examination requirements and called for free, unitary institutions (*Einheitsschulen*) from kindergartens to high schools for rich and poor alike. Socialists proposed that professional training be included in the curriculum and raised the then scandalous demand for coeducational instruction. Coeducation could help alleviate fears and misconceptions, and bridge the artificial gaps between the sexes.[53]

WORK, MARRIAGE, AND MOTHERHOOD: A RESPONSE TO EDMUND FISCHER, 1905

On the whole, socialist feminists concentrated on the goal of furthering the revolution and promoting class consciousness; they devoted less attention to questions of love, marriage, and family relations. They assumed that the self-aware, economically independent woman would marry solely for love and that common interests and mutual respect would provide a strong bond for husband and wife. Ihrer, Zetkin, and Braun, in part to meet a challenge launched within the socialist world against basic assumptions of their movement, offered more penetrating analyses of the changing relations between the sexes. All three recognized that the women's movement contained "a rebellion against the family." Braun declared perceptively: "The women's movement which began harmlessly, whose pioneers claimed that no tradition or custom would be affected, has proven to be revolutionary. And, instead of arriving at its goal with the realization of its first demand—the equality of women in economic, legal, and political areas—it only then begins to face the largest tasks."[54]

In 1905, *Sozialistische Monatshefte* published an article by Edmund Fischer, a reform socialist Reichstag deputy, which sought to prove that women's struggle for emancipation contradicted human nature.[55] Within a socialist framework, he reformulated traditional views of women's place in social life and offered a socialist "wife-mother-housekeeper" model for women in the future society. He questioned how one could free women from their domestic duties when "the first and highest goal in life for the woman, buried deep in her nature, [was] to be mother and live to educate her children." He blandly dismissed the Marxist belief in work as the vehicle for women's emancipation because, in his eyes, women's employment was "unnatural, socially unsound, and a capitalist misery that must disappear when capitalism is destroyed."[56] The women's question would not be solved by liberating women from men, he concluded, but by overthrowing capitalism and returning women to their families.

The reaction among socialist women was swift and biting, and it highlights a key issue in socialist feminism as it crystallized by the early twentieth century. The problem centered on the realization of equality while taking into account differences between the sexes. How could work—the liberator of the female sex—be reconciled with motherhood? Most leaders believed implicitly that a woman was not complete unless she was a mother, although, unlike Fischer, of course, they stressed the key role of gainful employment in achieving an ideal life.

Ihrer proved most unconventional in responding to Fischer.

She scorned his idolatry of the "home sweet home," calling such expressions of sentimentality "a sickness," and categorically dismissed the view that motherhood and childrearing were the highest goals for women. "To be a mother is as little a life's goal as to be a father. Women can find their life's goal only in general work areas or in solving social tasks that are in the interest of all."[57] In balancing motherhood and professional life, Ihrer leaned toward employment; however, society had to be reorganized so that a married woman could work without suppressing her desire to have a family. She developed an alternative model for the new woman. "The woman of the future will choose one occupation according to her capabilities and inclinations: she will be either working woman or educator of children or housekeeper, but not all three, as today's proletarian woman."[58]

Zetkin took Fischer to task for perpetuating the values associated with a particular stage of economic development and reminded him that socialists, above all, had no reason to halt historical change.[59] In her immediate response, as well as in later articles on related topics, she stressed the dialectical nature of capitalist misery that inevitably would be terminated. Women under capitalism, she admitted, suffered from the irreconcilable twin roles as workers and mothers. However, this was no reason to slight either function in the future socialist society. Within the womb of capitalism, the proletarian class struggle initiated the process of harmonizing work and motherhood; it forced reform on the ruling classes.[60] Women's labor, of extreme discomfort to Fischer, was equally as revolutionary. It dissolved the old form of marriage, bourgeois monogamy based on the subordination of women to men's desire for legitimate heirs, and spurred its evolution into a higher moral unit. Zetkin expected the marriage of the future to be a monogamous union, but one based on equality between husband and wife and fidelity as the moral ideal for both sexes.[61] The woman then could truly become a wife and mother, not as a "crippled creature," but as a free, strong, and fully developed individual while the man would help around the home. Fischer's perspective on child education that said, in essence, "my wife educates my child in my home" provoked her wrath. Only if fathers and mothers jointly raised children, she countered, could boys and girls learn to appreciate sex differences and later work together in life. She felt that a more realistic apportionment of home tasks, in turn, would help resolve the conflict between women's occupational life and their motherly tasks.[62]

With gross oversimplification, Zetkin asserted that since men and women in the working class had no wealth, they rejected men's privileged position in the family. To the extent that wives worked, male privileges disintegrated in working-class homes: "Legal dogmas cannot preserve what life's bursting surge destroys." Zetkin recognized that most proletarian couples clung to the bourgeois form of marriage, but felt respect for the institution had waned. "It is a small step from lack of respect for form to noncompliance with form," she predicted.[63]

Braun was less sanguine than Zetkin that the monogamous marriage would survive in the future, and she questioned the assumption of many reformers who predicted a lasting and successful union between two intellectually equal persons.[64] This view failed to recognize that "the instinct of the sexes [was] not identical with understanding." She feared that the complexity of modern life multiplied possibilities for conflict: men would find in their working wives the same intensity and nervousness as existed in the outside world, and women would experience the external world directly, not through an intermediary. Marital peace, Braun believed, required the subordination of women to men. Yet, she also felt that awareness of sexual needs made monogamy problematic and labeled her age a "turning point" in sexual relations. Prevailing Christian morality had made sexual release through prostitution inevitable for men, but women could find "love" only in marriage. She boldly stated that marriage destroyed love. "On the corpse of the martyrs of marriage speaks the priest of the religion of love with the words, 'faithful spouse,' " she wrote bitterly. With candor unusual for the times, she admitted that "since the women's movement has loosened our tongues, we see that the sexual drive is as strong in women as in men,"[65] and she sanctioned premarital sexual relations for both sexes. Yet, Braun rejected "universalizing" free love because it alone could not guarantee a woman independence; common-law marriage without economic freedom for women would bind them as tightly to men as the conventional marriage.

Braun's position on the women's question had changed over the years: her solution had become "a child and work." Women's independence that "liberated love" could not be secured through employment alone because women had a higher duty than work, the duty to become mothers. To insure a woman independence during pregnancy and the child's early years (Braun strongly felt that children needed their mothers until they went to kindergarten), she advocated universal maternity insurance for all women funded by a progressive income tax. She left the "form of love"—whether marriage or free relationship—unspecified for the future and stated only that it would correspond to the needs of individuals.[66] Braun's writings betray a strange blend of unconventional, radical, often contradictory ideas revolving around one constant: the belief that motherhood was a woman's highest duty in life.

In contrast to Zetkin, Braun felt that members of the working class were unreceptive to changes in family life promoting greater equality for women. She spoke of hearing complaints at meetings that men did not understand women's desires for education or public activity. Furthermore, she did not share the belief of most of her SPD comrades that the presence of men and women working together in public life or standing side by side in the economic struggle would be reflected automatically in more equitable familial relationships. On the contrary, the proletarian woman had to wrest from the man her personal rights because "the bourgeois philistine morality was so deeply ingrained in him." And, she declared that the socialist women's movement must educate her if she is unable to see this.[67]

The women's movement failed to take up Braun's challenge. In their official debates, socialist women omitted discussion of the family and its place in conditioning male and female role divisions. The question of the family was brought up before the women's conferences and SPD congresses in Imperial Germany, but only in connection with other issues such as education.[68] Consistent with socialist ideology, activists expected women's economic independence to be translated automatically into more equitable family relations, an evolution that would begin first in working-class homes. Since familial equality was seen as an inevitable byproduct of ongoing economic transformations, socialist ideology interfered with a thorough critique of actual family life in the working class. In the socialist subculture, then, the working-class family did not face a feminist onslaught and was better able to provide stability than if its specific composition and mythology had been under attack.[69] Such calculations, however, prevented socialist women from confronting the root cause of their own difficulty within German Social Democracy: the persistence in the organized working class of sex role expectations that confined women to the domestic sphere (part C).

German socialist feminists brought work and home into a novel combination that raised women's lives to new status. As seen by an examination of the politicization of eight leaders, their feminist outlook reflected personal experience with the existing constraints on women's development, whether in the labor force, in the family or in society. They subjected a whole range of social life to criticism and called for broad-sweeping changes that included improved educational and training opportunities in coeducational facilities; municipal reforms to ease the burdens on working mothers; and legal changes to facilitate more equitable family relationships. It was their pride in being women, however, that gave the vision its main thrust: women were not going to be molded into carbon copies of men. They saw women as nurturing creatures and sought to facilitate motherhood (if not the role of housewife) while reforming public life to guarantee women equal opportunities. This commitment to motherhood did not mean that German socialist feminists simply redefined traditional sex-role divisions; their view represented a far cry from the notion of separate but equal spheres for men and women as advocated, for example, by the remarkable Communard Paule Mink, champion of women's issues in French socialism during the early Third Republic.[70] Rather, women were to work in gainful employment in jobs commensurate with their talents and inclinations, find support in a marriage of their choice, and experience the joys of being mothers. Motherhood was to be made fully compatible with expanded opportunities in public life.

On some feminist issues the movement equivocated. While the leadership accepted family planning in principle, it refused to incorporate advocacy of birth limitations into the official program and thereby missed an opportunity to publicize a feminist goal. This controversy, too, showed clear conflict between socialist ideology and the life experience of some of the women who formed the movement's social base. As the next chapter documents, other feminist proposals went down in defeat, particularly those associated with the maverick Lily Braun. Braun was an ideal figure to question the orientation of the proletarian women's movement. Among socialist women, she symbolized their feminist consciousness. Her experience highlights aspects of the tensions that accompanied the union of socialism and feminism. While in the bourgeois feminist camp, Braun collided with Clara Zetkin and their debates revealed the fundamental differences between socialist and middle-class feminists. When Braun moved to Social Democracy in late 1895, the controversy simply shifted to the extent of feminism in socialist ideology and practice. Her difficulties both before and after her political reaffiliation testify to the prevalence of class loyalty among leaders and rank and file of the socialist women's movement and their relatively weak identification with the female sex.

CHAPTER V

CLASS VERSUS SEX IDENTITY:
CLARA ZETKIN AND LILY BRAUN

The depth of feminism in the socialist subculture was tied to the personal and ideological relationship between Clara Zetkin and Lily Braun. For over thirteen years, the two outspoken intellectuals collided over the most effective strategies in solving the women's question. Tactical differences reflected ideological divergences in such degree that feminist issues often became obscured in the clouds of debate. More often than not, it was the doctrinaire Marxist opposing the pragmatic revisionist, or Zetkin's "pride" facing Braun's "honor."

The controversy involved a struggle for power within the women's movement. Each contestant sought support from men and women in German Social Democracy. Zetkin was more successful and eventually forced Braun out of any decision-making positions. In Zetkin's victory, class loyalty triumphed over sex identity. The conflict also reflected the scope of the debates among socialist women. In part, arguments affected only socialist feminists, as exemplified by Braun's proposals for a "new orientation" in 1897; in part, discussions fed into wider issues facing the Party or unions. Braun's call for home cooperatives in 1901, for example, evoked the charge of accepting the possibility of socialism-within-capitalism, a major premise of Eduard Bernstein's revisionism.

BRAUN QUESTIONS THE MARXIST CONCEPT
OF CLASS STRUGGLE

Class struggle was a great divide—the central theoretical concept that defined and limited tactics in the political arena. It justified the SPD's noncollaboration policy in parliament, governed trade union behavior toward employers, and segregated socialist from bourgeois feminists.

With an iron fist, Clara Zetkin ran the women's movement in light of her perception of the nature of the class struggle. After 1896, she effectively used the Gotha resolutions to buttress her position. Collaboration with middle-class feminists was rejected decisively. Zetkin admitted that parallel action by socialist and bourgeois women was within the realm of possibility. Yet she was quick to point out that such collaboration in Germany would be a "retrogression" for socialists. "The German feminists up to now [1900] have proven to be so muddle-headed, wishy-washy, weak . . ." that they shun forceful pursuit of either their feminist or their general reform proposals.[1] In fact, an unbridgeable gulf existed between socialist efforts to liberate women in order to hasten the revolution and bourgeois programs designed to assimilate women into the capitalist state as equal and responsible citizens.

Proud of her role in the socialist movement, Zetkin once boasted to Karl Kautsky that "it is no exaggeration when I state that it was in large part my personal work that defined clearly the principles of our women's movement and its relationship to our general movement on the one hand and to the [bourgeois] feminists on the other."[2] She claimed responsibility for anchoring the proletarian women's movement in a firm Marxist foundation, and for removing the "rather vulgar feminism" that had plagued the organization in the early 1890s. Zetkin's self-image was correct; she was the key figure determining the early political thrust of the women's movement.

Zetkin's tactical efforts to restrict the scope of feminism to working-class action was challenged by middle-class reformers whose vision of change transcended class lines. The different perspectives emerged clearly in the clash with Lily Braun who was in the bourgeois camp in the early 1890s. Braun candidly confessed her inability to understand the Marxist phrase "standing on the ground of the class struggle."[3] In her eyes, the socialist goal of human liberation could not be reached through working-class efforts alone, an assertion she sought to prove by word and deed in subsequent years. This set her initially on a collision course with Zetkin on her left and the less progressive bourgeois feminists on her right.

In 1895 Braun helped write a petition for assembly reform and called on women of all parties to sign. That bourgeois women breached the class divide proved irritating to Zetkin, but the acceptance by socialists of joint ventures was much more disturbing. The leading socialist paper, *Vorwärts*, had reacted favorably to the petition, calling it a sign of the growing revolutionary aims in the women's world. In defense of their position, the editors claimed that women, disenfranchised and unschooled politically, should not be judged by the same criteria as men. Every step toward independence represented progress for women. Zetkin angrily took the SPD papers to task for supporting it. She dismissed the appeal as an expression of "vulgar feminist views" and as an offense to the class basis of the proletarian women's movement. Why should socialists abandon their principle of class struggle when a policy involved the female sex? She feared the fundamentals would be watered down if the women's question were no longer welded to the social question. Turning on bourgeois feminism, Zetkin declared that socialists looked not to individual persons nor to professed views, but only to action—if action corresponded to the socialist world view. The petition in no way met socialist requirements and socialists could only lose propagandistically by supporting it.[4]

From Zetkin's perspective, then, the equivocation in the socialist camp made it all the more important to differentiate clearly between bourgeois and socialist goals and tactics. She was particularly concerned with left-wing bourgeois feminism, typified by the Berlin club *Frauenwohl*, which Braun had joined in 1893. In its concerns and platform, it resembled socialist feminism and the lines between the two movements were often blurred in the popular mind.[5] The middle-class organization called for women's suffrage, female factory inspectors, and the abolition of the *Gesindeordnung*, vestiges of feudal laws that still regulated rural and domestic service relations; its members studied women's legal position in Germany as well as the problems of female labor.[6]

The club published a paper, *Die Frauenbewegung* (The Women's Movement), edited by Braun and Minna Cauer. The first issue in January 1895 summarized their purpose: to speak for all women regardless of political persuasion and fight for their common goal—full equality of the sexes. "We want to be as fair to the struggle for equal education as for equal wages." Zetkin, gifted in the use of language, caustically labeled the effort *Harmonieduselei* (feminist waxing over harmony). The proclaimed goal of working for all women was illusory and definitely dangerous to proletarian unity.[7]

The ensuing verbal battle between Braun and Zetkin captures both the tone and the substance of the different conceptions. Braun charged Zetkin with "blind Party fanaticism" in her refusal to sanction joint petitions or collaborate in the pursuit of common objectives. Equality of the female sex was a question for humanity, not the preserve of one party. She hinted that Zetkin's intransigence reflected perhaps her uncertainty over proletarian women's class consciousness. Zetkin retorted that German feminists showed all the symptoms of political decay characteristic of the bourgeoisie in general. True, Braun stood to the left of bourgeois feminism, but her program came from "the ethically coiffed and perfumed salon socialists"—those who knew Social Democratic ideas just enough not to repel the proletariat but who refused to join openly for fear of losing their foothold in bourgeois society. Animated by a vision of "suffering humanity," they offered only compassion. The proletariat did not need compassion but clarification: what are the reasons for social injustice and how can it be eliminated?[8]

If shunned on her left, Braun's efforts to bring socialists into feminist organizations met equally strong opposition on her right. Ottilie Baader had been instrumental in encouraging Braun to learn about the lives of proletarian women. They had met at an Ethical Culture lecture series when Baader questioned the speaker on his proclaimed identity of view with socialists: if you want the same thing as we do, why aren't you a socialist? As Braun recounted this experience, it made a deep impression. She tried to get Baader into the club *Frauenwohl* and the Union of Women's Associations (*Bund deutscher Frauenvereine*), an umbrella organization founded in 1894 to coordinate the various middle-class feminist groups in German politics. Baader, however, stressed two points. First, the bourgeoisie feared collaboration with the socialists. Time would prove Baader right as Braun fought in vain for official sanction to invite working women's organizations into the middle-class feminist union.[9] Second, socialists could ill afford the time and energy needed to reach the bourgeois world. "The area of our propaganda extends to the whole proletariat—large enough for the most strenuous efforts. Association with the bourgeois women's movement would have divisive and confusing effects. The great mass of our female workers are not yet so self-confident that they feel as equals vis-à-vis the society ladies."[10] The fear that working-class women would be intimidated by their bourgeois sisters to pursue purely feminist goals haunted working-class leaders.

Braun's move to socialism in late 1895 stilled but did not resolve her ambivalence toward the idea of inexorable class antagonism. She now began to defend bourgeois feminism in socialist circles, as she had championed earlier the socialist position among the middle-class feminists. In various articles and speeches, in her theoretical analysis of the women's question, *Die Frauenfrage*, and on tours she advocated cautious cooperation with middle-class feminists and tried to include bourgeois groups among socialist propaganda targets. She warned against involving bourgeois feminists in direct socialist agitation, particularly in the work place, and advised against any other direct contact between individuals in the two camps. Yet she had come to believe by the turn of the century that bourgeois feminism was "progressing": numerous middle-class activists were becoming concerned with and were proposing solutions to the specific problems of working-class women.[11]

Under Braun's prodding, the socialist women's movement,

at its first national meeting in 1900, sanctioned contact with bourgeois feminists or other middle-class activists, but only on an individual, informal basis and with the proviso that each comrade speak from a socialist perspective.[12] Braun felt that this option permitted socialists to spread their propaganda specifically among women teachers and clerks—in her eyes the backbone of bourgeois feminism. Their social situation, she claimed, resembled that of manual workers and this made them potentially receptive to socialist ideas.[13] Her views on the importance of attracting bourgeois elements were not shared by most SPD members. Earlier misgivings by socialist leaders that sex identity might transcend class loyalty were proving groundless; working-class women naturally kept a distance from women of the classes above them. Braun recognized her isolation from majority sentiment in the socialist subculture but pursued her course because, in her words, "I even consider it the first duty of a comrade to be critical toward one's own party and speak with the utmost conscience about what seems wrong."[14]

Braun's stance on bourgeois feminism went against the official Party position formulated by Zetkin who looked askance at any modifications of her guidelines of 1896. She regarded Braun's views as ideological heresy as well as a personal attack on her own leadership. Drawing on support from her radical socialist friends, Zetkin was able to preserve orthodoxy on this particular issue up to World War I: contact between socialist women and the middle-class feminists remained limited and informal. In 1900, for example, Zietz spoke before a Hamburg feminist club and stated that she believed collaboration was permissible in those cases where socialists faced feminists as human beings, not as members of political parties. Ihrer periodically addressed feminist meetings, speaking on the question of protective labor laws, and her presentations were warmly received.[15] Contact also was surreptitious, as the Sombart-Braun correspondence reveals. In November 1903, Sombart asked Braun to talk before his local chapter of the Society for Social Reform (*Gesellschaft für Soziale Reform*). This was less than two months after the Dresden Congress had censored Braun for collaborating on a bourgeois paper, so Sombart used great caution: "We are planning a series of evenings on the theme of domestic industry. . . . You talk with such warmth, passion, and fascination. . . . Since here in Breslau, we have a very good relationship with [SPD] comrades (Löbe is one of the most eager debaters), the deviation into the arena of bourgeois social politics won't hurt you in the eyes of 'your people.' "[16] In Imperial Germany, socialist women deviated only slightly from the political paths prescribed by the concept of class struggle.

CONTINUING CONTROVERSY IN THE WOMEN'S MOVEMENT OVER BRAUN'S REVISIONIST FEMINISM, 1897-1901

After her conversion to socialism, Braun embarked on an active public career, speaking throughout the country for Social Democracy as she had for bourgeois feminism. She attracted crowds by her reputation as a skilled speaker, as well as by her illustrious name. As Klara Haase Weyl reminisced, "When Lily Braun was billed, but couldn't make it and Frl. Haase replaced her, people were greatly disappointed."[17]

The first major test of Braun's socialist commitment involved her intended participation at an international (bourgeois) women's congress planned for September 1896 in Berlin. Socialist women, true to their ideological stance, had refused to participate. Zetkin gave Braun friendly advice: "You are an aristocrat—enough reason to regard you with mistrust and to hinder your activity in the Party of which I expect so much. Now you alone—against our decisions—want to participate in the congress that limits itself to the problems of feminism. Female comrades will never understand that. . . . Our female members will definitely resist your participating in inner Party work unless you prove your loyalty by submitting to our resolution."[18] Braun acquiesced and addressed the congress briefly to explain the official decision as well as to announce her personal reasons for shunning bourgeois feminism. Shortly thereafter, Zetkin wrote to Kautsky that she was very happy about Braun's "excellent" speech. "By her talk, she had done more propagandistically than by fifteen minutes of workmen's misery."[19] Zetkin's praise marked a unique departure from the usual conflict and antagonism. Her response reflected not only the general appraisal of the propaganda impact of Braun's decision to embrace Social Democracy, but also a feeling that "her [Zetkin's] ideas and courage had been transmitted to Lily." That she had convinced Braun to publicly chastise the feminist congress for its half-hearted stance clearly pleased Zetkin. In contrast, as Braun reminisced, the decision to subordinate her own views to the majority left her uneasy.[20]

Prior to her decision to work for Social Democracy, Braun had participated in an international gathering of bourgeois feminists in London. Her English contacts introduced her to a new work sphere that she then tried to import to Germany. Activists in England had formed the Women's Industrial Council to study the conditions under which working women labored as well as the impact of protective legislation. They sought to inform the middle classes of the position of working-class women and to provide statistical documentation for the latter's causes. In 1897, Braun raised the question of setting up a similar bureau in Germany and published her proposal in *Gleichheit*. In response, Zetkin called on the readers to reply to the proposal *as she conceived it*: can we afford to disperse our energies into scientifically based reform action, as Braun suggested, or would this hinder our main goal of propaganda among the now indifferent female proletariat?[21] The ensuing debate reveals considerable disagreement among socialist activists over the orientation of the women's movement.

Braun proposed the creation of a new organizational structure for the movement. It was to be divided into four teams that would deal with questions of immediate and practical value to women and operate in all major centers of Germany. The first team would be responsible for acquiring information on the situation of working women in Germany. The second, bibliographical group would collect and publish materials on the nature and extent of women's employment, compare the social and economic position of German and European women in general, and disseminate data to be used by activists on propaganda tours. The third team should be composed of women versed in legal matters who would publish all statutes affecting working women and advise their sisters in legal questions. The fourth group would prepare articles for the socialist press, write brochures, and support unionization among working women. The teams' work sphere would remain basically in the realm of empirical investigation; actual agitation for the unions or Party was outside its purview. Such an organization, Braun felt, met the needs of working-class women hemmed in by discriminatory coalition laws and police harassment.[22]

Ten women responded to *Gleichheit's* call for debate; six categorically opposed Braun; one, Martha Rohrlach from Berlin, modified Braun's plan; three women supported her ideas. The proposal never reached the stage of an official debate at the women's conferences partly because of the strong opposition voiced by Zetkin and Baader, although vestiges of the program reemerged periodically to haunt Zetkin at later meetings.

The major objection expressed by both Zetkin and Baader stemmed from their belief that the educational program would fail to awaken working-class women to proletarian consciousness. Zetkin wrote that the plan, while it furthered the education of socialists, did not educate to socialism, and Baader charged that Braun's proposal did not lead to socialist convictions.[23] Both felt that the program neglected the two vital areas necessary for a mature understanding of socialism— economics and history. The plan was a practical work program in a limited sphere that best could be left to already existing institutions—the educational clubs, the trade unions, or even to bourgeois social reformers. From a more pragmatic viewpoint, Zetkin thought that the women's movement lacked the means and leisure to devote official attention to such a project. It could ill afford the creation of a central leadership group to coordinate the investigations. Proletarian women could not perform their vital tasks and undertake Braun's program as well. Given the realities in the world of proletarian women, said Zetkin, one could only speak of "either-or" not both.[24]

In a personal slight, Baader wrote that only so-called educated women had the requisite training to carry out the proposals, and, although class-conscious comrades were found among them, "I do not expect much from their work." No one opposed their orientation, she added, but it was illogical to make activities suited to these educated women the guiding principles of the whole working women's movement. Shortening the workday, not a special organization, was required to promote socialist education.[25]

Personal motives underlay Zetkin and Baader's objections. Two revealing letters to Kautsky, whom Zetkin consulted for intellectual and moral support, betrayed her fear that Braun sought to create a permanent secretary and desired personal influence. "The real point of the plan is not contained in the article."[26] Zetkin called the proposal "woman's trash [weiberlich] . . . a translation of Heinrich Braun's collected works from the scientific-literary form into an effeminate, organizational, practical program," while publicly she had declared it "thoughtful." In her view, the proposal was written by one of the socialists "who lived a quiet bourgeois life, who cannot work in the propaganda struggle, unwilling to fight within the Party itself . . . but still . . . wanting to do something for her convictions and above all, eager to gain influence."

Kautsky shared Zetkin's sentiment, which greatly pleased and encouraged her. She confessed that, "I feel so very dumb."[27] His support, she added, gave her courage and confidence for the struggle she expected "because Lily's proposal hides a good deal of personal motives which will probably cause her to stick stubbornly to her project." Zetkin declared her willingness to take on not merely Lily but Berlin comrades, including Frau Ihrer and "some of the Party fathers, not to forget the much loved and admired August [Bebel] and still others."

Baader's conflict with Braun reflected the difficulties of bridging the gap in social origins. Baader's innate mistrust of the "aristocrat" Braun was fed not only by ideological differences but by personal animosity, illustrating the potential for tension between two leaders of diverse social backgrounds that is a theme in Robert Michels's sociological analysis of the German Social Democratic Party. According to Michels, it is not infrequent that "differences of principles . . . soon become personal and lead to a profound hostility."[28] Although Baader had been influential in converting Braun to socialism, she remained skeptical of the motives of intellectuals and "ladies" in the Party and publicly alluded to their social differences. At the women's conference in 1902, for example, she generalized that most academically educated ladies were "parade horses whom we don't need at all," although she carefully excluded Zetkin from the appellation. She also wrote cynically about women's desire to become "doctors" on some faculty, and when preparing her short and generally sketchy memoirs, Baader devoted a whole section to Braun's 1897 proposal. Clara Bohm-Schuch explains the Baader-Braun antagonism as a *Nichtkennen*—they were simply not attuned to each other. Baader, it appears, had the deep hostility of a worker against bourgeois ladies, and she was influential in thwarting Braun's effective participation in Party life.[29]

Approval of Braun's proposal came primarily from female unionists and most prominently from Emma Ihrer. This foreshadowed Braun's protagonists in later conflicts as well. Braun greeted the support with mixed emotions; she would have preferred other friends, although she had great respect for Ihrer personally. She mistrusted the trade union's "limited vision" and undue emphasis on organizational questions.[30]

The major article endorsing Braun's 1897 proposals was signed "A. N."; at its conclusion, Ihrer added, "It corresponds completely with my opinion on the subject," and stated she was not planning to add anything to the debate.[31] Braun's supporter declared that the plan was undoubtedly an important statement. A large movement needed to use each person's talents most effectively. The new organization would attract those unable or unwilling to agitate or tour the country but eager to work for the Party by pen. She approved of the practical orientation that Zetkin and Baader had criticized. Striking at the heart of the matter, the author praised the educational implications for the trade union movement: "For clearly, the trade union question must be the central point around which the proletarian women's movement revolves. Entry into her union is for most women the decisive step that elevates her from barren and sterile individuality to a higher form of community." Such views hardly pleased radical socialists who saw the central role of the proletarian women's movement as broadening and clarifying socialist knowledge and the unions' as preparing for the day of revolution.

A compromise solution was suggested by Martha Rohrlach, who modified the proposal by calling for a paid secretary, confirming Zetkin's fears. The other women participating in the debate responded briefly along the lines drawn by the pros and cons. Braun sought to win support by revising her proposal in ways resembling Rohrlach's views, but the modification met even less favor from Zetkin. Zetkin claimed that it was inadvisable for "the healthy development of a movement" to create a superorganization (*Spitze*) before a firm and broad foundation had been built.[32] With that, the proposal was buried.

The conflict engendered by Braun's educational plan had subsided by July 1897, and that month *Gleichheit* announced her responsibility for the paper's enlarged notes (*Notizenteil*). She performed that function for nearly four years until Zetkin summarily terminated their collaboration. Braun had come to alienate Zetkin and many other Party women on a host of issues since she was never shy in offering her novel views and suggestions.

In 1898, for example, Braun supported a resolution at the Stuttgart SPD Congress calling for the transfer of *Gleichheit* to the capital city and to the control of the Party press, a position that hardly endeared her to Zetkin. *Gleichheit* was independent of Party control until 1902, and Braun voiced misgivings over the paper's "very personal stamp."[33] At the 1902 women's conference in Munich, she supported an abortive resolution calling for a paid secretary for the women's movement. The proposal resembled her revised organizational scheme of 1897. Rejection of the plan, Braun later wrote, proved that anything new in the movement was being branded as "high treason."[34] She felt that opposition had come from members fearing a veiled attack on Baader, the official leader. At the conference, Braun had been very careful to speak highly of Baader's "great services," but nevertheless endorsed the proposal for a paid secretary. According to Ihrer, Zetkin was instrumental in insuring the plan's defeat. In a letter to the Bavarian SPD reform leader, Georg von Vollmar, in September 1902, Ihrer wrote that she would not be attending either the SPD congress or the women's conference that year. "Clara Zetkin has taken care that neither I nor any of my friends will attend. Just when five of us were on a trip, the women met and voted, for we had planned to make a motion to employ a secretary to coordinate propaganda and the movement."[35] Ihrer added that since she was being considered for the post of secretary, Zetkin had used all means "to avoid such competition." Zetkin was determined to maintain her dominant position against all challengers.

Braun at times steadfastly adhered to principles—surprisingly on some matters that most socialist feminists were willing to handle with flexibility. For example, in Hamburg where women could join political organizations, Braun rejected the separate women's representative system, saying "we are not feminists but Social Democrats." Here she equated feminism with separatism. In the same vein, she questioned why male comrades with mandates to the SPD congresses were disenfranchised from decision making at the women's conferences. This was contrary to the official position that the women's movement was an integral part of the organized working class.[36] Almost unconsciously, she unmasked a paradox that plagued socialist feminists in their effort to work out effective tactics for mobilizing working-class women. While officially part of the proletarian political and union structures, the women refused to be submerged totally into the larger organizations. As part C explores in detail, they had come to accept as crucial for their cause separate guidelines, committees

staffed by women, and, in the case of the Party, even measured institutional autonomy. Braun's interference in the early
twentieth century raised a sensitive issue that most would
have preferred to leave alone. Only on the personal level did
Braun demand freedom of movement and consideration given
to unique needs. Subordination of the individual to the "will of
the majority," or to the "Party's fundamental principles," as
prescribed on occasion by Zetkin and Zietz was anathema to
her.[37] If this were not enough to cause tension, she sought
also, as seen, to dilute the class basis of the movement.

In 1901, two publications by Braun, *Frauenarbeit und
Hauswirtschaft (Women's Labor and Household Cooperatives)*, a plea to alleviate women's domestic duties by organizing household cooperatives, and *Frauenfrage (The Women's
Question)*, a theoretical-historical analysis of the economic aspects of the women's question, aggravated her tense relationship with Zetkin. The two works engendered a debate among
socialist women that further impaired Braun's credibility as a
socialist and deprived her of effective influence in the
women's movement.

The experience of having a child prompted Braun to write
her book on household cooperatives, which called for apartment houses with one common kitchen (*Einküchenhäuser*). In
her memoirs she wrote, "After the birth of my son, the problems of women's liberation were no longer mere theories.
They cut into my own flesh."[38] The burdens of women as
workers (both manual and intellectual) and mothers had assumed new and immediate meaning, and from 1897, she was
determined to reconcile the two roles. Her fight for an extensive national maternity insurance was one response to her perception of the additional dimension of the women's question.
The call for cooperative living was another, reflecting her personal dissatisfaction with the added domestic chores after the
arrival of her son. She labeled the tedious housework as a "dis-
turbance of domestic peace," and resented the time and energy required to keep a household running smoothly. As one
of her biographers maintains, Braun "was unable to grasp what
she did not herself encounter and to feel what she did not ex-

perience herself."[39] Braun's proposal represented a translation of personal needs into programmatic form.

Braun based her call for communal household arrangements on the inevitable transformation of the single family unit under the impact of economic development. Industrialization had wrought changes in the family as a production unit as well as in women's economic roles at home. As early as 1896, she had proclaimed that economic growth would destroy the last bastion of traditional family life, the kitchen, and later wrote that the basis of marriage should not be in the kitchen, but in common intellectual and emotional ties and experiences.[40] Furthermore, the trend of female employment necessitated new institutions to reduce women's wifely, motherly, and housekeeping burdens. Cooperatives could become the foundation of women's emancipation; unless they obtained the leisure to develop harmoniously, their liberation would remain chimerical.[41] Home cooperatives, Braun predicted, would encourage feelings of brotherhood within the capitalist system and further the preconditions for socialism. She saw cooperatives as important building blocks in the future construction of a socialist society. According to Braun, capitalism would not suddenly disappear; she envisioned the gradual disintegration of the capitalist order concomitant with the slow ripening of the socialist system.

According to Braun's memoirs, the reaction to her proposal remained cool at best. Some women charged that agitation for communal households would divert the working class from its main political goals; others claimed she wanted to drive "all women from the intimate family life to the barracks." Quarreling and hatred were predicted if large numbers of families adopted a communal form of living.[42] The only favorable contemporary review came from Helene Block in *Sozialistische Monatshefte*, the revisionist organ, who wrote perceptively that even radical comrades favoring women's emancipation refused to apply their principles to their "four walls" and had a "good bourgeois fear" of a revolution in domestic life.[43] However, it was Zetkin's uncompromising opposition that destroyed any chance for official adoption of Braun's proposal.

In a letter to Kautsky, Zetkin described Braun's brochure as the "latest blossoming of utopianism in its most dangerous, opportunistic form."[44] By implication, she related Braun's proposal to the ongoing revisionist debate involving most Party members at the time. Underlying Zetkin's overt hostility was the specter of socialists adopting the erroneous view that socialism could be realized within the capitalist system, nothing but "amiable delusion."[45] This would imply a total rethinking of Social Democracy's concepts and tactics, she wrote publicly in *Gleichheit*. In reality, socialist goals could not be achieved contemporaneously with the political class struggle, and the only crucial tactic was preaching socialist ideas to the masses and organizing them for their historic role in opposing the capitalist system.

Zetkin detailed specific objections to Braun's plan. She agreed that economic change was revolutionizing the family and that improvement of the position of working women required an easing of their burdens as wives and mothers. However, she questioned Braun's solution, ostensibly because of the proletariat's living conditions. First, the major prerequisite, a secure, regular income was lacking; employment insecurity characterized the realities of life for most working-class members, and the unemployed could not maintain a smoothly functioning cooperative. Second, only a small percentage of the proletariat, those who were relatively well-off, could benefit from home cooperatives. Most women within this section did not work. Third, the psychological preconditions for communal living did not exist among these proletarian "aristocrats": they prized the single family establishment. Finally, striking at the heart of the matter, Zetkin believed that cooperatives would acquire revolutionary meaning only after the proletariat obtained political power. Cooperatives depended on radical change in thoughts, habits, and beliefs that, in turn, was based on transformed production and private property relations. She called cooperatives essentially bourgeois reform work, chastised Braun for failure to distinguish socialist from middle-class concerns, and dismissed the proposal as having no relevance for the agitational efforts of socialist women.[46]

In Zetkin's view, the municipal reform proposals of the women's movement or of socialist cooperatives, such as cooperative food stores or communal restaurants, bore no resemblance to Braun's plan. The existing communal experiments were not embryonic household cooperatives, as Braun asserted, but rather branches of industry assuming various economic functions of the former productive family. Zetkin held that the movement's call for municipal reforms corresponded to economic change and actually proved the bankruptcy of Braun's vision. Continuous industrialization of the family's former domestic economic roles, not the imposition of new structures such as home cooperatives, would supplant the single-family establishment naturally. [47]

This debate reflected a significant issue in the socialist movement of pre-World War I Germany: its attitude toward social reform. Zetkin's stance was consistent with Marxist thought as it was interpreted officially around the turn of the century. In a study of the relationship between reform and revolution and the implication for strategies and tactics in the political battle, Norbert Leser notes that "reform, according to Marxist thought, can in no way be a form of peaceful development into socialism."[48] Yet, this is precisely what Braun envisioned: reforms such as cooperatives would lead to the gradual emergency of socialism. She rejected revolution as necessary for the inauguration of socialism and resolved the tension between revolution and reform in favor of the latter.

In contrast, the orthodox position viewed reforms solely as a means of furthering the revolution. It accepted reforms if they served to promote the class struggle and prepare the masses for the revolution. Inherent in the stance was a belief in the inevitability of the revolutionary struggle once the objective preconditions had ripened, and the first and foremost task for propagandists was to organize the people and prepare them for the final day of reckoning. Hence, reforms for the sake of social progress alone were considered unnecessary distractions. With hindsight, it becomes clear that this position, so well exemplified by Zetkin's arguments against Braun's proposals in 1901, involved the consequence of social inaction. In

Leser's words, "the fixed gaze on the revolutionary goal hinders the optimal utilization of the situation in favor of reform because it encourages inactivity and standing aside, provides a theoretical alibi for this attitude, and also contributes the consolation that a future positive development will compensate for the frustrations of the present."[49] In short, belief in the inevitability of revolution and an assessment of the value of reforms in terms of their impact on the revolutionary goal engendered a fatalism and passivity[50] that hindered the employment of flexible strategies and tactics. Although in later years Zetkin became critical of the Party's tactics and, with Rosa Luxemburg, formed a truly radical wing demanding action against the more passive center, the 1901 debate reveals a characteristic prewar socialist attitude, one that leaned toward inactivity.[51]

Braun's plan clearly would not have hastened the revolution. Yet, it came from a deep concern for the position of women and would have eased the lives of those females living in the cooperatives. Braun's proposal envisioned transformed bases of existence—communal living—and a corresponding change in values and attitudes. Zetkin refused to accept Braun's proposition that cooperatives within the capitalist system could transform the members' bases of existence, presumably because the visualized communes would be solely consumption entities and leave work relations unaltered. Furthermore, her projection of cooperatives as meaningful institutions only under socialism served as an alibi for postponing action to some indefinite date. Zetkin's preoccupation with the economic preconditions for change made her unwilling to experiment with alternative life styles. By rejecting home cooperatives in the name of ideological necessity, Zetkin remained true to radical Marxism. At the same time, her position narrowed feminist options.

The publication of *Frauenfrage* coming on the heels of Braun's home-cooperative plan created a crisis. From the late 1890s, Braun had felt that the women's movement lacked a comprehensive, fundamental statement and thus was "groping about."[52] Her theoretical work was designed to fill the gap.

Part one presented the evolution of the women's question from antiquity through the nineteenth century, and the second part dissected the economic roots and major characteristics of the bourgeois and the proletarian women's movements. She planned to analyze the legal and moral dimensions of the women's question in a subsequent work.

Public reaction was mixed, although the book came to be used in the women's educational clubs and sessions.[53] Bebel called it "objective" and "scientific" and recommended that it be acquired by Party libraries. Georg Ledebour, writing in *Gleichheit*, was considerably less charitable, arguing that Braun failed to grasp the materialist view of history and introduced a false methodology. Braun's concentration on the economic sphere to the neglect of the superstructure (law and morality) distorted her analysis. He voiced amazement that Braun continued to propose home cooperatives in the book after the idea had been so thoroughly criticized by Zetkin. This "evokes the uneasy feeling that Braun is unteachable."[54]

Berlin women registered similar skepticism. Upon hearing of her plan to write on the women's question, Baader had responded that such a literary addition was superfluous. The movement had Bebel's "Frau" and Zetkin's articles in *Gleichheit*. Publication of the book precipitated reaction: in 1901, Baader sent Braun a letter from the Berliners formally excluding her from their meetings because she had proven "unreliable in the execution of Party duties."[55] In a letter of 1907, Zetkin voiced full support for the decision. "Berlin comrades have decided years ago that Lily Braun is unreliable, untrustworthy, and is not allowed to speak in their meetings and they refuse responsibility for her actions. . . . *Gleichheit* pledges its solidarity with the Berlin women. . . . My conscience agrees with this."[56] In 1901, she removed Braun from any association with *Gleichheit* and as subsequent letters indicate, refused to publish reports on Braun's activities in the Party or mention her name in the paper. For *Gleichheit* readers, Braun had become a nonperson by 1907.

Zetkin wrote a long and bitter letter to Kautsky after she had read *Frauenfrage*. How she analyzed her feelings toward

Braun documents the personal element in the ideological conflict. Zetkin's pride and self-image had been threatened by Braun's failure to acknowledge her role in the proletarian women's movement. It appears that Zetkin had agreed to review the book for *Neue Zeit*, but after careful reading wrote that "it is impossible for me personally to undertake the review." She complained, "The chapter on the working women's movement closes my mouth as a critic. I cannot criticize her [Braun's] partly unhistorical perception and her historically entirely wrong presentation of our German proletarian women's movement without contrasting them with my own personal lifelong Party activity."[57] Zetkin resented Braun's characterization of *Gleichheit* merely as the continuation of *Arbeiterin*, edited by Ihrer—a statement, she said, that totally neglected the important role of *Gleichheit* in training and educating female comrades. She complained that Braun only said she was the editor of *Gleichheit* and failed to discuss her role at Gotha in formulating the theoretical and practical guidelines to the women's question from a socialist perspective. "She managed to bypass my work completely," Zetkin lamented. In essence, "Braun has proven that she is a more narrow-minded person, dirtier, more malicious and above all, more stupid than those who know her well believe her to be." She hoped that someone in the Party who followed the true history of the movement would be propelled by a feeling for justice and truth to rectify the perverse picture. She claimed she could say in good conscience that she had never been motivated by jealousy, but stated it would be hard to bear that "a Lily Braun is dead-silent on my work because I know that it is alive in thousands and thousands of minds." Zetkin declared that she had broken off all contact with Braun. "As a member of the Party, I had the duty to do everything I could to help Lily Braun gain a position in which she could be of the greatest value to the Party. I did my best. But, after I recognized her dishonesty and her egotism, I saw it as my duty as a human being to limit my relations with her to the official Party work."[58] Zetkin said she insisted on "clarity and honesty" in personal relations. She owed this not only to herself, but to her children who must learn that to be a Social Democrat meant to be a human being who is better, more honest and selfless, and more ready to make personal sacrifices. They must not be subject to the duality between convictions and actions.[59]

While the public battle between 1897 and 1901 was waged around Braun's proposals for an information bureau and home cooperatives, a less visible struggle took place over the power of the written word. Zetkin sought to circumscribe Braun's function in the literary sphere and preserve her own dominant intellectual role. The exclusion of Braun from *Gleichheit* conformed with this aim. In addition, Braun found herself increasingly outmaneuvered by Zetkin, who thwarted her proposals for brochures and pamphlets on topics of interest to women. Zetkin countered several of Braun's plans with similar literary undertakings.[60] For example, in various letters to Richard Fischer, editor of *Vorwärts*, Braun wrote of her desire to prepare a propaganda brochure on women's employment in Germany that was to be based on the latest occupational statistics in the factory inspectors' reports. After corresponding with Zetkin, she learned to her surprise that Zetkin was planning a similar pamphlet and she withdrew her idea. At that time, Braun wrote that she did not want to get into a "race" with Zetkin. Complaining to Bebel in 1903 during the heat of the revisionist controversy, Braun referred to Zetkin blocking her literary activity in the Party and used the incident of the pamphlet to buttress her case. The pamphlet Zetkin had described as being "as good as ready" in 1901 had to date (March 1903) not appeared.[61]

AN ASSESSMENT OF THE ZETKIN-BRAUN CLASH

The controversy between Lily Braun and Clara Zetkin became public knowledge after 1901. Much was made of it in the contemporary press. After the Dresden Congress, for example, Zetkin complained to Bebel about the reactions of bourgeois papers. She wrote that the *Beobachter* asserted, "I pushed out Lily Braun from *Gleichheit* and paralyzed her party activities."

Somewhat disingenuously she denied the charge and added, "I can let them berate me because if anyone has a good conscience in relation to Braun, it is I."[62]

Several analysts, both contemporary and later historians, have sought reasons for the antagonism. Joseph Joos claims the origin of the conflict was Zetkin's realization that the proletarian women's movement was ideologically immature and that confusion could occur if she did not maintain tight reign. Both he and Anna Blos, a socialist deputy in the Weimar period, believe that Zetkin feared Braun as a competitor. Joos writes that Zetkin rejected Braun's proposal for a central information agency because she was determined to preserve *Gleichheit* as the main repository of data and analysis. And, Blos adds that Zetkin had been the undisputed leader prior to Braun's appearance, but she then faced a woman at least her equal, if not her superior, in many ways. Recent historians have dealt only peripherally with the controversy. Thönnessen simply notes, for example, that from the beginning "no love was lost" between the two women.[63]

There is probably no single explanation of a conflict as deep and personal as that between Clara Zetkin and Lily Braun. On one level, the controversy exemplifies the response of entrenched power to perceived threats from outsiders. Robert Michels deals with this phenomenon, and his theories of the autocratic leader able to perpetuate power because of institutional, material, and psychic advantages present in the leadership role serve as a partial explanation for the conflict and its outcome. As seen in previous chapters, Zetkin and her immediate followers dominated the women's movement, representing an oligarchy at the turn of the century, and as Michels claims, "every oligarchy is suspicious of those entering its ranks."[64] His statement of the "inevitable antagonism between the 'greatmen' [read: women] who have acquired a reputation in other fields . . . and the old-established leaders who have been socialists from the first" could have been written with Zetkin and Braun in mind.[65] Braun joined German Social Democracy as a well-known personage with a claim to a leadership role. Zetkin initially responded favorably because she felt she could mold Braun in her image. Once this hope was dashed and the independent-minded Braun asserted her individuality, Clara used often underhanded methods to keep Lily at bay. In the process, control over *Gleichheit*, her ties with *Vorwärts*, and her close contacts with leaders of the Social Democratic Party gave Zetkin a decisive advantage over Braun in the struggle for power. In 1897, Zetkin clearly feared that Braun sought to create a rival institution outside her control and successfully prevented adoption of the proposal. In 1902, for similar reasons, she maneuvered against Ihrer and safeguarded her dominant position. As seen also in the 1902 troubles, the new ideas were branded as an attack on the old, trusted national leader (Baader), and served to discredit the proponents in the eyes of the lower-level activists who supported their representative. The structure of the women's movement, in Michels's words, tended "instinctively towards exclusivism," offering the women prominent by virtue of their proven credentials, reputation, access to the press and chance for cooptation of like-minded individuals the possibilities to perpetuate their power.[66]

Apart from the issue of organizational power, the Zetkin-Braun antagonism reflected different images of the women's movement and its role and meaning in the socialist subculture. Braun was concerned with the needs of all women in the present society. She sought to weld together the broadest-based feminist movement (transcending class) under the socialist banner. She firmly believed that only socialism offered women both the analytic tools and the critical vision to begin the process of ameliorating sex oppression. Destruction of more and more barriers standing in the way of social equality would create the future socialist society. Yet, as exemplified by her proposal for household cooperatives, Braun's purview was the present. Zetkin's time horizon was far longer. To reach the future more quickly, she restricted her feminism to the needs of working-class women and willingly sacrificed at times feminism to socialism. Her concern with "all women" was intangible and projected into an idealized, egalitarian society. As the outcome of the controversy shows, large numbers of socialist women shared Zetkin's conceptions.

Different emphasis on feminism and socialism affected even the manner in which the two antagonists introduced proposals to SPD congresses. Zetkin explained her support thus: "When I feel the duty to speak in favor of a motion, it is not because I am a woman, but rather because I feel first as a comrade [*Genossin*], and recognize the importance of proletarian women for the movement." Braun exclaimed, "When I protest so energetically . . . it is not only as a comrade, but as a woman."[67]

The conflict was exacerbated by perceived offenses to each leader's self-image. Braun boldly challenged Zetkin's image of her role and importance in the socialist women's movement. As seen in the Kautsky correspondence, Zetkin felt hurt and angry that Braun bypassed her contributions to the emergence of a theoretically armed and tactically defined movement. Jealousy played a role despite Zetkin's assertions to the contrary. Yet Braun had wounded her pride as well. Without full access to Zetkin's letters and papers, only a tentative hypothesis may be offered for her vituperative reaction to Braun. In a letter to Frau von Vollmar in 1894, Zetkin revealed considerable inner uncertainty despite the strong, forceful, and clear exterior she presented to the outside world. Contrasting herself with Frau von Vollmar she said, "You are so intelligent and I am in many respects a big child."[68] Shortly thereafter, she wrote that she could not tolerate lack of self-criticism in people and added, "Maybe it derives from the fact that I am . . . forever dissatisfied with myself." Zetkin then tried to assess her own personality makeup and characterized herself as basically caught between the poles of "overestimation and uncritical dissatisfaction with myself."[69] In several of her letters to Kautsky to whom, as seen, she turned for moral and intellectual support (until ideological disagreements interfered with their friendship around 1910), Zetkin expressed great gratification over his agreement with her views. It seems, then, that Zetkin needed constant external confirmation and Braun threatened her by withholding it.

Braun had her own problems. She suffered, as previously indicated, constant tension between her personal desires and the necessity to adapt to the needs of the organization. In her memoirs and in articles, Braun raised the two requirements to polar opposites: one's own beliefs, the "I," versus the will of the socialist masses; individualism versus socialism; or self-assertion against self-sacrifice.[70] She failed to understand or grasp instinctively that organizations inherently limit individuals' options and require compromise and adaptation. Her reaction to increasing tension with Party comrades was also one of hurt: "I came to you out of love with a full heart and with all my strength . . . why do you rebuff me?"[71]

Another side to Braun's dilemma involved her firm belief in socialism and her gradual exclusion from socialist activity. After 1903, she found herself increasingly prevented from effectively working within the socialist world. By 1907, she all but withdrew from socialist work. Yet, practical as well as intellectual considerations prevented her return to the bourgeois world. She found herself suspended between the spheres of ability on the one hand and opportunity on the other, a source of extreme tension for one basically committed to action.

Braun's reaction to the conflict with Zetkin and other Party comrades corresponded to the dictates of the class into which she was born. She charged they had "slandered my honor," the ultimate social crime in aristocratic circles. Such an action required immediate satisfaction. Braun's emotional reaction to the Dresden Congress censorship reveals the difficulty of discarding the values of the social group in which an individual grew up. In her memoirs, she wrote that Bebel, "this ladies' knight, had the sad courage to proclaim me before the whole world as a woman without honor." Braun dreamt of shooting Bebel for offending her, and said she wished her father were still alive. "He would request restoration of my honor . . . with the trigger of a gun."[72] In 1907, Braun introduced a motion to expel Zetkin for slandering her honor by calling her an "embezzler" and a "swindler" in front of other colleagues. The executive forced Zetkin to retract her statements and Braun, in turn, withdrew her motion.[73] Prevention of a public scandal took precedence over personal grievances.

Braun's dramatic conversion to Social Democratic politics in late 1895 had created difficulties for women leaders already in the movement. Braun was an outsider, an independent and controversial figure whose understanding of feminism often ran counter to assumptions prevailing among insiders. She voiced her views openly and energetically and forced socialist women to come to grips with their own feminism and with what they expected of the women's organization. The conflicting positions were most fiercely contested in the astringent debate between Braun and Zetkin, and the outcome of personal battle had considerable impact on the place of feminism in the socialist world.

At the turn of the twentieth century, the balance of power in the movement still favored Zetkin. Feminism remained encased in a class framework. Its purview was limited to the needs of working-class women and its appeal was geared to their mobilization. The rank and file rejected Braun's plea to recruit among middle-class teachers and clerks or to work together with bourgeois feminists. Braun's educational plan was seen as too pragmatic and faulted for its failure to awaken women to socialism; as in the controversy over birth control, home cooperatives were rejected as diversionary and distracting undertakings, unrelated to the class struggle, and possibly inimical to the revolution. Preparation for the class struggle as well as the exigencies of socialism remained the major criteria for official acceptance of feminist proposals.

The feminist component in socialism was more than just a set of aims and goals. It carried with it unique tactics for realizing the stated objectives and for attracting working-class women to the labor movement. The feminist tactics, as the theory, were a product, in part, of hard experience; socialist feminists had to grapple with the question to what extent feminist calculations should determine their organizational relationships in the movement. As part C demonstrates, by the early twentieth century they had embraced a form of quasi-independence for their cause. Yet they faced the need to safeguard this choice in institutional structures becoming increasingly bureaucratized and uniform.

FEMINIST TACTICS IN
GERMAN SOCIAL DEMOCRACY

Socialist feminists' concept of sex equality was qualified in ways that directly shaped tactical issues. Prominent leaders such as Clara Zetkin and Luise Zietz stressed the point that men and women were different and applauded sexual diversity. They justified women's full participation in social life by pointing to unique female characteristics such as sensitivity, practicality, and warmth that benefited the human community. They believed that women's participation in Party and union life would introduce qualitative changes, not merely increase the numbers of participants in the class struggle.[1] These women went further and urged that special consideration be given women because of the centuries-long suppression of the female sex. They rejected the notion of absolute equality that might negate the realities of women's biological functions and different socialization experiences. Such equality only served to perpetuate actual inequalities. Appealing to "laws of necessity" as well as to women's peculiarities, they modified and reformulated tactical guidelines in ways applicable to recruiting their working-class sisters. They sought, in short, to carve out their own sphere of activity.

A three-pronged approach characterized the women's mobilization efforts. First, in the political sphere, they sought to win over females by advocating legislative reforms to remedy discrimination based primarily on sex. This was their feminist vision transformed into a concrete legislative platform. They also set up committees to deal specifically with women's needs and created increasingly complex bureaucracies that operated independently of the Party hierarchy until 1908. Second, they engaged in extensive unionization campaigns. Unionization assumed a strategic role as the legally sanctioned antidote to discrimination against women in the political realm. Third, an educational program to create new consciousness was devised in separate educational clubs, in the union hierarchy, and, after 1908, at Party-sponsored reading and discussion sessions. This effort focused on women as members of the proletarian class.

Part C examines women's role in Social Democracy, their impact on socialist institutions, and the degree to which both the Party and Free Trade Unions adjusted themselves to feminist demands. It seeks to assess the achievements of women within the socialist subculture as well as the limitations placed on them by that subculture.

CHAPTER VI

PARTY POLITICS:
INSTITUTIONAL AUTONOMY AND
DIVISION OF LABOR

Socialist women performed all tasks that fell to the organized working class. Under the motto "If we can't vote, we sure can agitate," they actively supported each electoral campaign and legislative proposal.[1] Working hard at recruitment, they undertook extensive speaking tours throughout the country, founded clubs, ran educational gatherings, joined committees, and canvassed city blocks and districts. At the same time, they claimed the special task of reaching the masses of women and winning them over for the class struggle. The female leaders, thus, worked doubly hard in the organization: they struggled alongside men for the general cause and they addressed the needs of working-class women as well.

Determined to counteract the debilitating political and psychological effects of sex discrimination, the leadership argued for freedom of movement and a degree of organizational autonomy. To suspicions that women would become a "state within a state," Zietz responded most graphically. "I do not want anything exceptional or even special rights but—as we are already second-class citizens—we refuse to be degraded to second-class comrades."[2] Working hand in hand with men, she stressed, should not preclude a beneficial division of labor within the socialist movement.

The arguments offered by women leaders to support their claim to a sphere of influence and the tactics used to mobilize working-class women reflected keen awareness of the different social worlds of men and women. Neither Marx nor Engels had studied women's "specific oppression"; woman was analyzed abstractly to assess the state of culture or it was assumed her function, role, and consciousness as worker would develop as did man's.[3] Because of the difficulties in reaching working women, German socialist feminists spent considerable energy investigating the social position of the working-class woman. The result was succinctly stated by Zetkin. It is the femaleness (*Weibthum*) of women, she wrote, which lay at the root of the problem.[4] Women's subordinate role in the family and in society hindered efforts at organization. Working women had an imperfect understanding of the implications of an expanding female labor force. They were "employed but without an occupation," questioned the importance of organizations, and feared that dues or similar contributions would deprive their families of necessities.[5] Alas, Zetkin admitted, the views of the masses lagged behind changed economic relations. Only the most careful attention to women's specific needs and unique experiences could bridge this gap between revolutionary changes and traditional conceptions.

ERECTING THE WOMEN'S ORGANIZATION PRIOR TO 1908

In the early 1890s, several immediate problems stemming from sex discrimination highlighted the need for special consideration. Legal restrictions on women's political activity were hampering their association with the SPD. One issue involved female participation at the Party's annual policy-making congresses, desired by leaders of both sexes. How could women be sent to the congresses in those areas of Germany that barred them from belonging to SPD organizations?

The first socialist congress after termination of the anti-Socialist laws in 1890 sanctioned special meetings where women would elect their own delegates if the (male) members in a given locality failed to support a woman.[6] Two years later, the clause was removed because, as leaders such as Ottilie Baader said, "We don't want privileges, but equal rights."[7] However, this decision was soon reversed. The next several years taught women a lesson quickly taken to heart: in the presence of real social and political inequalities formal equality could be discriminatory. Until the idea of sexual equality was accepted in law and popular behavior, women needed special privileges to secure their rights in the Party. These privileges allowed them to circumvent repressive laws as well.

Zetkin explained to the 1894 congress that removal of the clause had been an error. Since laws of political association discriminated against women, they had found it hard to compete during delegate elections. Ignaz Auer, a leading socialist, was even more direct in stating that the women's movement had to be represented at the congresses without being dependent on the good will of men. Men simply had not supported women delegates.[8] Bowing to practical necessity in 1894, Social Democracy reinstated special women's meetings with power to elect female delegates. Although this allowed women to attend the congresses without formally belonging to the SPD, German officialdom frequently made life hard for them. In 1894, for example, the Nuremberg Women's and Girls' Educational Club was dissolved for engaging in politics: it had sent a delegate to the Frankfurt SPD Congress.[9]

The hierarchy of representatives ascending from the local to the district and the national level formed the linchpin of the women's mobilization efforts prior to their incorporation into the Party. This organizational system conformed to the lesson of the early 1890s that had brought home the importance of institutional autonomy. Between late 1899 and 1908 Baader, "trusted and well-loved by Party comrades," headed the edifice in a central bureau.[10] Through her good offices, the leaders maintained close contact and coordinated propaganda throughout the country. They collected money to support their work, and were proud of a degree of financial independence. From 1900 on, delegates elected at open meetings met nearly every two years at national conferences to work out specific tactics and prepare resolutions. Conforming to their integral connection with the SPD, socialist women, at their own conferences, did not take an independent position on political issues facing the Party as a whole, such as revisionism or the mass strike. Rather, the gatherings handled questions of particular importance to women such as maternity insurance, children's education, or protective labor laws. The speeches were often published as pamphlets and were incorporated into the socialist library on women's questions available for general propaganda purposes.

In the 1890s, efforts were directed to reaching the industrial working woman, seen as relatively easy to organize. Soon, activists turned to those nonindustrial sectors such as domestic industry that were dominated by female labor. At the same time, the mobilization of nonworking women was actively pursued.

Socialist feminists sought to build their constituency by various methods. One or several political activists would establish personal contact with individuals chosen for their energy and competence who worked in factories or workshops. These women were politicized and then given the job of systematically continuing to spread socialist ideas among their female work colleagues. They often held discussions at the place of work. Public meetings for specific categories of working women or for all working women in a given locality were called, but never on Saturday evenings; even though by law women were required to quit work at five o'clock, socialists knew they usually did their housework Saturday nights. The initial propagandist as well as each speaker was well informed on the conditions of labor so that each individual working woman felt personally involved.[11] At the 1902 Munich conference, delegates agreed that the small gatherings of women in their work place were proving effective. Many future propagandists came out of these intimate sessions.[12] Socialists also sought to reach women at home by canvassing districts for the Party. They received names and addresses from the local leadership, distributed papers and brochures, and returned a few days later to win converts. Prior to large public meetings, the rank and file also engaged in house-to-house canvassing.[13]

A gap in the Prussian coalition law permitted women to form electoral clubs during the period set aside for active campaigning. Women made use of this right; in 1903, the Berlin club even gave the Party treasury 300 Reichsmarks (RM).[14] Members helped campaign for socialist candidates, arranged meetings, joined demonstrations, and sought to mobilize the economic power of the working class. They set up consumer boycotts against small businesses in working-class districts, threatening to take business elsewhere if proprietors supported nonsocialist candidates.[15]

Propaganda tours throughout the country also played an important role in the women's overall mobilization efforts. As a product of the travels, women wrote descriptive, as opposed to theoretical, articles on working and living conditions and sent them to the socialist press. The Party and union bureaucracy published lists of women speakers, and local organizations sometimes contacted the women directly. Tours were often coordinated by the central representative. Speakers were paid; in 1894, for example, a Berliner received six RM per lecture in the capital, and an additional four marks if she spoke in the province of Brandenburg. Either the local group or the national movement bore the cost. At the meetings, women would solicit money as well as new members.[16] Female speakers addressed general gatherings for both men and women or those called specifically for females on a variety of topics of interest to labor and consumers. Speakers capitalized on the high cost of living or on such grievances as women's disenfranchisement for the trade courts.

Between 1891 and 1914, *Gleichheit* recorded numerous tours that led directly to the founding of women's clubs, educational courses, or even union affiliates. The Liegnitz Women's and Girls' Educational Club, for example, was organized in the early 1890s after a talk by Ihrer. Zietz was sent on tour in 1900 by the Schleswig-Holstein district executive committee of the Unskilled Factory Workers Union. At Bremerhaven, her talk led to the election of a female representative, as it did in Saxony four years later. Grünberg's lecture to a women's meeting in 1904 in a small town near Frankfurt am Main resulted in the formation of an educational club for females.[17]

The agitational tours required stamina, dedication, and considerable skill in evading police provocations. A woman's reputation rested, in part, on her successes in eluding official harassment. Zietz was regarded as especially gifted in outwitting the police. At the women's conference in 1906, obviously very pleased with herself, she recounted how she had learned to get around the law: "In Thuringia, I was prevented from speaking. A [male] comrade then spoke for ten minutes, and I spoke in the discussion for one and one-half hours."[18] Thuringian laws severely restricted women's participation in political gatherings while no prohibition existed for men.

The police forbade women's meetings often on short notice, or they simply closed them down, as reported in a case involving Clara Zetkin, "who is known to preach . . . the overthrow of the existing state and social order." Ihrer faced numerous charges for violating the law, but used the opportunity to hold additional meetings in areas where her cases were being tried. Talks were often billed as "addresses" to "balls" sponsored by various worker groups. Activists suffered from petty to serious harassment. Once, Grünberg nearly found her meeting disbanded because she was introduced as "Frau" not "Fräulein." Since she was single, the police accused her of speaking under a fake name. Similarly, Zetkin experienced considerable difficulty using the name "Zetkin" because she had not legally married Ossip. For a time, officials insisted she be introduced as "Eissner" and occasionally prevented her from speaking. After they noted that she was known as "Eissner" only to law enforcers, "Zetkin" was accepted as her *nom de plume*.[19]

A cursory glance at the extent of tours that Ihrer, Zetkin, and Zietz undertook in 1892, 1894, and 1900, respectively, reveals the considerable investment of time and energy this role required.[20] In 1892, Ihrer spent most of January in Schleswig; February she spoke in her home town of Berlin; May saw her in Nuremberg, Mannheim, and Mainz; November in Leipzig; and December back home again attending meetings. Ihrer was childless and her husband ran a pharmacy near Berlin. She had both the time and financial resources to make the tours. Zetkin participated extensively in meetings near her home town of Stuttgart. Her job as an editor and her sole responsibility for her two children before her second marriage to the artist Zundell in 1899 kept her close to home. Nonetheless, in 1894, she spoke frequently in Bavaria, went to Switzerland in October, and addressed gatherings at Leipzig in December. One year of Zietz's active career saw her in late 1899 in Bavaria, Saxony, and Reuss; in February 1900, she appeared in Pomerania and East and West Prussia; in March in Magdeburg; and then she returned to Hamburg where she held union meetings to protest the buildup of the navy. At the end of March and early April, she was in Schleswig-Holstein; May in Halle; June in Anhalt; and in August and September, she took extensive tours throughout the Rhineland, Westphalia, and Saxony. In November, Zietz traveled to Brussels where she spoke on the struggles of the German proletariat and early December saw her in Lübeck. Zietz, childless and by then estranged from her husband, devoted full attention to the socialist cause.

An additional role performed by many women leaders involved their participation in several committees formed to oversee existing protective legislation. Beginning in 1898, socialist women set up grievance committees as intermediaries between working women and the trade inspectors. These bodies reported violations of protective labor laws to the inspectors on behalf of an unnamed plaintiff.[21] In an effort to insure compliance with a 1903 law governing child labor, socialist feminists also formed child-labor committees. These made known breaches of law to the police, secured aid for rural families whose children would otherwise be forced to work, and publicized cases of child exploitation in the hope of strengthening municipal law enforcement. Committee members worked with child-welfare bureaus, youth courts, teachers, and school doctors. They were trained in educational courses set up by female leaders. On numerous occasions, the members would search out children who were working illegally; in Hamburg early one Sunday morning in 1910, for example, they "caught red-handed" 1,921 children doing errands for businesses. Similarly, during one week in Berlin in 1911, members of the Greater Berlin child-labor committees (consisting of 58 supervisors and 800 aids) found 1,267 girls and 2,328 boys between five and fourteen years old delivering baked goods, newspapers, and milk.[22] Despite the opposition of many parents, the infractions were reported to the responsible authorities.

INCORPORATION INTO THE SPD: FEMINIST LOSSES

The 1908 reform of the coalition law legalized women's participation in political organizations. In the abstract, most socialists agreed that the reform helped bridge the gap between theory and practice: no longer would men and women need separate organizations to wage the proletariat's struggle against capitalism. In concrete terms, however, socialist women sought to preserve their own spheres. In some areas of Germany such as Berlin, separate political women's associations were set up parallel to and independent of the men's SPD locals. In other areas such as Hamburg, women's full integration into the local, which had begun two years earlier, proceeded smoothly. Partly to overcome the institutional inconsistency typified by Berlin and Hamburg, the "organizational question" became the main topic of debate at the 1908 women's conference in Nuremberg.[23]

The Nuremberg meeting decisively rejected "female separatism" (*weibliche Sonderbündelei*).[24] The Berlin model of organizational relations was abolished, although the sentiments underlying the women's desire for some institutional autonomy were not as easy to suppress. The new statutes directed women's separate political organizations to join the SPD locals. Each club was given the task of holding separate meetings and educational sessions designed especially for the theoretical and practical enlightenment of females. Also, at least one woman was to join each local and district executive committee and be responsible for propaganda among the female proletariat. The central bureau was transformed into a women's bureau and placed in the national executive; over the women's objections, only one of their members was admitted to the executive.

Baader had taken it for granted that two women would be asked to join the executive committee. Overburdened by work, she had been given an assistant in 1906 and felt the complexity of the job required at least two full-time people. At the Nuremberg conference, she proposed that Zietz be considered in addition to herself. The next day, clearly having received a reprimand from higher up, she explained that she had only expressed her preference: the SPD Congress, of course, would have the final say. When it became clear that the congress would only support one female, Baader graciously withdrew her name from consideration on the ground of her advanced age of sixty-one. Zietz was elected and Baader entered the women's bureau to help her and continued to enjoy "great trust and support."[25]

The statutes sanctioned the continuation of women's conferences. Socialist women had justified the independent meetings ostensibly because they did not wish to overburden the SPD congresses with special matters such as maternity insurance. In fact, the women's gatherings had come to serve important social, psychological, and political functions. Beyond contact and exchange of information, they provided a milieu in which sensitive issues such as the unwillingness of men to support the women's cause could be raised without embarrassment. What to do with the Pasha or Adam resting in men's souls was a nagging question, and a source of much serious reflection. Later, when the ideological antagonisms deepened, the women's conference served as a forum for radical socialist ideas. Also, the special provision for delegating women to the congresses was incorporated into the revised statutes, but Zietz made it eminently clear that its use would be viewed as a "demonstration against the [male] comrades." In fact, the clause that allowed women to elect their own delegates remained a dead letter, but behavior had not changed much from the early 1890s. Men were still unwilling to support women delegates. In 1911, for example, female executive-committee members in Greater Berlin met to discuss the disinclination of male members in two Berlin districts to vote for females.[26]

According to the bylaws, resolutions adopted by the women's conference became official Party policy only when passed by the full congress. The Nuremberg SPD Congress accepted the new relationship of women and Social Democracy, but made immediate use of its supreme authority; it diluted the women's resolution that had made it a "duty" for male comrades to bring their wives and daughters into the organization. The final statement merely "advised" men to enlighten their female family members so they would join the Party.[27]

The women's movement was transformed into a mass organization after 1908. Female membership soared: the Party gained roughly 150,000 women between 1908 and 1914; in the year 1911 alone, 22 percent of the growth in members was female.[28] Yet integration into the SPD cost socialist feminists freedom of action. For many, the price of increasing interference and loss of maneuverability was not offset by potential benefits in the form of direct financial, press, and administrative support.

Leaders of the women's movement openly discussed the pros and cons of the change. At the 1911 conference, Zietz talked about the new position of the bureau. "Earlier [she admitted] it had been the independent decision-making center of the proletarian women's movement, now it was a subordinate division of the executive committee."[29] Many women who had been active in dynamic locals of their own felt "hemmed in," she added. However, she argued strongly for the view that women could do so much more because they had greater means and more personnel at their disposal. Nevertheless, dissatisfaction rose with closer contact; as females became more familiar with the new situation, they noted the gap between the theoretical commitment to their cause and discrimination in practice.

Women were grumbling over the growing number of Party directives limiting their activity. For example, a decision to set up rest and recreation homes for women (*Frauenheime*) was postponed indefinitely. Berlin female functionaries were furious when they no longer received reports of national executive committee meetings.[30] Efforts in 1913 to set up special women's meetings in early spring were rejected by Party officials because of an alleged conflict with women's day. For their part, women made Party and union leaders uneasy over planned street demonstrations for women's day, set aside by the International socialist women's conference in 1910 to promote women's suffrage. Throughout Germany, coordinated meetings and demonstrations were prepared and propagandists went from the factory and workshops into neighborhoods passing out information. At a set time (after two o'clock in the afternoon to allow participants time to cook the noon meal), the women gathered, marched to a rallying point, heard speeches, and then organized larger street demonstrations. The plan hardly challenged what one historian has characterized as traditional patterns of behavior within German Social Democracy—the transformation of frustration into verbal aggression against the domestic enemy.[31] Nonetheless, the national Party and union leadership was fearful of those activities not directly under its control that could lead to violent skirmishes with police. Misgivings notwithstanding, the demonstrations were "controlled affairs"; in 1912, three to four hundred Berliners gathered to march into the city, but were stopped and dispersed by a cordon of police. Participants, it was said, simply were not interested in inciting political action.[32]

Integration in 1908 was soon followed by a process of functional segregation that reached its culmination in the Weimar period.[33] Increasingly, women came to dominate one sphere of activity: child-labor committees and their related municipal welfare tasks. Police reports reflect the change: although the committees owed their origin to the women's 1904 conference, as late as 1909 they were still sexually integrated. By 1910, the reports show that "as leaders, supervisors and aids, women have created a work sphere in which they clearly [outdo] men." By 1912, the committees had become women's preserves; over 200 had been set up throughout Germany in 1913.[34] This evolution toward separate areas of activity violated the spirit within which women leaders had raised their feminist demand for division of labor. It meant that they were being kept out of positions of responsibility and authority on other matters or were often mere decoration, as Baader indicated in 1909.[35] That women would gravitate to the rewarding role of child-labor reform was natural, but, with hindsight, it helped to limit their feminist perspectives.

In 1910, a bitter debate was provoked by the executive committee's refusal to call a women's conference for that year—a breach of the tradition of biannual meetings, as many women charged. The refusal reinforced anger at men's lukewarm attitudes toward the women's efforts. Also, it added to the fears of Zetkin and like-minded radical socialists that they were losing influence within the women's movement, since integration had elevated Zietz to a position of Party leadership.

In January, *Gleichheit* raised what at first glance appeared to be an innocuous question: should a women's conference be held that year? The article sounded eminently moderate, noting how important the conferences had been in promoting women's political maturity and in bringing advantages to both Party and unions. The query evoked six months of intense and vitriolic debate.

The initial responses, all from south and middle Germany, favored convening the conference that year. Grünberg, surprisingly militant when the subject involved safeguarding women's role within the organized working class, demanded that the number of women in leadership positions be proportional to their total membership in the Party. Election of one woman to the executive committees had been insufficient to ensure effective recruitment of women. She even went so far as to say that trade unions should initiate a separate woman's conference; unions suffered because many talented women lacked the requisite attention and education. The issue was a "burning one."[36]

The debate became heated in March. Two of Zetkin's supporters, Mathilde Wurm and Fride Wulff, attacked the women's bureau for its failure to take a stand. Wurm chastised both Zietz and Baader for getting entrenched behind Party statutes and neglecting to call Berlin women together, even informally, to debate the question. She demanded to know if the high office (the executive) would or would not call the con-

ference. To Wulff, the issue involved the question of male supremacy: should decisions affecting women be made by men?
She feared relationships between males and females in the
Party had deteriorated since 1908; men were patronizing; and
since women had become Party members, "close contact
among [them] does not exist the way it did."[37]

Baader and Zietz were quick to take up the challenge.
Baader explained to Wurm that regular meetings of Berlin
women had to be sanctioned by male comrades: "we can't call
them."[38] Zietz walked the tightrope trying to please all sides.
Echoing the excuse most often used by men, she said that they
were overworked and therefore might appear negligent; male
attitudes did not reflect "bad will." The arguments of the
executive committee had been persuasive, she claimed. The
committee hoped to send women to the 1910 International
socialist congress in Copenhagen, and felt that most districts
could not afford female delegates at both an international and a
national meeting. It agreed to convene a women's conference
next year. Thus, Zietz reinterpreted *Gleichheit*'s question to
read whether to hold a women's conference this year against
the wishes of the Party hierarchy or next year with its support.[39]

Zietz's reformulation introduced a new element into the
discussion. Up to then, all socialist women responding to the
Gleichheit article had favored holding a conference in 1910.
Thus perceived, radical socialists and reformists could join
hands; in fact, Zetkin and Grünberg had spoken in harmony
defending their feminist tactics. After Zietz's statement, however, it became clear that the call for a 1910 conference meant
opposing the Party leadership, a step many refused to take.

Ten women went on record supporting Zietz after April;
five opposed her as did two districts, Heilbronn and Düsseldorf. One advocate of the leadership position, Johanna Reitze,
would later join the majority socialist group that inherited the
SPD women's movement in 1917. The same position, however, was also defended by several future independent socialists such as Linchen Baumann and M. Böttcher.[40]

It was Clara Zetkin who found herself outflanked on this

issue by an alliance of reform and radical socialist groups. Zetkin had reached the pinnacle of power by the sheer force of her personality, her grasp of Marxism and ability to formulate socialist thought in pithy, catchy phrases, and her editorial control of *Gleichheit*. Her authority had also rested on an intimate connection with Party affairs (she was a member of the control commission beginning in 1895) and close ties with Bebel, Kautsky, and, until the revisionist controversy, Bernstein. However, ideological disagreements were interfering with her personal relations; by 1910, her ties to Bebel and Kautsky had become frayed. Her close personal and political friendship with Rosa Luxemburg caused misgivings among the Party leadership and evoked latent antifeminist sentiments. Kautsky called them "those women" (*die Weiber*), complained to Bebel that they were staging an attack on all central institutions—the executive committee, *Vorwärts*, and *Neue Zeit*—and warned "to be doubly on guard." Bebel, on hearing that Zetkin had proposed her son, Konstantine, for a position in the Party school in 1910, generalized about the feminine character. "It is an amazing thing with women. If their beloved hobbies, or their passions, or their vanities are questioned and not considered or even violated, then even the most intelligent woman is beside herself and becomes hostile to the point of absurdity."[41]

Zetkin participated in the 1910 controversy with characteristic vigor, but her position elicited only limited support: the women's conference was postponed until 1911. She took the women's bureau to task for its antidemocratic stance and its willingness to sanction "decisions from above." Female comrades should have been called to battle if their representatives succumbed to the "spirit of bureaucratic autocracy." She favored solidarity between the various branches of Social Democracy, but not at the price of submersion. What good does it do to have a bureau without a voice? Always sensitive to criticisms of *Gleichheit*, Zetkin declared she owed the women's movement no explanation of the delay in publishing Baader's reply; when another woman commented that *Gleichheit* should have agreed with the executive, Zetkin scornfully replied that she refused to transform her paper into a mere "yea machine" (*jasagemaschine*).[42] The 1910 controversy fore-shadowed growing difficulty. That year, the Berlin local, in Zetkin's own words, "took the wrong path," and failed to elect Luxemburg as delegate to the International congress. Previously, Zetkin had counted on the unswerving support of organized women in Berlin.[43]

THE EXTENT OF WOMEN'S EQUALITY
IN GERMAN SOCIAL DEMOCRACY

The 1910 controversy as well as other tensions between men and women in the SPD after 1908 point up the gap between the theoretical commitment to sex equality in the socialist subculture and the actual position of women and their cause in the Party. Evidence overwhelmingly supports the view that women were not seen as equals and were, in fact, the butts of jokes and ridicule. Blatant as well as latent antifeminism was a fact of life in the socialist organizations, as it was elsewhere. Women had to fight not only capitalism, but also sex discrimination in the organized working class itself. Yet, this is an incomplete assessment, for the socialist subculture provided at the same time the most supportive milieu in Imperial Germany for women seeking to improve their economic, social, and political position. The efforts of both male and female feminists had brought about measurable change in attitudes toward women.

The male working class that emerged after the mid-nineteenth century had been clearly antifeminist. It attached the label *Fabrikmensch* ("factory girl") to the working woman, saw her as morally depraved, and demanded her return to the family. These views became more strident during economic crises when unemployed males vigorously protested the employment of women, "competitors and too ignorant for the struggle."[44] Although the organized working class never shed antifeminist sentiments completely, its attitudes were softened and modified in the course of time to the point where the socialist movement emerged as a benign environment in comparison to German society as a whole. This development warrants more detailed analysis.

German Social Democracy represented a union of two parties that, among other things, diverged over the women's question. In the 1860s, the group around Ferdinand Lassalle was decidedly antifeminist. Lassalleans rejected women working outside the home, called for their employment, if necessary, in domestic industry, and looked to improvement of men's condition as the solution to the women's problem.[45] In contrast, the Third Congress of the Federation of German Workers' Associations at Stuttgart in 1865 advanced a more positive view on the women's question that the Social Democratic Party (*Eisenachers*) inherited. The 1865 meeting recognized capitalism's need for female labor and the futility of rejecting the phenomenon of working women. It recommended the founding of female industrial schools and trade unions and self-help associations for women; and it welcomed plans to form a bourgeois feminist association. The congress adopted as one of the organization's main tasks the education of women and their material and moral support to the same degree as for men.[46] Increasing antisocialist sentiment in Germany caused the Social Democrats and Lassalle's group to join forces in 1875 at Gotha. Unification brought a clash between the two opposing positions on the women's question. The result was a compromise. Advocates of women's rights squashed a resolution calling for an end to female employment, and opponents succeeded in having the explicit mention of "both sexes" in the Party's suffrage reform proposal voted down.

The conflicting views that produced compromise in the mid-1870s gave way to a more positive commitment to women's equality in the following decade, at least on the surface. Socialist propaganda was becoming more sophisticated: it forcefully challenged the notion that wives did not belong in factories, extolled the virtues of organization for women, and related problems of preserving family life not to the presence of women in the labor force, but to the capitalist mode of production. These theoretical justifications for women's rights were being reinforced by the actual changes in the social and economic position of the female sex. The year 1885 was decisive. Spurred on by the success of Emma Ihrer and others in Berlin, numerous working women's clubs were founded throughout the country with the active moral and financial support of SPD national and local leaders. A circular from the Prussian chief of police indicated that officials felt the Social Democratic Party had set "the whole women's movement in motion."[47] This development sent shudders through bourgeois feminism. "Socialists' messing with women's rights threatens to set us back decades," moaned a leading feminist journal in September 1885.[48]

In the spring of 1886, the police mounted a coordinated effort and closed many working women's associations as covert political clubs. Their ties to the socialist movement had become too flagrant. A secret meeting of socialist deputies and Berlin proletarian women's movement leaders in May 1886 set guidelines for future action, but SPD officials promised to refrain from meddling in the affairs of the women's movement. Male socialists were sensitive to women's needs as well as to political reality.[49]

Feminist ideas became acceptable to sufficient numbers of SPD leaders after 1890 to prompt statutory changes proclaiming women's equality in the Party; in turn, women leaders were championing feminist interests with increasing forcefulness. As seen, separate women's meetings were set up for delegate selection; symbolically, the SPD in 1892 substituted "Vertrauens*person*" for "Vertrauens*mann*," neutralizing gender; and the Party's legislative plank incorporated radical feminist reforms. Socialist Reichstag deputies themselves (all male at that time) were the objects of derision when they pleaded for reforms to improve women's lot.

A report on socialist activity prepared for the Imperial Ministry of Interior in 1893 highlights the serious socialist commitment to women's equality. The report stated that after the end of the anti-Socialist laws, SPD leaders were careful to avoid public arrest, but noted one glaring exception: they challenged the provisions of article 15 of the Bavarian laws of assembly that prohibited women's political activity. "Social

Democratic agitators in various cities stubbornly directed their efforts to drawing women into the socialist movement."[50] The leaders insisted that women could attend political meetings if called by an individual, not a political club.

There is enough evidence, then, to document increased efforts of male leaders to win over female working-class members. In part, this was a matter of socialist self-interest; the unorganized woman was seen as a threat to both the economic and the political struggle. Yet such a cynical interpretation obscures the real concern over the hardships of working-class women's lives. Altogether, it seems best to characterize the attitude of male socialists toward their female counterparts in the movement as ambivalent. What lay at the root of the ambivalence? How did socialist feminists themselves perceive the problem?

Socialist women objected mainly to symptoms without examining causes. Their criticism revolved around two major issues. First, the Party too often focused its attention on those groups whose power could be expressed through the vote (i.e., men), to the neglect of both women and children. Women's disenfranchisement made their effectiveness less tangible; hence, many men failed to appreciate their key role in the family or their importance in the work place.[51] In this conception, women's traditional roles as guardians of the family could be placed in the service of socialism. Second, men made only feeble efforts to encourage their wives and daughters to join the organized working-class movement. Beginning in 1911, women leaders themselves undertook a vigorous program to reach the wives of SPD comrades and pressure them into joining the movement. They went to their homes, brought literature, and talked to the females in the household, and tried, at least, to interest them in voluntary work on child-labor committees.[52] Although hardly neutral observers of Social Democracy, the police in this case correctly uncovered the difficulty of this tactic: men questioned political life for their wives and daughters. As one officer noted: "Most male comrades are not at all convinced of the future society with its abolition of the private home and prefer to keep their wives in the family and the domestic sphere, rather than see them step into the political arena to the neglect of their home."[53]

In his analysis of the socialist leadership, Robert Michels supplemented this assessment. According to Michels, a questionnaire sent to organized Social Democrats asking if their wives belonged to the Party would have produced a shattering response. Michels enumerates the reasons: double membership imposed a financial burden; the woman's domestic duties often prevented her from attending evening meetings; and because of the limited education of females, their family orientation, and the conservative influence of the church, women generally were more hostile to socialism than were men.[54]

Michels omitted an extremely important factor: the persistence of sex-role expectations, reinforced by family norms critical of women's public activity. Although socialist feminists recognized manifestations of antifeminism that reflected these norms, they could not break the barriers to their emancipation that were inherent in the generally accepted roles assigned to the female sex. They themselves hardly subjected role divisions to penetrating and unambiguous critique. They clearly wanted women to be out in public life in challenging jobs of their choice. The difficulties came over domestic and motherly duties that socialist feminists generally described as women's work even if men could be encouraged to help or society reorganized to perform. In fact, the delicacy with which female leaders approached family life contrasted markedly with the militancy with which they fought ideological opponents. Several reasons account for their reluctance to tackle the issue of family life more forcefully. Socialist feminists, deeply concerned with the development of class consciousness and class solidarity, were probably fearful of threatening proletarian unity by attacking the existing family structure in the working class too harshly. Their class loyalty dampened a feminist offensive.[55] As seen, their ideology, too, interfered with a thorough critique of family life, since the activists expected women's economic independence to be translated into more equitable family relations, beginning first in the working class. Finally, socialist women underestimated the degree to which male comrades, even those supporting the women's struggle, had retained bourgeois expectations of sex roles. The tenacity of these expectations is vividly illustrated in a passage from the memoirs of August Bebel. Bebel was a staunch champion of women's equality, but he described his marriage in these terms: "To the man who fights in public life against a world of enemies, it is not unimportant what kind of spirit lives in the wife who stands at his side. . . . I could not have found a more loving, a more dedicated, a more self-sacrificing woman. If I achieved what I accomplished, it was primarily possible through her untiring care and assistance."[56] Despite his clear theoretical and, in general, practical commitment to the struggle for women's equality, Bebel implicitly extolled the virtues of the divisions of labor between men in public life and women supportive at home. Karl Kautsky expressed similar sentiments in his eulogy to Julie Bebel: "All that Bebel did as a pioneer and leader, we owe to him. . . . But also to the strong support which he found in his wife, the intelligence, untiring dedication with which she kept the small daily worries away from him. . . . Her ambition was to rule over an area which was cut out for her."[57] Although he added that Julie was also August's comrade and advisor, Kautsky stressed how well she had performed the traditional roles assigned to women.

In general, large numbers of male comrades failed to regard their wives as equals or help them grow and mature. Gertrud Bäumer, in the middle-class feminist camp, analyzed a random selection of workers' autobiographies that, she claimed, reflected prevailing ideals. She noted the indifference with which men—particularly the politically active and enlightened—regarded the intellectual life of their female family members. For example, the autobiography of the trade union leader Bromme vividly juxtaposed the exciting intellectual world of a worker to the "emptiness and drudgery of a woman's life." As "beast of burden," his wife had made it possible for him to pursue his "high ideals."[58]

It was only after World War I that socialist women began to

recognize and lament this gap more openly. In 1921, Helene Grünberg, disillusioned over the political behavior of women in the early Weimar Republic, bitterly charged, "People are criticizing women that they are not using the vote correctly. Big brother scolds little sister. If, in the thirty years that we labored . . . more practical socialism had been promoted in the family, then women would have had more love and understanding for socialism."[59] Only after World War II did public attention focus on the nuclear family as a key obstacle to women's real emancipation, once they had achieved political and legal equality. Marie Juchacz, who returned to Germany after exile during the Third Reich, foreshadowed the growing consciousness among mid-century women of their subordination in the private sphere. At the SPD congress of 1952, she called on men and women comrades to recognize that "the cell of work is in the nuclear family. . . . The position of men to one another, between men and women, must be based on real equality. . . . It is true that in the family the man is still a Pasha."[60]

Women's position in the SPD reflected ambiguities never resolved under any of the changing institutional arrangements within the Party. Ambiguities beset the women's own perception of their role. As socialists, they toiled diligently to promote the working-class movement. As feminists concerned directly with the lot of working women, they demanded special rights within the SPD and a division of activities commensurate with their unique concerns. Real equality, they believed, rested on a degree of organizational independence and on special rights and privileges. Ironically, the women's full integration into the Party in 1908, a victory for formal equality, tended to hamper real equality by reducing the freedom of action for the women's movement. Among the causes of interference by the Party hierarchy, none provoked more controversy than the seemingly trivial refusal to approve the regularly scheduled women's conference of 1910.

As the organizational integration brought male and female functionaries into closer contact, the women activists became more fully aware of ambiguities among socialist men as well. The men's theoretical commitment to sex equality was not matched by their behavior in practice. This dichotomy appeared not only in the leadership, but also among the rank and file. Latent and overt antifeminism and the persistence of traditional family norms and sex-role expectations in the working class hindered the efforts of female activists to mobilize working women and the wives of male socialists. As the next chapter shows, strategic controversies and antifeminism combined also to thwart greater rewards in the economic sphere. Although progress was made in unionizing female workers, the uneasy relationship between the political and union wings of German Social Democracy involved women in jurisdictional conflicts and dissipated energies.

CHAPTER VII

PARTY AND UNIONS:
COMPATIBLE AND CONFLICTING
LOYALTIES

The ties between the political and trade union wings of German Social Democracy tested that part of socialist feminist strategy that closely joined the political and economic struggle in the service of women and the revolution. These relations posed unique problems for Party women whose movement, due to women's subordinate legal status in Germany up to 1908, rested midway between a political and a union orientation.

The women's movement lent its considerable expertise and empathy to the overall effort to unionize working women. The character of the German female labor force increasingly directed these efforts toward the nonindustrial sectors. Females dominated the home industries as well as domestic service. In the early 1890s, socialists launched a sustained campaign to organize workers in domestic industry; by the turn of the century, they were focusing on servants. Both undertakings proved only marginally successful by 1914.

Party women, at times, collaborated harmoniously with the trade union hierarchy. For example, in the move to abolish the domestic industry system as well as during a garment workers' strike in 1896, unionists and Party members worked with minimum friction. Similarly, Emma Ihrer's union for artificial-flower makers received the financial and moral support of both the general commission and the Party leadership. More typically, however, the effort by Party women to unionize female workers was a source of tension with the union leadership; it also divided socialist feminists among themselves. The controversy between the moderate Helene Grünberg, founder of the Domestic Servants Union, and more militant women reveals considerable ideological antagonism within the women's movement itself. The genesis of the Servants Union set SPD women on a collision course with the union hierarchy and illustrates the sensitivity of the various wings to perceived challenges to their power and influence. By straddling the fence between political and union activity, socialist feminists experienced both the rewards of successful collaboration and the pitfalls of encroaching on spheres of influence.

COLLABORATIVE EFFORTS
TO REACH WORKING-CLASS WOMEN
BY PARTY AND UNION MEMBERS

The commitment to the incorporation of women as equal members in the Free Trade Unions came in the early 1890s. Prior to 1890, the discriminatory laws had necessitated sex segregation: leaders founded unions for females that were modeled on the male pattern of local association.[1] After the end of the anti-Socialist laws, a debate over a localist or centralist form of organization for unions had grave implications for women. If the unions had continued to exist as local clubs recruiting for the class struggle and engaging in political matters, women would have been excluded from union life as they were from Party activity in several important German states. At early trade union congresses, Emma Ihrer and Helma Steinbach, in particular, fought for centralized, nonpolitical unions to be oriented primarily toward wages and working conditions. In pleading her cause, Ihrer used both the existence of legal discrimination against working women and the harm of unorganized females to the overall effort to improve conditions of labor. For similar reasons, Party women strongly supported the centralist, nonpolitical position. Its victory secured women an official place in union life.[2] The Halberstadt Congress in 1892 specifically directed the craft unions to transform themselves into "mixed craft" organizations, admitting unskilled female labor with male workers in a given occupation.

Socialist feminists took advantage of the statutory changes in union rules, and the importance attached to the economic battle can be seen in the numerous union functions performed even by those socialist feminists who identified themselves primarily as Party women. Clara Zetkin, for example, worked closely with the trade unions, often touring Germany on their behalf. For twenty-five years, she was a member of the Bookbinders Union in Stuttgart. As a radical socialist, she was concerned, ultimately, with schooling workers for the class struggle—a political struggle; this did not preclude accepting union jobs. Zetkin played an active role in the Tailors Union, attending many of its congresses. In 1896, together with Ottilie Baader and H. Stühmer, she represented German tailors and seamstresses at their second international congress in London and was elected the union's provisional international secretary, a post she occupied until overwork forced her resignation in 1900. Zetkin's educational background and gift for languages facilitated international contacts and accounted for her willingness to act as translator at trade union congresses and other working-class meetings.[3]

Luise Zietz's career reflected a similar pattern. She worked as hard for the unions as she did for the Party and, even after her election to the SPD executive committee, continued to promote union efforts and collaborate with Gertrud Hanna in the general commission. Zietz had joined the SPD as a member of the Unskilled Factory Workers Union and while living in Hamburg participated in the St. Georg local. She was often chosen secretary of the union's congresses. In general, Zietz saw her role as pushing for women's equal rights within the organization. For example, she sought to raise women's dues so that during strikes they would receive compensation equal to that paid to men.[4]

Ottilie Baader coupled her leadership role as socialist women's central representative with union activity for the Tailors and Seamstresses Union. She saw her task in the unions, too, as promoting and when necessary defining women's rights, but she was conscious of union activity performed by essentially Party women. Participating as a guest at the 1905 Cologne Trade Union Congress, she stated that, *"even* politically active women gladly support unions with their propaganda," and added that, "politically active women have worked with and for the unions for years."[5]

In the early years, those women whose primary time was spent in union life extended their energies to the performance of Party roles. Emma Ihrer was representative of Nieder-Barnim women in 1902 and for years local Party representative for Pankow near Berlin. As occurred in the movement generally, however, growing specialization of function came to characterize women's activities prior to World War I. Gertrud Hanna's career shows that the trade unions were being depoliticized as fewer unionists—men or women—assumed additional Party posts. Furthermore, those leaders such as Helene Grünberg who held both Party and union functions increasingly tended to identify with the unions.[6]

Socialist feminists, trying to broaden the base of the class struggle and attune to the needs of their constituency, sought to extend unionization to areas of female labor dominance. This took them outside the mainstream of Free Trade Union influence, the labor force in the urban industrial sectors. In the decade before World War I, for example, Zietz sought to direct the women's movement to the plight of rural working women who fell under the jurisdiction of her union. In 1906, she addressed the Mannheim women's conference and spoke on "propaganda among rural working women." The title notwithstanding, Zietz really offered participants a general description of labor in the countryside—the extent of poor housing, low pay, long work hours, the competition introduced by foreign workers, and the functional diversity among rural laborers. She characterized working women as the "real underdogs" in rural life, doubly, even triply, exploited. Her concern for women, however, was incidental to her interest in them as workers. Thus, she failed to raise the issue of whether a women's question existed among peasants and the potential this might offer for socialist recruitment. The official definition had excluded rural workers; Zetkin at Gotha had stated that the women's question was a product of capitalism and exempted the peasantry, with its noncapitalist economy, from

such concerns. Zietz's analysis neither refined nor challenged
Zetkin's views. Her message, as Kautsky's eight years earlier,
was pragmatic: it would be a "grave mistake" to neglect rural
workers because agriculture was the domain for strike breakers and wage depressors.[7] In vain, Zietz tried to cement rural
workers to the Unskilled Factory Workers Union; she feared
jurisdictional conflicts would emerge with her own union if a
separate rural workers' union was founded. Rural labor often
undertook seasonal factory work in sugar producing or in dis-
tilling. Nonetheless, under the guidance of the general commission a union for agricultural workers was created in 1908.[8]
The women's movement never became committed to reaching
rural working women. Its position reflected the ambivalence
of German Social Democracy toward the peasantry and the
rural question generally, since socialist ideology was a product
of and geared to an urban environment.

No such ambivalence existed about the domestic industry
system. It was seen as posing serious and immediate threats to
the whole labor movement, and socialists carefully watched
and bemoaned its growth. National occupation statistics of
1882 and later years confirmed the continued presence of the
system. Originally a preindustrial phenomenon, domestic industry had survived into the industrial world, but in a transformed condition. Observers in Germany noted three main
sources that contributed to its growth under capitalism. First,
in technically unsophisticated or economically weak industries, factory production often regressed to the home of workers, as happened with the manufacture of artificial flowers.
The stimulus here was a determination to circumvent existing
and costly legislation regulating conditions, wages, or hours in
the industry. Second, the government or individual entrepreneurs often exported home industry production to depressed
areas in the hopes of maximizing profits through low wages
and reduced overhead. Third, domestic industry emerged in
large cities by attracting female members of all classes endur-
ing a marginal existence. In these urban areas, it took two
forms: in the workers' home or in workshops.[9] It flourished
generally in primitive industries not requiring a division of

labor and where human labor costs were sufficiently low to preclude the widespread adoption of machinery.

The cause of domestic industry workers offered a meeting ground for the leaders of various branches of Social Democracy; none regarded it as its own preserve. Socialist feminists for their part were involved because of the extent of female labor and the maxim that women had greater success in reaching other women. In 1892, Baader had toured Germany speaking on the domestic industry system. Home employment was the "worst form of exploitation," oppressing the most vulnerable in society: women and their children. Her tone reflected her own personal experiences as a domestic industry seamstress. She mocked the dominant view that the system preserved traditional family life. Arguing that long work hours, poor pay, and cramped quarters left little time, energy, or even desire for domestic tasks, she called for extension of protective laws to embrace workers at home. Zetkin, at the Berlin SPD Congress that year, submitted Baader's call as the first in a series of resolutions sponsored by socialist women on the need to reform the industry.[10]

Socialists adopted two broad tactics to meet the challenge. The first was the incorporation of domestic industry workers into their occupational union. The second involved legislative reforms to contain, control, and eventually abolish the entire domestic industry system. It was not only detrimental to working-class solidarity and organizational strength, but it also excessively taxed its workers. The inherent dangers were greater still: since controls were nonexistent, consumers in German society (whatever their class membership) faced the possibility of contracting contagious diseases when buying unhygienically produced goods. For the sake of national health, socialists admitted, domestic industry reform offered an opportunity for collaboration between them and the middle class.

A strike of domestic industry garment workers in 1896 demonstrates clearly the difficulties of realizing the goals set by the organized working class. The strike was defensive in nature, prompted by pay reductions in the apparel industry during the price depression. Home industry workers who bore the cost of production were facing growing poverty as their net incomes declined.

Piece rates had plummeted in the decade prior to the outbreak of the strike. In two years, between 1893 and 1895, the pay for boys' jackets had fallen from 2.50 marks to 90 pennies. The fact that Gerson's, a large apparel firm in Berlin, paid its middlemen 10 marks for men's jackets and they turned over only one-third of the sum to their female workers was a source of discontent, as was the average 75 percent differential between the sums accumulated by middlemen and working women involved in the production of boys' suits. Around 1895, it was estimated that a female home worker in Berlin earned 364.95 marks in thirty-four weeks. After deducting costs of sewing machine, yarn, needles, rent, light, and heat, she was receiving 8.46 marks per week for a fourteen-hour workday, or roughly 10 pennies an hour. The net weekly income in the men's apparel branch of the industry in 1895 was only 3.45 marks. In January 1896, *Vorwärts* estimated that a couple in a large city spent approximately 5.65 marks per week for food.[11]

The Tailors Union sought to transform these grievances into concrete demands for change. Its propaganda committee formulated specific proposals, and throughout 1895 held meetings to propagandize the demands. It called on employers to set up workshops (which subsequently became the key demand of the strikers); accept secure wage contracts, weekly payments, and additional monies for overwork; and recognize referral agencies. The SPD Breslau Congress in October directed its Reichstag deputies to pressure for extension of legal protection to domestic industry workers and supervision of home industry establishments by official male and female personnel. It also called for an end to the middleman system, for erection of workshops, and for wage security.[12]

In January 1896, the issue became critical as garment workshop and factory workers demanded a 25 percent wage raise for those in domestic industry. The Tailors Union stood at the forefront of this action, although it had organized less than 1 percent of factory apparel workers. Domestic industry, primarily female labor, too, remained distant from the union. The 1895 census estimated that about 116,479 persons worked in the garment trades either at home or in middlemen's workshops, although the treasurer of the Tailors Union claimed that in Berlin alone around 81,000 women were engaged in the various branches of apparel.[13] The union set up a five-member strike committee to represent the workers and sought to negotiate with the middlemen and the employers.

For the sake of "the wife of the worker," who would be torn from her home and children, the middlemen rejected the workers' demands, particularly the call for workshops. Although many employers agreed to a minimum-wage scale, they refused to negotiate, fearing the proposals would diminish the competitive power of the German industry.[14] A strike was called in seven cities in early February 1896; at its height, it embraced in the capital alone over 20,000 male and female workers.

Within two months, it was over. Financial support for the strikers had run out despite collections at public meetings and loans assumed by the strike committee. In contrast, employers could have continued the strike, but, as the new season approached, they were unwilling to forgo income and accepted negotiation. An agreement produced a 12 to 18 percent pay rise for workers, paid for by the middlemen, and enjoined the manufacturers not to continue business with the middleman if he reneged. A minimum wage was set for the men's and boys' branch, and wage rates were to be displayed openly in workshops and businesses.[15] The strike failed to achieve its main goal—the immediate erection of workshops to end employment in workers' homes. The Tailors Union, furthermore, could not translate worker support and sympathy into permanent gains. During the strike, membership in the Berlin local, for example, rose dramatically: in early 1896, male membership stood at 9,423 and female at 7,886; by the end of the year, the numbers were 7,563 and 1,956 respectively.[16] The drop in female membership was striking and conformed to the hesitancy of working women to join organizations, a sentiment aggravated in this case by their isolation from fellow workers.

The plight of domestic industry workers aroused the bourgeois conscience. The strike publicized the harsh conditions of employment and produced an apparent about-face among nonsocialist deputies in the Reichstag. The National Liberals even entered an official inquiry concerning laboring conditions in the garment industry. They advocated extending those provisions of the Industrial Code that protected child and female labor to domestic industry workers and workshops, abolishing night work for children and overtime for women, and supervising the ordinances by inspectors aided by female assistants.[17] The final measure, however, fell far short of these demands. A May 1897 law extended the Industrial Code to workshops of the garment and linen industry manufacturing on a large scale, but excluded tailors' workshops producing on order, family businesses, and workers' homes. The law regulated child labor and prohibited night work for women. In 1898, payroll books for the industry were required.[18]

Passage of the feeble legislation reinforced socialists' inherent mistrust of middle-class reformism. During the strike, leaders had warned the working class not to place its faith in future parliamentary decisions.[19] The caveat was proving correct. In late 1897, Ottilie Baader sent a questionnaire throughout Germany inquiring into the effectiveness of the law of 1897. The results were negative, she reported to the tailors' Mannheim Congress in 1898: women continued to work at night and particularly during the season took work home to circumvent prescriptions governing length of their workday.[20]

The nature and extent of damage to worker and consumer alike moved socialists to keep working with the middle classes in reforming the industry, although most felt, like Zetkin, that only the proletariat would "set the spark for the struggle."[21] Ihrer and Zietz sought to involve bourgeois and working-class women in a joint campaign. They called on women as consumers to use their purchasing power to curtail domestic industry production by boycotting home industry goods. Ihrer advocated clear labeling of wares to facilitate such an action. Production of goods would be forced into clean, regulated workshops.[22]

In 1904, the general commission invited nonsocialist groups to participate in a Congress to Protect Domestic Industry Workers (*Heimarbeiterschutz-Kongress*). The meeting was designed to dramatize abuses of the industry and focus public attention on the need for reform.[23] Only a small cross section of progressive bourgeois reformers responded; the government "politely refused," and the Ministry of the Interior remained silent. Two representatives of the Progressive Party (liberals) participated, and the Catholic unions sent no representative. Of the Hirsch-Duncker unions, only the Düsseldorf local, known for its advocacy of the need for liberals to unionize female labor, appeared. Bourgeois feminists from the Progressive Women's Association, the Club *Frauenwohl*, and the Berlin Women's Association documented their concern as did sixteen socialist women, six of whom were female unionists.[24] Of 179 delegates, twenty-eight were women. Zetkin, Ihrer, and Braun joined the committee that prepared the congress's resolutions.

The meeting reaffirmed the necessity of legally protecting domestic workers. It prepared an exhibition displaying domestic industry products and the conditions under which the articles were produced. The metal, tailoring, artificial-flower, shoemaker, and bookbinder industries presented their domestic industry goods, indicating time needed to produce the articles and wages received. The exhibition became institutionalized, and in subsequent years socialist and bourgeois women worked together in the planning and execution stages. In 1905, for example, Ihrer, together with two bourgeois feminists, Else Lüders and Alice Salomon, comprised a section of a committee to prepare the display.

The major reforms demanded by socialists remained unrealized in Imperial Germany. Despite continuous coverage of abuses as well as pressure in parliament by SPD deputies, the government remained "cool, hard, and untouched"; a 1910 law stipulated only that wage lists or books containing price information must be available to domestic industry workers.[25] The organized working class was unable to overcome the complex and interrelated barriers posed by domestic industry and its female workers.

These barriers are graphically evident in the case of the union that Emma Ihrer founded in 1901 for workers producing artificial flowers, feathers, and dusters. The industry, singled out at the *Heimarbeiterschutz-Kongress* as an example of a trade fighting a losing battle against domestic industry encroachment, was located primarily in Berlin, Schleswig, and Saxony. By the turn of the twentieth century, the home industries contributed half the output in the trade and were blamed both for the 50 percent fall in wages that had occurred over several decades and for the surplus of cheap mass-produced, poor-quality articles (*Schleudergeschäft*). Production was overwhelmingly a female occupation (90 percent). About 19,000 female and 1,000 male workers were employed in factories; it was estimated that between 20,000 and 25,000 females worked at home.[26]

In the industry, working-class women faced competition from lower-middle-class females, and the latter were determined to maintain their social distance from the working class. Young girls generally worked in the factories and workshops, and among their number were daughters of lower officials and artisans who regarded their employment as transitional, their income as supplementary, insisted on being called *Fräulein* and referred to their compensation as salary (*Gehalt*), not wages (*Lohn*). The workers spent, on the average, eleven hours a day in the factory, but often took up to six hours of work home at night. The domestic industry, in contrast, was comprised of married women, recruited from former single factory and workshop women or those who were forced to begin work after marriage and motherhood. Often, as in Berlin, they lived in the suburbs and villages where life was less expensive. The average wage in 1904 for a female worker in a flower factory was 7.50 RM per week; for a domestic industry worker, only with a longer work day, 4 RM; a factory binder made 10 RM per week while her counterpart at home received 6 RM and bore extra costs.[27] Production in urban areas, such as Berlin, suffered from competition of rural areas as Sebnitz near the Bohemian border that drew on cheaper labor, or from the Erzgebirge where, in 1905, employers began introducing domestic industry flower production to gain the advantages of a depressed labor market.

In the middle of the nineteenth century, mechanized weaving mills introduced in Sebnitz had attracted cheap Bohemian labor known for its production of artificial flowers. These workers displaced the indigenous hand weavers who moved to outlying villages. Bohemians continued their former trade and intermarried, and sons of weavers often inherited the artificial-flower businesses. By the early twentieth century, peasants owning a home and garden were moving into the industry working for a trifle (*Bettelpfennige*). The middleman system had also appeared. The intermediaries were often females who accepted large orders, took four or five young girls between fourteen and sixteen years old into their homes, and paid them three to five marks each month. The girls worked seven days a week and helped with the housework as well. The opening of a trade school in Sebnitz to train women aggravated conditions in the industry by creating a free labor source. Students paid twenty RM for a six-week state-supported course during which time they produced flowers sent all over the country. This production tended to depress wages because of the low price such products commanded. In addition, the school often provided the new designs to businesses without charge. As seen previously, socialists opposed these specialized institutions and proposed instead obligatory continuous education to give working-class girls and boys needed labor skills.[28]

Ihrer faced an uphill battle in attempting to unionize workers in the industry. A series of tours in Schleswig and Saxony and meetings in the capital led to the formation of local unions; in 1902, they centralized under the auspices of the general commission, published a small monthly, *Blumen-Arbeiter*, offered limited health insurance, and geared dues to jobs within the industry, not to sex. By 1904, the union had 304 members.

Female membership exceeded male for the first time in 1911, 597 to 540. The union suffered severe fluctuations in membership reflecting, in part, the peasant-worker character of much of its labor force. Over 600 factory workers in Dresden, for example, joined during the season, but then disappeared to the countryside for the harvest.[29]

Male factory workers were the most stable members and the union centered its mobilization campaigns on men who, in workshop meetings, were directed to bring in factory working girls. These single women, however, tended to shun the entreaties. From that base, an effort was made to attract working-class wives in the home industry. Ihrer admitted that "even the strongest funds [were] drained when used systematically for organizing home industry workers."[30]

The union was active in the socialist campaign to abolish domestic industry. Ihrer decried as "unnecessary" the encroachment of domestic industry in the production of artificial flowers. It was a luxury trade that hardly need turn to workers' homes to reduce the price of its goods. Consumers of luxury items did not ask price but looked to quality and elegance. Her union, too, chastised the Party and other Free Trade Unions for purchasing domestic industry wares for May Day or other workers' holidays. This practice undercut the struggle to improve conditions of the very poor. In 1913, the leadership asked that artificial flowers be purchased only through its unions that would order them from those employers who accepted union wage rates. In this way, the middleman system would be eliminated.[31] As the experience of socialist feminists has shown in challenging antifeminist sentiment in the organized working class itself, the battle often had to turn against attitudes and behavior in the socialist subculture.

The high proportion of women workers, as a reflection of the extent of domestic industry, convinced Ihrer that her young union should join a more powerful group. She turned to the hat makers, who were organizing in a related industry that faced similar problems of domestic industry encroachment, and proposed incorporation. The plan had the blessing of the general commission. Paul Umbreit, its spokesman, endorsed, in principle, the amalgamation of smaller unions that "served the general trade union movement." Above all, however, he felt that working women must be supported in a larger organization more capable of sustaining their struggle. A whole group of small unions, he said, came together regularly to devise ways and means to organize female labor and he praised Ihrer for her leadership role. Yet he questioned the results: working women who entered small and weak unions could not receive the requisite attention and support.[32] Perhaps because of Ihrer's untimely death in 1911, the hoped-for amalgamation with the hat makers did not occur. The Artificial Flower Makers Union eventually joined the Unskilled Factory Workers Union.

That domestic industry remained indifferent to socialist wooing did not go unnoticed by government officials. The Imperial Government saw the whole system as a crucial bulwark against socialism. Thus, although it admitted the existence of "grave abuses," efforts to reform the industry ran up against determined opposition. A memo prepared in the Ministry of Trade and Commerce in 1906 noted pointedly that domestic industry workers were more immune from political propaganda than factory workers. It judged that for this reason above all socialists wanted complete abolition of the system.[33] The ruling classes feared reforms would work only to socialists' advantage.

FRICTION OVER FEMINIST TACTICS

Socialist feminists were conscious of the problem of legitimate spheres of activity. The claim to a division of labor within the Party even after 1908 was based on women's special role in reaching the female proletariat. Party members were careful to distinguish between political and union decision-making competence. Theoretically, at least, they rejected a voice in union policy formulation. In preparing for the 1900 women's conference, for example, *Gleichheit* noted that the agenda omitted collaboration with unionists, "one of the most important tasks of the proletarian women's movement."[34] This implied no slighting of union efforts, the paper wrote, but meant that the specific ways and means to unionize working women stood outside the conference's purview.

Despite efforts to distinguish jurisdictions, women leaders' feminist tactics opened the possibility of encroaching on union domain. Members of the women's movement sat officially on the local union coordinating bodies, the "cartels."[35] Yet they jealously sought a place on other union committees. At the 1904 women's conference, Zetkin summarily closed a discussion on the establishment of women trade union commissions. She stated, somewhat mendaciously as it turned out, that "to take a position on this . . . is up to the trade unions and not to the women's conference."[36] Shortly thereafter, in an apparent about-face, she published an article that called on women to assume the leading role in the formation of the commissions. Zetkin had obviously feared provoking an open controversy at the conference. Her written statement rested on the strong belief that the key ingredient for successful mobilization of working women was the presence of women leaders. They were needed to supplement trade union leadership efforts.[37] Furthermore, the commission's designated function to train a cadre of female unionists added urgency to the issue of leadership. Zetkin seemed determined to lodge instruction in radical socialist hands or, at least, under Party women's direction who would educate for the class struggle. By 1904, the question of who controlled education—and decided the degree of harmony between theory and practice—was hardly academic.

The grievance committees founded by socialist women as part of their campaign to reach the employed female operated in a gray area between political and union activity. They evoked suspicion among union leaders, and Baader admitted to the 1911 women's conference that the committees' function actually belonged to the unions.[38] Nonetheless, numerous resolutions had been passed at earlier conferences supporting Party women's move into legislative supervision while, at the same time, calling on them to collaborate with the cartels. Despite the official appeal to cooperation, misgivings were voiced that women might bypass the unions. In turn, Party women complained that the unions "unfortunately show little interest" in the grievance committees.[39] The blurred jurisdictional lines led to mutual recrimination. By 1911, the bodies had fallen under union direction. Hanna addressed the women's conference that year and sought to balance union independence with the accepted dictum that women worked more successfully with women. Since the union movement did not have enough trained females, however, she said it would accept Party women's help. But she warned that grievance committee members had to be well informed on working conditions in each industry.[40] Hanna spoke as a unionist who felt uneasy with the feminist tactics when they seemed to challenge union autonomy.

In their effort to define legitimate spheres, Party women adopted a concept that proved ambiguous in practice. Their 1900 conference called on activists to approach the employed women (without neglecting the housewife) and prepare the ground for union propaganda (while paying attention to political enlightenment).[41] The conference introduced a delicate and subtle distinction between preparatory work and actual unionization efforts that led to added conflicts with union leaders.

The various problems that women encountered in the socialist movement were apparent in the controversy between the leadership of the women's movement and the Free Trade Unions over founding of the Domestic Servants Union in 1906. Four sources of discord converged: the ideological antagonisms in the women's movement itself; the tension of dual loyalty when one woman embodied both union and women's movement leadership roles; union determination to free itself from Party control; and the difficulty of mobilizing women workers in a nonindustrial sector.

Domestic servants in Germany stood outside the Industrial Code, working under special laws (*Gesindeordnung*).[42] The hard conditions of employment coupled with higher wages in industry accounted for the general downward trend in total numbers of servants beginning in the last third of the nineteenth century, although the proportion of women in the occupation rose. In 1895, there were about 1.3 million servants, the majority of rural origin. Most urban-born women rejected domestic service. According to socialist analysis, the young girls who migrated to the city were poorly educated, lacked knowledge of the working-class movement, and accepted employment at any price.[43] Demand for servants exceeded supply. This situation offered them the opportunity to improve their position once they became aware, through socialist propaganda, of the potential for change.

As a member of the Nuremberg workers' secretariat and political representative of the city's women's movement, Grünberg worked with servants and began publishing their complaints in the local paper. Soon the expression "a revolution in the kitchen" came into vogue. In February 1906, Grünberg called a public meeting to discuss unionization; one month later, the first Servants Union in Germany was formed that rested on Free Trade Union principles: it rejected the possibility of harmony between employers and employees. The union sought to "raise the legal, economic and social position of servants" through meetings, their own employment agency, limited health insurance, social gatherings, and the reading of *Gleichheit*.[44]

A similar movement in Nuremberg had erupted in late 1903 sparked by news that contributions to the health insurance scheme would increase by 2 to 3 percent; housewives in Bavaria paid the contribution, but refused to assume total costs. They demanded that their maids bear half the contribution for the first two years of employment. The servants, aroused, coupled their rejection of this plan with calls for higher wages, better clothing, and more leisure time. The movement floundered for lack of leadership and coordination.[45] Grünberg provided both ingredients in 1906.

Grünberg outlined her general goals to the Mannheim women's conference. The movement aimed to abolish the *Gesindeordnung*, incorporate servants under the Industrial Code, and institute obligatory continuous education for girls up to eighteen years of age. Through education, the leadership hoped to "change consciousness" and open servants' eyes to the working-class movement, the potentials for advancement, and the dignity of their profession.[46] In socialist analysis, this would terminate a vicious circle: the problem of unenlightened female servants who, after marriage, opposed their husband's efforts for socialism, worked in domestic industry, or joined the unaware mass of factory working women, often serving as strike breakers. Unschooled domestics were perceived as potentially harmful to the organized working class.

The response to Grünberg's endeavor was immediate and positive. Within two years, she had sent information to forty-eight German cities to help found similar unions. The next several years witnessed the proliferation of Servants' Unions. In many cases, as occurred in Fürth, Munich, Cologne, Bremen, Hamburg, and Kiel, Party women, with the backing of the union cartels, were responsible for the foundation of the unions. The Mannheim and Wiesbaden unions, in contrast, owed their genesis solely to trade union leaders' efforts. One reporter claimed, however, that only after the Mannheim women's organization had become involved in the servants' movement did the young local make progress. Prussian police keeping tabs on the socialist movement regarded women SPD members as the prime movers in the effort to mobilize domestic servants. Launching of the Nuremberg local provided the stimulus for socialists to take over a Servants' Union in Berlin headed by middle-class women. In 1907,* the Berlin trade union commission announced, "it is now in our hands."[47]

In November 1906, the harmony among socialist women seeking to unionize domestic workers was marred by the publication of a model contract. Central to the contract was the sentence, "The regulations of the Servants' Code (*Gesindeordnung*) do not apply for the contractual relationship."[48] By private agreement, the contract sought to remove servants from working under the special, highly restrictive laws. In addition, it provided for free housing, free room and board, weekly or monthly cash wage, a furnished room, eight consecutive hours of sleep, time off, and it carefully stipulated the conditions under which each party might terminate the agreement. Positions on the contract reflected divergent attitudes among socialist feminists toward union tactics, the degree of militancy in the trade union movement, and the efficacy of raising radical demands for mobilization purposes.

The Nuremberg union, under Grünberg's leadership, rejected the contract as a "future dream." Betraying her basic moderation, Grünberg claimed that servants represented the most unenlightened stratum of the working class, and the first task for the leadership was to awaken and educate girls and solidify their organization throughout the country. "We must gather our ammunition . . . and then go into battle. We must first assemble our troops."[49] Win members through social activities and festivities, and only later create new consciousness, she prescribed. Above all, Grünberg feared that the contract would scare servants off and impede organizational success.

Zetkin and radical socialists in general strongly disagreed. Zetkin believed that the Nuremberg local had misunderstood the intent of the contract. It sought to establish a work relationship that would guarantee the maid basic rights since she labored under difficult, dehumanizing conditions. The contract was a means to promote the organization, above all an agitational weapon, not a danger to it. The crucial decision involved accepting the contract in principle. It could then be modified to suit local conditions and used, not necessarily in battle, but to attract domestics to the union and awaken them. If girls were unenlightened and lacked the courage to propose the contract, then the union's propaganda efforts should be geared to overcoming, not succumbing to, these feelings. Grünberg's question if *Gleichheit* should have been involved in the internal affairs of a union struck a raw nerve. *Gleichheit*, Zetkin lectured, not only had the right as the organ of women comrades, but the duty to take a position on issues involving principles and political strategy. Since Nuremberg published its rejection of the contract, *Gleichheit* had to see that other Servants Unions did not "blindly follow."[50]

Ida Baar, president of the Berlin Domestic Servants local, criticized Grünberg for her interpretation of union tactics and her claim that the contract "went too far." What if the trade unions had waited for workers to become enlightened, Baar queried? *Correspondenzblatt*, the Free Trade Union mouthpiece, walked the tightrope. It accepted Grünberg's basic premise that the union was not strong enough to propose the contract, but felt it could be one of several means to improve the position of servants.[51] The Hamburg, Jena, and Frankfurt unions accepted the contract; more typically, union members either substantially rewrote it or adopted their own model. During the controversy, *Gleichheit* employed its own tactics to undercut opposition. Whereas, previously, news from Nuremberg had been signed either with Grünberg's full name or her initials, beginning in November 1906 the reporter remained anonymous. The importance of publicity, exposure, and public acknowledgment of responsibility cannot be underestimated.[52]

Grünberg's stance during the burgeoning conflict between Party women leaders and the general commission provoked additional hostility. To coordinate agitation and prepare guidelines for eventual centralization of Domestic Servants Unions, Baader called a special women's conference in 1907. Grünberg initially agreed to speak, but withdrew after the general commission made known its opposition to the whole undertaking. The union leadership clearly was skeptical of the women's intentions. It affirmed the key role of the union cartels in preparing the necessary preconditions for centralization, and pleaded for restraint and time to see if the groundwork were strong enough to support a new edifice. In some cases, it admitted, women comrades had been active in founding Servants Unions, but the general commission stressed those examples where the "whole propaganda and organizational work" was done solely by the cartels. Carl Legien, general commission spokesman, rejected being drawn into a "petty struggle over jurisdiction" but wrote sourly of leadership henceforth resting with the women's central representative. Although both a trade union leader and political representative, Grünberg stood with the union hierarchy and announced that Servants Unions owed their loyalty to the union executive.[53]

Baader chastised Grünberg for attempting to patronize the Servants Union as well as the socialist women's movement. She claimed that the Nuremberg leadership had overstepped its bounds by acting as advisor and judge over the whole women's movement. Baader felt that success in reaching servants derived from the efforts of both women and union leaders. In fact, reversing union emphasis, it was largely socialist women who had brought life to the movement. The aim of women comrades, she claimed, was to promote centralization and eventual incorporation into the Free Trade Unions. A women's conference could only further this goal.[54]

The conference met as scheduled. It affirmed the importance of the employment agency and declared that the contract was an agitational tool to be transformed, eventually, into a weapon in the struggle against employers. A five-member committee was created of representatives from Berlin, Leipzig, Frankfurt am Main, Hamburg, and Nuremberg (after Grünberg refused to participate, a member was appointed from Munich). The committee was instructed to improve relations with the general commission. Party women had never intended to found a union independent of the trade union structure. *Gleichheit* was designated the organ of the Servants Unions.[55]

During the next few years, female leaders and the union executive collaborated in founding a central union. But success eluded the young organization. The initial flush of enthusiasm gradually gave way to disillusionment. The main goal, the abolition of the *Gesindeordnung*, had to wait until the German Revolution in late 1918. The social position of servants hindered lasting mobilization. Servants were isolated from one another and labored under the special laws that forbade strikes and upheld patriarchical ideals. Furthermore, theorists argue that continuous contact with members of higher classes tends to undercut radical political action.[56] Turnover at the local level was excessive and prevented administrative continuity. Several locals were closed by the police for violating laws prohibiting persons under eighteen from joining "political clubs." Although in Nuremberg conditions were improved, wages raised, and employers, as part of the contract, permitted their maids to attend Sunday union meetings, "organizational stability did not match the propensity to organize."[57] The Nuremberg union attracted roughly 4 percent of the city's servant population although membership fluctuated greatly. In 1914, the president of the central union complained that men in the union cartels refused sufficient support. She shamefully contrasted membership in the Catholic Servants Union, which stood at 17,000, with the mere 6,000 members in the Free Trade Union.[58]

Tensions continued, surfacing periodically. Grünberg remained sensitive to the union chain of command as witnessed by a verbal dispute with Zietz at the women's 1908 conference. During the general discussion, she corrected a statement made by Zietz that Servants Unions stood under Social Democratic leadership. "I emphatically maintain that is not the case at all, [they] operate as pure trade union organizations." Zietz replied that Grünberg had misunderstood her: "I said that from our discussion sessions we get people who have taken over propaganda among servants as well as the leadership positions. If that should mean our servants' movement has a political character, that must be true for the whole trade union movement. For at its head stand convinced Social Democrats, and I wish ardently this were true for all the members."[59] Zietz engaged in wishful thinking. Reality revealed a sharper differentiation between political and trade union orientation.

Divergent orientations were manifest in two additional, although abortive, challenges to radical socialist women leaders by female unionists, among them several prominent members of the Printers' Aids Union. In 1904, Ihrer publicly questioned the need for women's conferences and stated that the decision to hold official meetings had been made against the wishes of a strong minority. Her group feared that public debate would remain superficial; only women with oratorical talents would be chosen as delegates to the possible neglect of those performing the essential day-to-day routine work. It had hoped to institutionalize private channels of communication to facilitate voicing of grievances or offering suggestions.[60] Discontent smoldered and erupted in 1911 when Paula Thiede, president of the Printers' Aids Union, carried Ihrer's ideas one step further. She called on Party women to adopt the union model: women union leaders performed functions geared to reaching working women, but never held special trade union congresses for females. She questioned the efficacy of meeting every two years and hearing lectures when decisions reached at the conference had to be ratified by the SPD congresses. Thiede advised women comrades to be flexible and not perpetuate customs after the preconditions had disappeared.[61]

By 1911, the position of radical socialist leaders in the Party, generally, had become insecure. They continued to exercise a strong although divided voice in the women's movement due to the entrenched position of Zetkin and her followers. In an effort to maintain control, radicals were orchestrating speakers' lists at the conferences as evidenced by an undated letter from Baader to Klara Weyl around the spring of 1911. Baader, together with Margaret Wengels, Zetkin's faithful radical supporter, requested that Weyl "definitely" appear and alluded to troubles with Thiede.[62] The women's conference had assumed great importance as a forum for radical ideas as well as a meeting ground to renew and expand contact. Thiede's critique struck at one pillar of radical strength.

In 1908, an attempt by the Textile Workers Union to promote the founding of a trade union working women's paper to replace *Gleichheit* challenged another radical institution. The bid received the lukewarm support of Gertrud Lodahl, Printers' Aids Union secretary, who wrote that large numbers of unorganized working women required the whole gamut of trade union propaganda efforts, including a women's trade union paper. Ihrer, however, using her considerable prestige, closed the discussion by claiming that union women had no intention of founding a second women's organ. Not until World War I created unbridgeable strains in the organized working class did the unions launch their own paper, *Gewerkschaftliche Frauenzeitung*, edited by Gertrud Hanna, to counterbalance the radical socialist stance of *Gleichheit*.[63]

SOCIAL DEMOCRACY'S PERFORMANCE
IN THE UNIONIZATION OF FEMALE WORKERS, 1897-1914

Socialist feminists had tangible results for their efforts to unionize the gainfully employed woman. The Free Trade Union record improved steadily throughout the Imperial period. From a small beginning of 2.8 percent female membership in 1897, or some 11,600 persons organized in nineteen unions, the proportion had risen to 8.3 percent by the second quarter of 1914.[64] This represented 223,020 females, although one-third of the unions were still exclusively male. By the outbreak of World War I, the Free Trade Unions had mobilized both absolutely and relatively more women than their German competitors, the liberal (Hirsch-Duncker) and Catholic unions. The dominant role of the socialist unions in mobilizing female labor is shown in Table 5. While less than a

TABLE 5   Women's Participation in
German Trade Unions in 1912

	TOTAL MEMBERSHIP	FEMALE	PERCENT
Free Trade Unions	2,553,162	222,809	8.7
Hirsch-Duncker	109,225	4,950	4.5
Catholic	350,930	28,008	7.9

SOURCE: *Anhang zum Correspondenzblatt: Statistische Beilagen*, 30 August 1913, pp. 174-175 and 196-197, including members of the Domestic Servants and Rural Workers Unions.

percentage point divided the socialist and Catholic unions in terms of their female composition, the Free Trade Unions had eight times as many female members. In the prewar period, furthermore, Germany ranked second in Europe behind England in total female union membership. The independent British Women's Trade Union League and its offspring, the National Federation of Women Workers, had won over 430,000 members by 1914, a majority drawn from the textile trades.[65]

In Germany, female membership varied a great deal from one union to another, depending on the sex distribution of all workers in an industry or occupation, or the extent of unionization generally in a particular trade. In 1914, unions in four trades out of forty-eight reporting in *Correspondenzblatt* recorded a majority of women: Domestic Servants, Trade Clerks, Printers' Aids, and Hat Makers. Other unions with large numbers of women included the Bookbinders, Tobacco Workers, and Textile Workers. These were the female-dominated occupations that accounted, in part, for the high proportion of women members. But in addition, with the exception of servants and clerks, ongoing mechanization of the trades had encouraged high worker concentration in factories, a work situation on which socialists capitalized. Although the work force in the garment industry was dominated also by women, only 17 percent of the Tailors Union membership was female. The decentralized, small-scale nature of production made it extremely difficult to reach these workers. Similarly, only 6 percent of the unionized apprentices in the inn-and-restaurant business, often run along traditional patriarchal lines, and just 5 percent of the unionized workers in agriculture were female.[66]

The number of unionized women compared with the total number of working women in individual trades offers perhaps the best perspective on the extent of organization. In 1903, only the Bookbinders and Shoemakers Unions had mobilized as many as 20 percent of women in the industry, the Printers' Aids Union and Metalworkers Union had 15 percent and 13 percent, respectively, while female membership in the rest of the twenty-one unions responding to an inquiry fell considerably below 10 percent. In overwhelmingly female occupations such as the textile or garment industries, the Textile Workers Union had won only 2.11 percent and the Tailors Union a minuscule .87 percent of working women.[67]

Generally, unionization of women in nontraditional female jobs fared much better than organizational efforts in conventionally female occupations. In many of the latter type, such as domestic industry or domestic service, the structure of work itself thwarted organizational success. This mode of work minimized opportunities for mutual consultation and retarded the emergence of a sense of solidarity that is at the heart of union life. Employment in factories, which was more typical of nontraditional female jobs, enabled union organizers to do their job wholesale at the entrance gates or surreptitiously in the work place. Internal communication of grievances and similar matters was easier. Paradoxically, some unions such as the Servants Union, with the largest share of women in their membership, were also the most powerless because they represented only a small part of the workers in a given occupation. In isolated cases such as the Metalworkers Union, the share of unionized women relative to that industry's total female work force was high by 1914 (over 44 percent). This reflected the nontraditional nature of women's work, its manageable proportions (from the union perspective) as well as the fact that male workers drew their wives into related jobs.[68] Similarly, the Printers' Aids Union had relative success due, in part, to the elite character of the printing profession but also to the sensitivity of the female-dominated union in meeting the needs of the semiskilled workers.

Women came into the unions handicapped by female socialization and a work experience subordinate to men. The rules established by the Free Trade Unions for its own membership and the members' work life confirmed these existing negative assumptions about what the woman could do and what kinds of demands she had on life. One of the obvious issues in the unionization of females was to determine the scales for union dues. The prevailing solution provided for dues differentiated by sex. Most typically, fees, insurance, and strike money as well as dues were geared to sex not job function or wage, although women employed in larger cities often made more money than men in similar occupations in towns and villages. This meant that the financial support during strikes and lockouts or for insurance purposes was proportionately lower for women. The only exceptions were Paula Thiede's Printers' Aids Union, which geared dues to wages, and Emma Ihrer's Artificial Flower Makers Union and the Tobacco Workers Union, both of which tied dues to job. Proportionate dues for women reflected the failure of the Free Trade Unions to press seriously for the principle of equal pay for equal labor. In vain did female leaders time and again at union congresses decry this unequal treatment and argue for raising female dues not only so the woman could receive more sufficient compensation but as an important step to a higher valuation of female labor generally.

The official trade union policy of incorporating women as full and equal members never was met fully. Role expectations that reinforced antifeminist sentiments in the Party were also present among unionists. This lay at the root of common complaint that male union leaders, too, were not supportive of the women's causes. It helps explain the unwillingness of unionists to encourage their female members to join the *Frauenbewegung*, although the "automatic" step from unionization to political activity, which the socialist feminist analysis had predicted, itself failed to materialize. As seen in chapter two, unionized rank and file comprised but a small proportion of women's movement members: the unionized women typically came from nontraditional jobs, such as metalwork, or they were unskilled or semiskilled workers in small trades with a long history of unionization, such as the bookbinding, wood, and printing industries. Their political activity, however, apparently stemmed from such influences as membership in a family involved in socialism or from age and personal inclinations rather than directly from the work experience. Yet the union hesitancy to encourage the step to politics also reflected its sensitivity toward the Party as well as the presence of ideological and strategic disagreements in the organized labor movement. In their special effort to mobilize females, socialist feminists could not break these jurisdictional barriers nor reconcile the divided loyalties that permeated the socialist subculture.

Legislative reform through Party pressure as well as the incorporation of women into the political and union structures were two of three key tactics to winning over the working-class woman. The third involved the effort to create a higher consciousness through a specifically socialist education program and rested on a different plane: ideally, it was the crowning touch to the whole mobilization effort. Once the working-class woman was politicized, she needed to anchor her commitment in a firm theoretical foundation. The educational curriculum in separate clubs prior to 1908 and the instruction programs sponsored subsequently by the Party were designed to make the socialist world view a living reality. Unions, too, were committed to continuous education for broader training and greater understanding of conditions of labor, protective labor laws, and historical perspectives on the present-day struggle.

CHAPTER VIII

THE UNSOLVED PROBLEM OF
WOMEN'S SOCIALIST EDUCATION

Socialist women saw the economic and social changes around them as proof that the objective preconditions for the triumph of socialism were ripening—economic development was revolutionizing the women's world. They regarded feminist reforms as necessary steps in the preparation of women for the ever-sharpening class struggle. Education had a high priority among the reforms. To awaken women to a sense of their subordinate position, to point up ways to improve present-day conditions, and to sketch more equitable social relations in the future would serve both the feminist and the socialist cause. Considerable attention was given to educating working-class women in special evening meetings and in education clubs, as well as in trade union and Party courses.

The decision to found educational clubs independent of Party affiliation was motivated by the legal position of women in Germany. On the surface, the clubs engaged in purely intellectual nonpolitical pursuits; in reality, they were designed to raise women's class consciousness and anchor their political commitment in a secure understanding of Marxist ideology. The clubs owed their origin only partially to political discrimination, however; women leaders were determined to continue separate educational efforts even after 1908 when there was no longer any legal reason for them. Socialist women recognized the vital role the independent clubs played in educating future propagandists. Accustomed to deferring to men, women learned more easily to express their own views and overcome shyness when instruction was sexually segregated. Besides, education by women for women was conceived to serve a dual function: it not only formed class-conscious but, equally important, sex-conscious proletarians. As Ihrer put it in 1892, men tended to view women "not as equals, but as append-ages,"[1] an attitude that stifled women's personal and political maturation.

WOMEN'S EDUCATION PRIOR TO 1908

Emma Ihrer led the fight for separate educational institutions. In 1892, she had called for independent working women's schools, but the idea seemed dangerously feminist from a con-temporaneous socialist viewpoint. Baader, on the executive committee of the Party's Berlin educational school, strongly opposed the proposal. Women should join the existing educa-tional institution that opened its doors to both sexes.[2] Just as extant sex discrimination in German society persuaded women leaders in the early 1890s to reinterpret equality to read "special consideration," the legal barriers to women's political participation made the idea of separate educational arrangements more compelling. Ihrer prodded the movement along. Numerous associations were formed in the 1890s since women activists realized that public meetings were not suffi-cient to transmit the needed education and enlightenment for informed socialist activity. In 1899, Ihrer noted that "the de-sire to form educational clubs is the wish of women and girls who have no opportunity to join trade unions and who find themselves unable to join political clubs."[3]

By 1900, the adverse reaction of Party and union leaders to separatism in education had largely evaporated. Experience showed opponents that their fears had been misplaced: the women's educational institutions had not become competitors of Party and unions nor had they degenerated into "gossiping and bickering societies."[4] Most women present at the Mainz conference expressed great sympathy for the organizations. Zietz's about-face was typical. "A few years ago, I did not favor them," she wrote. However, after observing the clubs in ac-tion, Zietz felt that they could work effectively, particularly in encouraging women to voice their views and in imparting self-confidence.[5] Zietz also had come to believe that the clubs were useful in offering women leaders a sounding board and a forum for discussion of new ideas.

Most women leaders in the Party or unions had ties to the educational movement by the turn of the century. Zietz, for example, ran the educational club in Hamburg together with two other women. Discussions ranged from the female proletariat and Social Democracy to relations between mothers and children to the education of youth. Zietz felt that the function of these clubs was to teach logical thinking through the use of the Socratic method—raise a series of questions and let the participants uncover the answers and theoretical connections themselves. "Pride in being able to do something, leads to self-confidence and to further desire to learn." Zetkin gave lectures on cultural history at the Stuttgart women's educational club, and Baader was active in the educational movement in Berlin.[6]

Since women could join unions throughout the country, independent educational clubs for female unionists never materialized. Rather, in 1905, when *Correspondenzblatt* opened a discussion of trade union educational courses, union leaders started to gear classes within the existing educational structure more specifically to the training of women union leaders.

Grünberg's experience documents the union commitment to continuous education. Two years after assuming her position in the workers' secretariat, she began an educational course for unionized working women to supplement the information participants obtained at meetings and in the press. Her intent was to promote agitation among working women by educating propagandists who would seek prospective members among their work colleagues. The first course dealt with such themes as the trade union movement in general, employers' associations, and protective laws; thirty-three women participated, most from the Metalworkers, Unskilled Factory Workers, Printers' Aids, and the Domestic Servants Unions. The Nuremberg school councelor brought charges against Grünberg for holding classes without official permission, but the court ruled in her favor on the ground she had not founded a school because she only held lectures. Grünberg joined a union educational committee in 1908 and continued her course under its direction, expanding the topics to include a comparison of the Free Trade Unions with other German unions and those in England, France, Austria, Switzerland, and North America. She supervised weekly sewing evenings run by two seamstresses and set up a special course in 1910 to explain the industrial code (*Gewerbeordnung*) to working women.[7] The union educational idea clearly was directed to practical subjects.

Women who went through the educational institutions assumed key roles in the bureaucracy. Participation was the springboard to official posts within the women's movement as well as to membership in the various committees sponsored by socialist feminists. In 1907, for example, the women's movement had 407 representatives; most had been elected in the educational clubs. In Berlin, in 1908, child-labor committee members were drawn from those attending the evening lecture series. Leadership positions were interchangeable: in 1912, for example, Frau Jacob, head of the second Berlin educational session switched places with Frl. Seyfahrt, leader of the local child-labor committee. The educational clubs often prepared lists of delegates to congresses that were later voted on in open membership meetings.[8] Future propagandists for both the Party and unions were trained in courses set up especially for that purpose.

In 1908, when women obtained direct access to the Party, the continuance of the separate educational clubs was called into question. The new organizational statutes stipulated that the men and women of each locality should make the decision. Membership in the educational associations, however, could not replace the women's obligation to join the SPD.[9] *Gleichheit* came out for preserving the clubs, although with stringent modifications, and Zietz reaffirmed the paper's position at the women's conference. *Gleichheit* called for divesting the clubs of their political and "deep theoretical" functions, which the Party could take over, and for transforming them into institutions to instruct mothers in child care and the supervision of compliance with child-labor and school laws.[10] They were to perform functions geared specifically to women as mothers; their transformation implied no slighting of the importance of theoretical training for women. The tasks of preparing socialist consciousness would be left to the Party in special educational sessions (*Leseabende*). These sessions would be held in addition to existing instruction sponsored by Party affiliates that had been open to women beginning in the early 1890s.[11] Acceptance of this proposal by the SPD congress formalized a previously initiated evening lecture series for women, as an examination of the Berlin case reveals.

THE *Leseabende*:

A CASE STUDY OF GREATER BERLIN, 1904-1914

The Berlin women's movement had a long-standing commitment to continuous education for its rank and file. Interest in systematic instruction for members of German Social Democracy tended to be restricted to metropolitan areas, while socialists in towns and villages either were apathetic toward or passively opposed to education.[12] For large cities, therefore, the Berlin case illustrates the content and method of instruction as well as interest in and participation at the special educational sessions set up for female members. It also demonstrates barriers to the dissemination of socialist knowledge among the organized female working class.

The initial response to the official closing in 1894 of the Berlin propaganda committee (*Agitations-Kommission*), the organizational forerunner of the women's representative system, had been the creation of special educational sessions for women. They were to meet twice monthly in various districts of Berlin, and each group supposedly listened to a reading from either a newspaper or a political tract, followed by discussion. Seven leaders of the sessions were appointed.[13]

What became of this early effort is unclear; not until 1904 do the women's educational sessions reappear in the records of the Berlin police. That year, Ottilie Baader instituted a reading session for factory and domestic industry working women who were involved in the trade union movement. Emphasis on union members corresponded to Party women's hope of playing a vital role in training and molding union propagandists. Fifteen women attended and heard weekly lectures on such practical issues as the housing question in Berlin, the eight-hour workday, domestic industry, and children's education; they read also Social Democratic Party literature. Baader brought in leading representatives of various Berlin unions and agencies: Frau Rösner from the local health insurance bureau, Anna Kuhlike for domestic industry workers, Frl. Kadereit and Frl. Baar for metalworkers and sales clerks respectively, and a spokeswoman for the Berlin grievance committee.[14]

In the fall of 1904 Baader shifted gears. To a new lecture series she invited only those participants who would be of "direct benefit" to, and who could secure advantages for, the political wing of Social Democracy. After the course, each individual was expected to found a small club, and in turn, educate additional propagandists for the women's movement. Until September 1907, admission was by invitation only. Thereafter, any Party woman who was interested in continuing her education could attend.[15] Prior to the meeting, leaflets indicating time, place, and topic were passed out around Berlin.

Themes now centered mainly on political questions. The literature studied included the *Communist Manifesto* and the Party's Erfurt Program of 1891. Among the subjects analyzed in some detail were the history of industrial development as well as Social Democracy's position on suffrage and particularly on the women's vote. The discussions also included health care and insurance laws. Particular attention was given to providing children's education with a specifically socialist content. In 1911, the Executive Committee published a manual for the sessions, containing themes and materials for discussion. Leaders generally followed the guidelines, except when current political issues intruded, such as the 1910 campaign to reform Prussia's three-class electoral law.[16]

The participants were grouped into classes of not more than thirty persons. If no speaker was scheduled, each participant read out loud a short passage from a particular work. The rest asked questions, encouraging the reader to give her interpretation of the section. It was "education of all by all"; as *Vorwärts* proudly described it: "everyone participated." The director of the session was often called upon to explain difficult passages. The sessions were held monthly in clubs, halls, or the homes of the leaders. As the sessions grew in size, districts subdivided the meetings to keep attendance small and manageable. The structure, too, shifted from discussion to lecture.[17]

The meetings were set up for women, and men were requested to stay away. Several males, however, played an active leadership role in the educational structure. At the outset, attendance was weak; in some cases, only three women showed up; for a number of years, the average hovered between seven and twelve and in 1907 rose to twenty-five to thirty. With the elevation of the sessions to official Party institutions in 1908, participation increased considerably, reaching roughly one-third of a district's female membership. The number of sessions also grew quickly after 1908; there were 95 meetings held each month in Berlin in 1910; 110 in April 1912; 158 in November 1912; and 170 in April 1913. Table 6 breaks

TABLE 6   Berlin Women's Educational Sessions in 1910

ELECTORAL DISTRICT	TOTAL FEMALE MEMBERSHIP	AVERAGE ATTENDANCE	PERCENT OF MEMBERS ATTENDING	NUMBER OF SESSIONS PER MONTH
First	104	25	24	1
Second	363	85	23	2
Third	284	60	21	1
Fourth	2,796	1,050	38	41
Fifth	220	60	27	2
Sixth	3,509	1,100	31	13
Teltow-Beeskow . .	3,899	n.a.	n.a.	19
Nieder Barnim . . .	1,591	n.a.	n.a.	16
Total	12,766			95

SOURCE: Staatsarchiv Potsdam. Pr. Br. Rep. 30, Berlin C, Tit. 95, Sek. 7, Nr. 15852, Bl. 37-38. "Sozialdemokratische Frauenleseabende und Unterrichtskurse in Gross-Berlin."

down the number of sessions by district and shows the relationship of attendance to total female Party membership in the Berlin movement in September 1910. It was estimated that throughout Germany that year, 150 localities had instituted similar women's educational sessions.[18]

In January 1909, an effort was made to modify the institutional structure in light of what was regarded as generally weak and sporadic participation. Grass-roots support favored a proposal to consolidate sessions so it would be worthwhile inviting a speaker. A year and a half later, weak participation was diagnosed as a result of scarcity of skilled, available speakers. Time and again, the heads of the sessions asked for male or female speakers only to be told that none was available, or, compounding the problem, that speakers refused to address such small groups.[19]

To help solve the problem of obtaining speakers, the women's bureau set up a special course for female functionaries and leaders of the educational sessions. The course was designed to offer additional oratorical training and more sophisticated analysis of socialist thought. It was expected that the women with advanced training would run better-organized, more interesting sessions, fill the speakers' gap, and bring more intelligence and experience to their Party positions. Each participant was elected at district meetings; forty-four attended the first course held exclusively for "women who staffed positions in the Social Democratic Party." The themes were drawn from both the theoretical and practical sections of the Party program and emphasized militarism and the Reich's financial history. By reading the Party Bulletin, the group also kept abreast of current political issues. Each woman was instructed about the literature she should read, on where to find it, and how to gather an adequate collection in order to have sufficient materials on hand to prepare lectures. At each of the eighteen meetings, three women presented talks and the others offered criticism. The sessions included also the teaching of composition and good writing.[20]

These special courses became a standing institution. Marie

Juchacz participated in one and reminisced: "Numerous women who had moved beyond the level of the educational sessions . . . nevertheless had a strong need for more education. For this reason, continuing courses . . . were set up . . . in which we read Marx, Engels, and Lassalle."[21] Although poor, Juchacz continued, each woman willingly paid a few marks for Bebel's *Women under Socialism* or thirty pennies for a brochure, knowing that a good grounding in the literature was needed to work effectively for socialism.

Käthe Duncker's lecture series for women in Teltow-Beeskow in late 1913 documents the degree to which theoretical training was sought. The course centered on one theme: the scientific foundation of the modern working-class movement. Participants were introduced on such topics as the relationship between social reform, democracy, and socialism; idealism and materialism; and utopian and scientific socialism. These materials were followed by analyses of precapitalist economic development, the origins of the capitalist mode of production, the formation of the proletariat, and the nature of capitalist exploitation. After eleven weeks, the class ended with a discussion of the method and the goals of the class struggle.[22]

Some women openly questioned the use of such sophisticated concepts and theoretical themes, particularly for the new members. A 1910 meeting of leaders of the Berlin educational sessions, for example, voiced considerable sympathy for introducing converts to practical questions of immediate interest to women as mothers and workers. Proponents of this view rejected the radical socialist emphasis on theory and some of the critics, among them Anna Matschke, were later found in the majority socialist camp in 1917. In one district, attendance was said to have improved since the meetings had begun dealing with more practical issues such as hygiene and child care.[23]

In the course of time, internal dissatisfaction with the training of socialist women was increasing. The leaders in Berlin admitted that their educational sessions were less than glowing successes. Similar conclusions were drawn in other parts of the country.[24] Problems were pinpointed, but solutions remained elusive.

Beginning in 1911, complaints were raised that the sessions in the capital lacked coordination; there was no uniform propaganda, no personal contact between the district leaders, and insufficient opportunity to share views or exchange experience. The independent educational clubs of the pre-1908 period, it was said, had maintained close contact and coordination, and leaders wistfully spoke of the good old days. To meet the criticism, periodic district and interdistrict meetings of the sessions' leaders were instituted to discuss issues of mutual interest and the thematic manual of discussion topics was issued.[25]

Far more intractable was the problem of weak and sporadic participation. Police records provide interesting insights into the question. The police that watched the educational activities with great care were quite realistic in their negative appraisal of the extent of women's interest in socialist training. At the same time, the reports reveal the prevailing attitudes in Germany toward the female sex. By police accounts, women were politically immature and indifferent. They were also bored by the meetings. They would sneak out of the rooms, politely, but resolutely; appear once, and then fail to show up again. Usually, the same old Party members would make up the audience and new converts simply stayed away. Officials stated time and again that working-class women were intellectually "not far enough along" to be able to follow the lectures.[26] One report generalized that women would rather participate in street demonstrations, "large stormy meetings," electoral struggles, or routine work than attend the educational sessions.[27] Police annals stereotyped women as emotional (easily caught up in large, exciting gatherings), conscientious, and hard working, but not at all interested in developing their intellect.

Stereotypes aside, the verdict of the police on women's reaction to the educational programs was not much different from that of the socialist leadership. Despite extensive efforts over a long span of years, attendance at the educational meetings did not increase. In the years immediately preceding World War I, female membership in the Party rose, but membership in the educational institutions did not; in some districts, the number of participants was declining significantly.[28] Time and time again, meetings were called to discuss the reasons for the lack of interest. In the desperate search for solutions, the sixth electoral district came up with a ludicrous plan to employ comedians (for low wages) to "help make things more interesting."[29]

The women's educational programs operated in a difficult ambiance. The schooling of working women did not at all prepare them for logical and analytic thought, and family norms in the working class more often than not excluded females from participation in political discussions. The primary schools that working-class women attended offered inadequate instruction. Juchacz repeated the fourth grade four times because her small village school went no further.[30]

In view of the poor intellectual foundation of the clientele, it became a major problem to generate interest if not enthusiasm. The solution depended on the character and competence of the speakers as well as the position of the educational sessions within the Party structure. By many accounts, lecturers were second-rate: monotonous, poorly trained, and unable to keep the audiences' attention for the whole evening.[31] As has been brought out, it was often impossible to get a speaker. At best, only two-thirds of the lecturers were women; the sessions had to rely on men. However, in Berlin, as well as elsewhere, men were less than eager to address women's educational groups. It was an activity with low priority, and many men felt ambivalent about broadening women's horizons. One policeman called the unwillingness of men to speak before women's groups and the hesitancy of Party institutions to assign men to the lecture route for the women's sessions "passive resistance" against the whole educational effort.[32] In July 1913, session leaders met to discuss what to do in light of the poor support for their educational institutions by male colleagues. They planned to close down the first district's educational sessions in protest, until the objection was raised by the women themselves that such a strike would accomplish nothing since "men admit they prefer their wives at home."[33]

The negative attitudes of a number of male speakers and Party functionaries were reinforced by similar sentiments among family members. Husbands or fathers dissuaded women from attending the "useless" educational sessions.[34] Thus, powerful forces combined to work against the spread of socialist education to females. Women leaders in Berlin simply were unable to devise counterstrategies to neutralize the inhibiting assumptions.

SOCIALIST VERSUS TRADITIONALIST VIEWS: SHORTCOMINGS OF THE EDUCATIONAL GOAL

If the strenuous efforts of Berlin women to promote interest in socialist education proved only marginally successful, the results conformed to a more general pattern. Leaders of the socialist movement found it difficult to evoke interest in education among the rank and file generally. For example, in 1910, the Party's national educational committee coordinated 272 lecture series throughout the country; roughly 4 percent of the total membership in the SPD attended, and even that figure might be inflated since the statistics failed to distinguish between Party and union members in the audience. In 1909, only sixty persons out of a total membership of 8,600 attended a course in Offenbach.[35] Similarly, less than 1 percent of the members of the Berlin socialist movement joined the Workers' Educational School, an association dedicated to the spread of socialist knowledge. In 1908-1909, the school had 1,585 members, of whom 11 percent were female.[36] Those most interested in education tended to be skilled workers such as the mechanics as well as designers of instruments and machines who hoped to improve their living standard by acquiring new skills.

In the reports that differentiated by sex, women showed less interest than men in education. For example, the Party instituted "itinerant orators" as part of its effort to increase interest in education; for years, Hermann Duncker and Otto Rühle crisscrossed Germany, speaking in hamlets and metropolitan areas on a wide variety of topics. Between 1907 and 1912, an average of only 9 percent (some 7,600) of the participants were women.[37] Even at these highly popular series only one-half of the male and female participants attended all the lectures.

The national educational committee saw its main task as instituting courses on economics and scientific socialism. A cursory glance at lecture topics shows that natural science rivaled, and in two years, surpassed economics in attracting audiences; general history fared well, as did more practical questions of social-political reform.[38]

An added difficulty faced by socialist leaders was the effective communication of an alternative set of values and beliefs through the spread of specifically socialist literature. Two studies undertaken in Imperial Germany indicated that interest in socialist works among organized working-class men and women was limited. In 1911, Hertha Siemering analyzed book-borrowing patterns in trade union and Party libraries in Berlin as well as the yearly reports of the Party's schools. She concluded that, generally, while workers supported the SPD, with few exceptions, they were not interested in scientific socialism. Gertrud Hanna, in 1913, corroborated the finding and noted that women in particular did not pick up socialist books.[39]

In libraries run by trade unions, socialist materials remained on the shelves; workers preferred books dealing with geography, peoples, and foreign lands. Similarly, in the SPD libraries Siemering noted a small turnover in books dealing with politics and economics, while interest centered on science, geography, travel, or health. The only exception was Bebel's "Frau," an extremely popular work. Workers shunned "modern" naturalist literature that depicted the realities of life and preferred German classicial authors such as Goethe, Schiller, and Heine.[40]

Hanna bemoaned the typically aimless choice of library users despite lists of recommended literature. Workers showed a preference for entertainment. She found that most working women concentrated on sentimental novels or romantic poetry. Women in the working class seemed to be largely indifferent to more serious issues or matters beyond their daily concerns. Hanna felt this apathy greatly inhibited the struggle for the liberation of the working class.

A lack of consensus as to the purpose of education in the socialist subculture also hurt the program. After the turn of the century, the question of education as well as the nature and function of the press became divisive issues. Debates at several conferences reflected growing ideological tensions. Delegates divided over the question of practical or theoretical training. Grünberg, for example, questioned the wisdom of introducing newly won comrades to Marx's *Das Kapital* or the Party's Erfurt Program. They would be bored instead of intrigued, she predicted. On another occasion, Agnes Fahrenwald also claimed that works on scientific socialism were too difficult; women came once or twice to the sessions and then stayed away. She recommended the use of pamphlets, calling Ihrer's publications "excellent" and applying the same adjective to Braun's, "even if they aren't quite what we would like" (a statement that produced mirth among the delegates).[41]

Zetkin felt that it was erroneous to differentiate between simple and difficult themes; even the most abstract idea, if handled properly, could be effectively communicated. She believed that the function of the educational evenings was to clarify the socialist world view and to educate revolutionary fighters, although she warned against presenting socialist principles as bloodless, abstract theory. The concepts were to be related to the capitalist system that directly impinged on the life of the working class. Zietz supported Zetkin fully on this issue and urged the delegates to educate "revolutionary class fighters" not "social reformers."[42] The decentralized system of instruction, however, precluded control. Courses could not help but reflect the individual leaders' ideological predilections, their choice of subjects and reading materials, and the socialist climate of the particular area.

Gleichheit's abstract, theoretical bent came under considerable criticism. Dissatisfaction grew more intense after 1900. Adversaries hoped to popularize the paper ostensibly in order to reach larger numbers of women who were indifferent to socialism. The controversy over the orientation of *Gleichheit* paralleled the conflict over the content of the educational program. Zetkin refused to lower *Gleichheit*'s standards for the sake of greater appeal. The paper, she emphatically stated in 1902, was an educational organ directed at women already in the movement and designed to teach them theory and the relation of theory to political action.[43] She upheld the Marxist emphasis on the unity of theory and practice. Socialist women, Zetkin held, needed an intellectual organ to help them relate current events to the larger context of the exploitative capitalist system.

Zetkin found a consistent supporter in Baader and although Zietz admitted some of the opponents' charges, she wholeheartedly agreed to the basic thrust of *Gleichheit*.[44] Zietz conceded, however, that the level of the paper precluded it from "bringing the completely indifferent woman to socialism." As Zetkin intended, it spoke well to "convinced Social Democrats." Zietz advocated in 1900 publication of another, more popular paper dealing with themes and concepts the masses of women could understand and focusing on concrete issues drawn from daily life. Such a paper, she wrote, could be published as a weekly supplement to the Party press and was particularly relevant for women unable to attend political meetings, as in Mecklenburg or Braunschweig.[45] Through the supplementary women's paper, Zietz sought to extend recruitment beyond the groups reached by *Gleichheit*. Her proposal, ostensibly inoffensive to Zetkin, was not adopted; the 1900 women's conference agreed with Ihrer's position that it would be better to leave the task of education to women who could influence the editors or join local editorial boards.

Others were more adamant. Grünberg questioned Zetkin's theoretical presuppositions and sought not to supplement but reform *Gleichheit*. She jibed at the 1911 women's conference that *Gleichheit* was "loved" not for its main content but for the children's supplement. It was written for propagandists, not for the people. Growth in subscriptions was unimpressive if no one really read the paper. To the considerable merriment of the audience, Grünberg urged *"umsatteln"* on Zetkin. This was a clever double entendre, for the German verb could mean either that Zetkin change her ideas or that she change professions. Grünberg found some support for her position, and Zetkin was forced, once again, to hold forth on the importance of elucidating theoretical concepts and broadening understanding among the enlightened female comrades. Grünberg, sensing the specter of a confrontation between "radicals" and "revisionists," defended her views: "I want women to have a paper they understand and read. One shouldn't talk from a certain position on this. I am a socialist. . . . Zetkin's sensitivity against criticism of *Gleichheit* is inappropriate. . . . I come into daily contact with working women and know they don't read *Gleichheit*, even the popular articles which are in the paper . . . and even SPD women . . . don't read it because they are used to seeing things in *Gleichheit* which have no meaning to them."[46] With this latter point, Grünberg demolished the radical edifice built on the interconnection of theory and practice. The integration of the women's movement into the Party indeed tended to favor a reorientation of *Gleichheit* away from its preoccupation with theory. In 1913, Zetkin agreed to "change views" and gear the paper more to the women sympathetic to but unschooled in socialist thought.[47]

The educational ideal of socialist women remained unrealized in Imperial Germany. Their goal of disseminating learning to benefit the political struggle and insure the triumph of alternative values proved largely abortive. The socialist subculture was separate from the dominant society, but not quarantined. From a very young age, working-class members were exposed to nonsocialist values and views. Many even preferred traditional German classics or sentimental poetry to theoretical reading in history or economics. Others stressed the importance of practical learning in such areas as health or child care. These findings support the conclusions of other historians interested in the degree to which the socialist subculture was able to keep traditional values at bay. Guenther Roth finds that German socialists generally were "unable to transcend the major political and non-political values of the dominant society."[48] To the extent, then, that German values encroached on socialist ideals, traditional views governing sex roles and expectations barred the spread of those that upheld the equal worth, rights, and capabilities of women.

Yet, even though the educational goals were far from being reached, the endeavors were not spent in vain. During the wartime crisis, socialist feminists proved loyal to the prewar radical ideal of creating "revolutionary class fighters." Good numbers rejected the center-right alliance that took over leadership of the Social Democratic Party in 1914 and they shunned the call to "relearn." A group of women more interested in practical rather than theoretical matters fell heir to the women's movement of the SPD in 1917. Their ascendance spelled the end of an era.

PART D
THE END OF AN ERA

CHAPTER IX

WARTIME DIVISIONS:
FROM SOCIALIST TO SOCIAL
FEMINISM

World War I confronted socialist leaders with a series of challenges that changed the face of Social Democracy and profoundly altered the relationship of men and women in the movement. When the SPD adhered to the *Burgfrieden* (cessation of party strife) and suspended internal opposition, it sacrificed those principles that had made German Social Democracy the envy and hope of the Second International: anti-militarism, internationalism, and noncollaboration. The war curtailed the Party's independence and encouraged a center-right alliance of socialist forces for the war effort.[1] Backed by most Free Trade Unionists, the alliance managed socialists' new relationship with government forces and only gently criticized official action. It oversaw the massive influx of working-class women into industry and, to meet social dislocations, channeled organized women into municipal welfare activity. In 1917, however, prewar ideological antagonisms and wartime strains combined to demolish proletarian unity. The center-right coalition crystallized into majority socialism (old SPD); a disparate group of oppositionists formed independent socialism (*Unabhängige Sozialdemokratische Partei Deutschlands* USPD), a smaller but more radical party committed to the principles of international socialism and revolution.

Many prewar activists in the socialist women's movement supported the USPD. Why did females tend to join the opposition? Do the divisions shed light on their overall political commitments and priorities? These are some of the questions this chapter seeks to answer. Its main focus, however, is on a new group of female leaders who inherited the old movement.

These majority socialist women modified four basic aspects of feminism's prewar alliance with radical socialism while USPD women maintained the original analysis. For majority socialists, preparation for the class struggle gave way to a new emphasis on immediate, practical efforts to further the triumph of socialism; women's role in the socialist movement in specific and society in general was restricted primarily to municipal welfare activity; the women's question was no longer related to the social question but was considered a human problem (*Menschheitsfrage*); and, finally, the relationship of socialism to bourgeois feminism came under more pragmatic review. Who were these new leaders? What factors could help explain the adoption of a more modest interpretation of the women's question and why did they evolve from socialist into social feminists?

SOCIALIST FEMINISTS RESPOND
TO THE HARDSHIPS OF WAR

World War I brought a major transformation in the employment of women. The closing of luxury industries and the strangulation of the textile trades requiring imported raw materials freed working women for war-related jobs. The exigencies of war, too, required ever larger numbers of females for the production process as was true throughout Europe. An emergency law of 4 August 1914 suspended protective labor legislation and opened categories of jobs in mines and foundries that had been barred to female workers in the prewar period. The law also relaxed the various controls over work conditions and night employment for women and children. Hanna noted a shift in female employment from prewar, unskilled occupations to more skilled jobs such as supervisors, foremen, and managers. Yet she also remarked on the growth in domestic industry as well as the fact that women seldom used the employment offices and continued to accept employment for low piece wages.[2] Thönnessen compares the 1913 and 1918 figures for men and women employed in mining, handicraft, construction, and in industrial establishments with more than nine workers. He finds that by the end of the war, only 71.6 percent of the prewar numbers of male employees were working while the numbers of females had risen by 152 percent.[3]

Conditions of employment deteriorated as controls were removed and wages fell. It is estimated that the average daily real wage of workers in war industries declined 21.6 percent between March 1914 and September 1916, while real wages in nonwar related industries in the same period plummeted 42.1 percent.[4] The rising cost of food—in the five months following the outbreak of hostilities prices for food skyrocketed—added fuel to an already explosive situation. Pressured by the SPD, the Free Trade Unions, and urban groups, the government sought to impose price ceilings, initially on wheat. The effort was unsuccessful: food riots, strikes, and demonstrations became the response to hard times. In May 1916, the government created a war food office that allocated food premiums to workers according to "need," but army procurement remained outside its competence and numerous national and state officials were less than sympathetic to its activities.[5]

The educational sessions run by socialist feminists recorded growing discontent with wartime conditions. Complaints over "poor food and the character of women's work" were common themes, and speakers never tired of depicting women in munitions factories carrying seventy to eighty pounds of shells. In February 1915, a special session for the third Berlin district was held to protest the rising cost of bread and potatoes; numerous meetings on similar topics subsequently were called throughout the country. The government, Junkers (East Elbian nobles), peasants, and war racketeers all were blamed for the shortages. In Königsberg and nearby areas, wives of drafted SPD members were attracted to socialist meetings to protest the level of state financial support in light of the higher costs of living. After a well-attended women's meeting in Stuttgart in November 1915, eight women called for a demonstration to protest rising prices: 400 showed up in front of the mayor's office.[6] Increased burdens on women as workers and consumers provided a context for a growing spirit of rebellion.

To ameliorate conditions and ease wartime strains, the SPD and union leadership directed organized women into city administration. A circular of 7 August 1914 called on them to perform vital functions: secure assistance for the unemployed and for families whose fathers were at the front; provide health care for new mothers; staff the job referral bureaus; join orphan institutions and pressure for day nurseries and kindergartens; set up communal kitchens; and help procure food and establish maximum price levels.[7] Self-interest prompted the decree: SPD leaders hoped that through municipal work, socialist women would maintain personal contact with their constituency since mass rallies and other former recruiting and propaganda tactics had been suspended by law. They also expected female members to handle important jobs in the organization since the war was depriving the movement of thousands of skilled male functionaries.

Bourgeois women, too, moved into municipal administration. They formed a national women's service (*Nationaler Frauendienst*) and organized a women's auxiliary army for municipal officials. In her capacity as head of Social Democratic women, Zietz spoke before middle-class groups in Berlin to explain socialists' welfare efforts and raised the possibility of collaboration. Socialist feminists followed the Party in suspending the class struggle. The actual decision to cooperate with bourgeois women was left up to the local clubs, but the war had created new political options.[8]

All over Germany, female socialists accepted the challenge. The reaction to contact with middle-class women varied greatly. In Berlin, over six hundred socialists joined together for municipal work and remained independent of the middle-class organization, as did females in Leipzig and Breslau. In Hamburg and Cologne, by contrast, socialist and middle-class women harmonized their efforts. In Cologne, a national association of women was formed and the founders called on women of all political persuasions to join. After contacting the leadership in Berlin, Marie Juchacz, secretary in the local SPD organization, entered the organization. She reminisced, "At first, I was greeted with much often painful curiosity and benevolently made welcome. We [socialists] were appointed to city commissions. I was asked to join the food committee which the mayor himself ran. . . . I also made it my task to visit two or three families each day . . . to help them. . . . We learned that not everything was reactionary on the other side."[9]

The experience of Helene Grünberg in Nuremberg was much less positive. She battled local administrative officials at every turn, challenging their attitude toward welfare and decrying tokenism. A women's office had been established to promote female employment in munitions factories. Grünberg bitterly reported that its advisory board was staffed with bourgeois groups—representatives of all middle-class women's clubs in the city as well as women drawn from church-affiliated unions—and "as decoration" she herself. On one occasion, the city's welfare councilor challenged her right to represent workers' grievances in the welfare bureau. Calling her a spy (*Spitzel*), he sought to prevent her from entering the public office and attending meetings. A court decision favored Grünberg, but a climate of bitterness and mutual hostility characterized the contact between Nuremberg socialists and the middle class.[10]

Despite adherence to the *Burgfrieden*, propaganda critical of the SPD's official position began to circulate. In December 1914, Zetkin wrote of growing opposition to the Party's stance and added, "Do I have to explain why I am with the opposition? I think my whole life's work tells the story."[11] The conflict was between those socialists who rejected complicity in an imperialist war and charged betrayal of the principles of international socialism and those who claimed that socialists had a duty to defend a wronged nation. It split the women's movement since females raised their voices in support of one or the other camp.

Life was especially difficult for the opposition, which operated in a hostile environment replete with censorship, house search, surveillance, and the threat of arrest at any time. Survival depended on anonymity and surreptitious behavior.

To some extent, dissemination of radical propaganda rested

with females since officials drafted those men suspected of leftist leanings. Radical sympathizers were warned not to mention names if caught with illegal brochures or flyers: "persons unknown stuck them under doors" was the proper response. They were told not to greet each other at demonstrations to prevent the police from linking participants together. To encourage silence, the case was mentioned of a woman who confessed in order to gain her husband's release: surprising to none, the man still languished in jail.[12] Meetings often lasted only minutes and the full message, relayed in stages, came after several such furtive gatherings.

Those interrogated would feign ignorance. Rosa Huith, a Stuttgart radical questioned by the police in September 1915, said she thought the meeting was to have discussed savings institutions; another woman, Minna Lorenz, claimed she had "just arrived when the police entered the room, wasn't really listening and didn't understand a thing, anyway."[13] Rather than openly bill a well-known radical, the coordinator of a meeting would ask if any one had anything to say. The speaker, who had been sitting quietly in the audience, then would address the meeting. Stuttgart radical women met under the pretext of holding "knitting evenings." The police who, in late 1915, had labeled their meetings "gatherings of radical Social Democracy" changed the heading accordingly: *Strickabende*. The women would knit and talk "in an apparently aimless fashion." When questioned, they said they simply had discussed the feasibility of setting up such a knitting group in the old city. The topic, in fact, had been the effort at Bern, Switzerland, to resurrect the International.[14]

DISINTEGRATION OF THE WOMEN'S MOVEMENT IN 1917: AN EVALUATION OF THE SPLIT

How did the socialist *women's* movement divide on the issue of support for or opposition to the official position of the SPD? The secondary literature has argued that women by and large favored the opposition. It has offered as evidence the move by prominent national leaders such as Clara Zetkin, Luise Zietz,

Margaret Wengels, and Mathilde Wurm into opposition; the complaints of majority socialists that the split deprived their camp of officials; and the wartime reports in *Gleichheit* recording local organizations' vote for or against the SPD.[15]

The analysis is correct with one important qualification. The war years brought an extremely high attrition rate for women members. Estimates vary: Margaret Wengels and Frida Wulff called for a women's conference in September 1916 in light of a 39 percent loss of female membership; Mathilde Wurm at the conference estimated that 100,000, or about 57 percent of the prewar figures, had left the Party since August 1914.[16] It can be surmised that the deeply politicized and committed women remained in the movement, giving an edge to the radical wing.

The proportion of members who went over to the USPD is difficult to establish with precision. Much of the evidence is impressionistic. The press division of the army General Command in September 1918 noted that the USPD was "systematically" and "eagerly" working in the area of the women's movement and "majority socialists apparently are unable successfully to counter the effort."[17] Majority socialists were aware of the appeal of the opposition and decried the loss of leadership to the USPD. During the war, they tended to explain the divisions by adopting a stereotyped view of females as more emotional creatures. In July 1917, *Gleichheit*, under majority socialist control, editorialized: "Women are more influenced than men by their emotions. In this lies their strength and also their weakness. In this case, the strength is a passionate opposition to war. . . . Their weakness is that, due to emotionalism, they are more susceptible to the erroneous view that majority socialists favored war."[18] In the immediate postwar period, majority socialist women spoke of problems in creating an effective women's movement because of insufficient numbers of skilled leaders. At the June 1919 conference Juchacz complained, "We don't have qualified female speakers because the Party divisions robbed us of many people." Wilhelmine Kähler, at the same conference, perhaps initiated the facile generalization that "women have always stood to the left in the Party and thus, to many, the USPD was more attractive." In addition, Klara Bohm-Schuch, writing in 1922, admitted that "the split . . . weakened us."[19]

The steady diet of antiwar articles in *Gleichheit* had provoked the first controversy. In May 1915, the paper reported that women in Harburg called on the executive committee to reform the paper. At the same time, five hundred women in Bremen met to declare their full agreement with *Gleichheit*'s political stance. Battle lines were forming.

The trade union bureaucracy dispensed with talk and acted. It founded a biweekly in January 1916, *Gewerkschaftliche Frauenzeitung*, edited by Gertrud Hanna. Although Hanna would later deny the charge that the paper "has been founded only as a substitute for *Gleichheit*" and claim it descended from Ihrer's more union-oriented *Die Arbeiterin* of 1890, the new paper was clearly the union bureaucracy's response to *Gleichheit*'s unacceptable political position. It faithfully toed the union line and presented the views of the majority while "shunning an extreme patriotic tone in order not to alienate the uncommitted." It emphasized practical questions of importance to working women, sought to educate them on the operation of the economy and, in particular, was geared to winning and keeping women for the trade union movement. *Gewerkschaftliche Frauenzeitung* was popular although "too abstract and not styled to the ways of the readers," a fact that was regretted in majority socialist circles.[20] In fifteen months, subscriptions reached over 100,000; by December 1918 the numbers had doubled.

The decision of the national executive committee to oust Zetkin and Zietz from their positions irrevocably split the women's movement. The leadership removed Zetkin from editorial control of *Gleichheit* and Zietz from the executive committee, and it reorganized the women's bureau by locating Baader in a menial position in the Party's correspondence section. Radical socialists were outraged, although a few said that Zietz should have resigned rather than let herself be thrown out. Zietz held meetings in Berlin and whipped up sympathy for her side by detailing ugly attitudes toward women on the executive: Philipp Scheidemann, she charged, actually substituted *"ninny"* for *woman* on circulars.[21] Other socialist feminists saw the SPD's leadership action against Zietz and Zetkin as a direct challenge to their movement. Friedrich Ebert, leader of the SPD, admitted that, "most female comrades hold the view that disciplining their leaders and disbanding the bureau cannot further the women's movement." He promised that the SPD would devote time to women's causes in the future.[22] The impression had been created, however, that the executive was reneging on its former promises to the working-class woman. An unconscious feeling that the women's question should have transcended Party divisions and that the executive had no right to expel the democratically elected representatives of women made many female Party members uneasy. Socialist feminists were proud and possessive of their paper and their bureau and found it difficult to accept the decision by their male comrades. Zietz recognized the potential of these sentiments for her side. She stated that "no one has the right to throw us out of the Party. . . . Many left it in opposition to the executive. We must win them for us."[23]

Why was the left able to attract goodly numbers of socialist women? The answers fall basically into wartime and long-term causes. Food scarcity and high prices engendered consumer outrage, a sentiment skillfully exploited by USPD propaganda. This tells as much about mobilization potential as political ideology: in both the prewar and war periods women were mobilized as consumers to protest economic hardships. The USPD played on war dislocations, but also on the growth in female labor and the ever more urgent desire for peace. Zietz and Wurm organized peace demonstrations in the courtyard of the *Vorwärts* building to coincide with Party meetings.[24]

USPD propaganda also fully exploited long-term reasons for discontent among socialist feminists: agitation lay in the hands of prewar leaders who knew well the problems women had faced in the SPD. As seen, the USPD profited by the anger many women felt after Zetkin and Zietz had been deprived of influence within the women's movement. Also, the discrepancy between the Party's adoption of the theory of women's equality and its discrimination against women in practice worked to the advantage of the left. The USPD sought not only to preserve the radical socialist theory of female liberation, but to safeguard women's interest with new vigor. It affirmed the principle of participatory democracy and recognized that statutory equality did not guarantee equality for women; the new Party rejected egalitarianism (*Gleichmacherei*) and established special institutions and designated work spheres for women. Separate channels of communication bypassing the normal routes were created. Zietz at the founding congress declared: "I hope women's demands will be more highly valued than in the old Party. . . . We must act differently. . . . Greater independence within the Party . . . makes possible collaboration among women . . . for women's rights."[25] Due to the upheavals of the time and the Party's demise in 1922, the commitment was barely tested; but many women in the stormy days of 1917 must have viewed their position and responsibility in the USPD as an improvement.

A greater tendency toward radicalism was reinforced by the fact, as noted in previous chapters, that activists in the socialist women's movement were older women, many of whom had experienced double exploitation as workers and females. Prewar efforts to awaken consciousness played on these dual aspects of working-class women's oppression. Also, because of their sex, women activists in the socialist movement had not been as nationalized as men. In general, the male worker had acquired a certain vested interest in society. His position had been raised by the Party and unions willing to work for immediate, short-term goals, and he sent delegates representing his interests to most legislative bodies in Germany. In contrast, as Gerhard A. Ritter cogently argues, in the prewar period women were prevented from participating in national, state, and many municipal organizations.[26] Their disenfranchisement distanced them from legislative bodies and perhaps from obsession with the Party's parliamentary tactic and electioneering emphasis.[27] Furthermore, proletarian women's organizations in the pre-1908 era had been subject to considerably more official harassment and inconvenience than was true for the movement as a whole. In short, politically active women could feel more alienated from "the system"—a sentiment that reinforced radicalism.

On the basis of a cursory analysis of the immediate postwar period in Germany, the above observations must be interpreted with caution. First, the socialist women's movement had only a minor impact on the German working class in general. Thus, the reasons presented above for potential left-wing socialist sympathies pertain to groups of organized women; in no way do they imply a long-term radicalization of working-class women or even an ability to engender socialist support: in the Weimar period working-class women tended to vote nonsocialist.[28] Second, socialist feminists themselves were unable psychologically to fight for their own rights if the struggle meant actively opposing their male colleagues. They paid a heavy price for their fundamental reluctance to adopt a more forceful feminist stance. At stake in the early postwar years was women's "right to work"—the vehicle of their emancipation according to their own analysis. Yet once again feminism bowed to other considerations during an internecine struggle that routed large numbers of women from the labor force. The official demobilization orders decreed by the *socialist* government after the November Revolution of 1918 sacrificed women to the claims of men returning from the front: women whose husbands were employed headed the list of those to be removed from their jobs, next came single girls and women, then those supporting one to two persons and, finally, all remaining females.[29] Enforcement provoked an outcry from women leaders who charged that "in industrial areas, thousands of married women are simply being thrown out of their jobs." Hanna complained that the discharge of women in many cases had occurred callously and often unnecessarily. She admitted that some unionists were now singing "home sweet home" to women. Lacking an independent power base, she could only plead with her male colleagues for restraint, decency, and fair play, and she vent her frustration on other women who were failing to safeguard their interests. The consequences of so few women joining unions are clear, she moaned, and then admitted, pathetically, that she had no solution to the controversy. Similarly, the radical socialist women were politically bankrupt on this issue.[30]

Thönnessen, analyzing unemployment statistics, concludes that the complaints raised at postwar congresses concerning the removal of women from the labor force were justified. In 1923, Hanna noted that only a few women remained in those wartime jobs that had been prewar male sanctuaries; the old pattern of female employment had reasserted itself, with perhaps a slight rise in the numbers of skilled workers.[31] The crisis emphasized the unwillingness of organized male workers to support the woman's right to work when the Marxist principle was seen as conflicting with their own interests. The number of working-class women who had been radicalized was not large enough to cause traditional concepts of their relations to men to be changed. Moreover, socialist feminists were trapped in the logic of their former choice since their world view had located the enemy not at home but in capitalism. Although a significant proportion of them had voted for the mass strike in 1913, five years later they could not fight for their own rights in the labor market.[32]

MARIE JUCHACZ AND
THE SECOND-GENERATION FEMALE LEADERSHIP

The split in the socialist women's movement stripped much of the existing leadership from the SPD organization, but gave rise to a new group willing to reconstruct the movement. These women differed in several ways from the prewar leaders; they were younger, less ideological, and more pragmatic, and they introduced a new tone and focus to the fight for women's emancipation.

The new SPD leader most typically was a second-generation woman who rose to prominence within well-defined working-class organizations.[33] Nineteen SPD women were elected to parliament in January 1919; parliamentary handbooks and articles in *Gleichheit* presented short biographies of these women.[34] (See appendix.) Eleven of the representatives had been born in 1875 or after and probably had begun their political activity around the turn of the century. Three women, Louise Schröder, Elizabeth Röhl, and Frieda Hauke, were born in 1887, 1888, and 1890 respectively.

Second-generation leaders experienced a different political milieu than their older sisters, a fact that might account for the variance in leadership skills, motivation, and conceptions. The skills needed for prominence during the anti-Socialist laws (1880s) or the 1890s, when an informal structure loosely bound women together, differed from those necessary in the bureaucratic organization that had emerged in 1900 or after women formally joined the SPD in 1908. Older women such as Zetkin, Zietz, Ihrer, Braun, or Baader can be characterized as dynamic orators, possessed by an almost religious belief in socialism and its redeeming powers, morally outraged at existing conditions, innovative, creative, and basically uncompromising. Not all the older leaders had each trait, but the characterization serves as a general portrait.

The younger women rising to leadership when the organization already existed were more talented administratively, less committed to doctrine, more compromising, and more concerned with day-to-day questions. Among the nineteen SPD women parliamentarians, twelve had been functionaries in the Party or trade union organizations. A similar preponderance of Party functionaries characterized the second-generation male counterpart in the SPD. One need only think of Friedrich Ebert or Philipp Scheidemann, men who also had "grown up in the political machine,"[35] to recognize the role of bureaucratization in conditioning leadership skills and orientation. Furthermore, seven of the women—Marie Juchacz, Elizabeth Röhl, Minna Schilling, Anna Blos, Klara Bohm-Schuch, Frieda Hauke, and Elfriede Ryneck—had worked with municipal welfare officials or in the Party's child-labor committees prior to World War I. Their functions within the organized

working class brought them into contact with German officialdom and increased their sense of identification with the nation.

An additional perspective on the new leadership is gleaned
from a comparison of prewar and postwar lists of delegates to
SPD congresses and women's conferences.[36] For example,
eighty-five women appeared at the SPD women's conference
in June 1919. Sixteen delegates, or 19 percent, had been present at similar prewar *women's* gatherings. Of these sixteen
women, 56 percent had attended the meeting for the first time
in 1908 or later. Eleven delegates to prewar *Party* meetings
attended war and postwar SPD congresses, and 81 percent
had participated for the first time only after women were incorporated officially into the Party. Zietz had recognized this
general phenomenon as she greeted the delegates to the 1911
women's conference with a reference to "many new faces."[37]

Contemporaries stressed generational differences. Juchacz
wrote: "At the beginning of the century, a rather large number
of women of my generation were interested in the development of economic, social, and political life and participated
in the debates and struggles at the time. This generation,
however, rested already on a definite tradition. Men and
women from a previous generation had awakened us: Ihrer,
Zetkin . . . Bebel. . . . And we women at the turn of the century . . . ? We found our own form for our struggle."[38] And
Paul Löbe, Reichstag president in the Weimar Republic, corroborated this view. "The first women in parliament were the
second generation *Frauenbewegung* personalities. Juchacz
headed . . . [the] Social Democratic women delegates.[39]

The second-generation women who gathered with Marie
Juchacz at the SPD's women's conference in 1917 advanced a
series of ideas that, when taken together, formed an alternative to the theory of women's emancipation as formulated by
Clara Zetkin. Central to the new theory was the rejection of
the concept of class struggle as the guide to political action and
substitution of "practical activity in the service of socialism."[40]
The new commitment to practical activity was restricted to social welfare at the local level, an area regarded as especially

suitable for women. Juchacz, at the conference, stressed an additional motive in the reorientation. "Everywhere where women engage in welfare activity they win the affection of working women. . . . [W]here we offer help we get trust. . . . Then it is easier to approach them with our ideas."[41] The war, she emphasized, has estranged the masses of women from the SPD. She believed that majority socialists could win converts best through the personal contacts and relations that were a natural part of social work.

Juchacz amplified her views in a subsequent article. The prewar movement had shown that "women talk best to women" because of the psychological and emotional differences between the sexes. In the female creature lived a strong drive for useful, daily activity, Juchacz generalized; nature predisposed her to care for the downtrodden. For proof she pointed out that "before the war our politically organized women had worked in child-labor and action committees," neglecting to add, however, that the socialist women's movement had been infinitely more variegated.[42] Similar themes reappeared at postwar women's conferences. In 1921, for example, justifying the importance placed on social welfare, it was maintained that "women are the born protectors of humanity and, therefore, social work corresponds so well with their nature. Women have more understanding of how to protect and safeguard human life."[43] Majority socialist women modified the traditional conception of women as wives and mothers inherently concerned with the welfare of husbands and children by extending it to the municipal level.

A loose link only tied the majority socialist women's movement to its predecessor. The prewar movement had regarded welfare and municipal activity as only one of many spheres within which female members could fulfill their tasks. Not until 1901 did Zetkin extend their demands to include municipal change.[44] She wrote then that a reformed city administration could offer needed welfare services to the working woman as housewife and mother. Pressuring for reforms offered women a "rich" and "worthy" sphere and a meaningful content to their lives. Zetkin even maintained that such activity was ideal because it allowed them to experience their true nature: motherliness (*Mütterlichkeit*). These sentiments, which underlay majority socialist women's justification for their new orientation, were not absent from the prewar literature. In fact, they appeared more pronounced in the immediate years prior to World War I. Zietz in 1912, for example, explained that women were turning to the youth movement "where they can activate all their warmth, motherliness . . . and [that] their warmhearted . . . sensitivity" made them especially suited for child-labor committees.[45] In contrast to their heirs, however, the prewar leaders relegated such activity to a minor role and hoped it ultimately would facilitate the working-class woman's participation in the struggle for socialism. Although a common denominator—an acceptance of unique female qualities—was present in the leaders of both generations, the conclusions drawn for political action differed greatly. In prewar Germany, the appeal to women's peculiarities was used to jusitfy their full participation in all aspects of Party and union life and to reinforce the claim both to special feminist propaganda tactics for working-class women and to self-government. After 1917, the same ideas served to restrict women's role in Party as well as in social and political life.

In the prewar period, the German municipality had proven more willing to admit women into bureaus and institutions than the government at the state or national level. This partially explained the growing pressure on the local level. In 1910, for example, Württemburg accepted women on school boards and Oldenburg gave women the passive vote for city elections; in 1911, Grünberg reported that the Bavarian state legislature had passed a law permitting women to join a bureau for the care of the poor and infants and "we are turning [our women's] attention to municipal affairs." She entered the Nuremberg committee for the poor that year; in 1913, joined an infant-welfare bureau that set up meetings addressed by doctors; and as the social worker for juveniles was admitted to the youth court.[46] Not until the war curtailed former political options, however, did socialist women turn in large numbers to such welfare work in city administrations. The political reality within socialist organizations, too, had encouraged this direction, as witnessed by growing emphasis in the prewar period on health and welfare in the women's educational sessions and by female socialists' gravitation to child-labor committees.

Women in the USP tended to feel that once the war ended they would resume their former, multifarious tasks in furthering the socialist revolution. Majority socialists, in contrast, projected wartime activity into the postwar era. Their position culminated in the founding of the *Arbeiterwohlfahrt* (workers' welfare bureau) in December 1919. Women leaders overcame the initial skepticism of the SPD's "old guard" toward creation of a Party institution devoted to welfare. According to John Caspari, one of the initiators under the spiritual guidance of Juchacz, Party leaders had regarded "welfare as something bourgeois—the rich giving to the poor."[47] Juchacz fought hard to win acceptance of her proposal; in November 1919 the leadership handed execution over to female members. The bureau was designed to help the working class influence the "conception, direction, and impact" of welfare legislation. The underlying philosophy held that the "social organism has a duty to care for its members and the individual . . . a duty to work . . . for . . . this goal."[48] Welfare was no longer to be the preserve of the daughters of the upper classes.

The creation of a welfare bureau within the SPD in the postwar era irrevocably welded women to municipal reform activity. The founders, according to Juchacz, had intended to create a sphere of activity primarily for socialist women. They hoped an exchange of personnel and activity would take place between the women's movement and the bureau; as head of both institutions Juchacz symbolized the organizational intermarriage. A questionnaire sent out in 1926 confirmed the expectations. Typical answers to the ties between the women's movement and welfare activity read as follows: "*Arbeiterwohlfahrt* is the soil on which our women's movement grows and prospers. . . . One cannot report on the Social Democratic women's movement without thinking of this branch. . . . Through social work, which touches on the innermost female interests, many women can . . . be placed in the service of the working-class movement."[49] Although majority socialist women were encouraged to participate in daily political questions and general Party affairs, the evolution of the women's movement had carved out a separate functional sphere for female comrades.

Analyzing the postwar era, Thönnessen concludes that the restriction of women to social work represented a continuation of discrimination by different means. His argument basically is correct; the division of labor within the SPD produced a "new form of political discrimination" that limited women's influence to areas traditionally neglected by men.[50] A subtle, but important addition to Thönnessen's argument might characterize the situation more completely. The evolution was a product of changes that began in 1908. The division of labor, a prewar feminist demand, had, as seen, encouraged increasing segregation of Party women into child-care and municipal spheres of activity. The educational institutions prepared women for roles in child-labor committees, and the emphasis on practical education as well as the continuance of the educational clubs had meant, in part, training in hygiene, nutrition, and child care. A whole generation of new leaders had grown up who, like Juchacz, confined their primary political role to social welfare. Thus, Thönnessen's claim that women were pushed into municipal work neglects the change in consciousness that explains their willingness to walk. While not denying that this limitation was greeted favorably and promoted by male comrades determined to preserve their political dominance, social work had come to represent leading SPD women's self-image of their contribution to the general struggle for a more just society. Majority socialists were resembling social feminists.[51]

Majority socialist women modified other tenets of the socialist theory of women's emancipation. Marx, Engels, Bebel, and Zetkin consistently related the women's question to the social question: women and workers were victims of the system of private property. Yet an alternative view had gained currency that cast the question into a new yet more general context. Since women bore the nation's future generations, it was argued that the conditions under which they lived and labored concerned society as a whole. Females had assumed a large part of the national defense during the war and were destined to play an ever greater role in social and economic life. Thus, issues affecting the female sex ranging from maternity insurance to suffrage were a concern for all.[52] The women's question was, in essence, a problem for humanity

Appeals to humanity did not translate into willingness to collaborate fully with nonsocialist feminists. The exigencies of war had opened the door to joint activity and most majority socialists, as expressed at their 1917 conference, felt that "in practical matters, we can learn many new things from bourgeois women."[53] They did not, however, fully embrace their bourgeois sisters. The conference declared that in the struggle for women's political equality, socialists should join with existing bourgeois suffrage groups; the decision for other forms of collaboration would depend on the issue and context, and it required leadership sanction. Juchacz expressed their misgivings: socialists must not just work with the bourgeoisie, but must influence the spirit and character of work.[54] Although the new leaders left socialist-middle class cooperation for common ends more flexible than in the prewar period, class identity intruded to precluded ongoing and wholehearted collaboration for the cause of women's rights.

The years between 1914 and 1918 had a profound impact on the socialist world. The dislocations of war, the triumph of nationalism, and the suspension of the class struggle aggravated prewar tensions and irrevocably destroyed proletarian unity. An era had come to an end for socialist feminists. Future battles would be changed by the new context of republican Germany, and for many, by a reformulation of the socialist theory of women's emancipation.

CHAPTER X

CONCLUSION

The aims of two great egalitarian movements—socialism and feminism—converged in the nineteenth century in a union for social and sexual liberation. Each ideology expressed the Enlightenment optimism and faith in progress and human betterment. Socialism could offer feminism a world view and set of analytic tools with which to dissect critically the women's question, while feminism could proffer greater sensitivity to interpersonal relations and to non-work-related factors in the formation of human consciousness. Yet to forge these complementary movements into a balanced alliance proved difficult in practice. Two identities competed in the minds of adherents and two sources of loyalty—class and sex—vied for allegiance. Crucial questions had to be answered. How did feminist reforms relate to the class struggle? In what ways would socialism liberate women? Should working-class women join with the men of their class against male and female capitalists? Or should they enter a purely feminine coalition designed to counter male domination and oppression? The choices made and priorities set in solving these problems comprise the fabric of a hitherto neglected aspect of European left-wing politics.

The fusion of the two social movements found its clearest expression in the careers of women associated with European Social Democracy. From Petersberg to Milan, Paris, and Berlin these socialists grappled with issues of liberation and sought an end to both class slavery and sex oppression. They envisioned a truly human revolution that would integrate the woman for the first time into mankind and simultaneously restructure the whole of economic and political life.

The common aspirations of socialist women, however,

masked profound differences in feminist conceptions, tactics, and strategies, as well as various degrees of socialist receptivity to feminist pressures. During the heyday of the Second International, from 1889 to 1914, it was German socialist women who developed the most far-reaching program for change, followed, perhaps, by their Austrian sisters who modeled themselves after the German pattern. In terms of sheer numbers, Germany had the largest socialist women's movement by far. Its feminist plank was the most progressive, in some ways even now seventy years after its formulation a model of feminist questions and answers. Also, German socialist women apparently were unique in their insistence on a measure of autonomy and freedom for their undertakings[1]—what has been called in this volume their feminist tactics.

The German experience can be appreciated best through a comparison with other continental countries. Feminist theory and practice were more suspect among socialists outside of Germany.[2] Several examples can document this finding. In Russia, Aleksandra Kollontai, who did the most to bring feminism to Bolshevism, experienced the visceral response of socialists to feminism in its extreme form. Women's emancipation, of course, was part of the inherited ideological package of Russian Marxists, but the Bolshevik wing—disciplined, serious, and dedicated to revolution—had no intention of letting itself be sidetracked onto feminist paths. Prior to World War I, it rejected Kollontai's plea for a special bureau of the party and for reformed guidelines to reach working women. Kollontai found herself isolated on the issue and open to the charge of dividing the working class.[3]

In Italy, an extensive socialist feminist platform never materialized. In the 1890s, this failure reflected careful, pragmatic political calculations. In the effort to transform the conservative, trade unionist labor movement into a Marxist party, potentially divisive issues were played down and feminism was one victim. Thus, Anna Kuliscioff could appear at the International Congress in Zurich in 1893 and speak eloquently about the need for protective laws for women, but when a similar amendment was proposed for inclusion into the Italian party program, she accepted indefinite postponement on the ground that the issue was detrimental to unity. Marriage reform had a similar fate.[4] While after the turn of the twentieth century, separate papers were published for women workers and in 1912 a national organization of female socialists was formed, the Italian party never fully committed itself even to the central feminist goal of the era, women's suffrage.

France was the home of the original socialist feminist synthesis but in the years intervening between the Utopian Socialists and the founding of the Third Republic, Proudhon had injected strong doses of antifeminism into the ideology of the French left. His notions were challenged in the last third of the nineteenth century by the Marxist faction (*Parti ouvrier français*, POF), which in 1879 accepted women into the movement. Arguing against the Proudhonists who sought to straightjacket women into the domestic role, the group declared it did not "assign any particular role to woman. She will assume in society the role and the place which her vocation dictates."[5] But the division of French socialism into a variety of factions exacted a heavy toll on females determined to unify socialism and feminism. They became caught up in socialist rivalries, at times pressed more against opposing groups than for their own causes, and generally were used to gain advantage in the struggle for power but denied concrete support for their own ends. In the 1890s, when the parties turned more toward parliamentarism, the commitment to feminism weakened as groups feared losing votes by championing contested feminist issues.[6] Unification of French socialism in 1905 actually undercut organizational gains that French women had made in the preceding years. Predicated on a uniform federated structure, the new party refused to admit separate women's organizations, although it accepted individual women as members. This spelled the end of the Feminist Socialist Group, for example, an organization that on the surface had been designed to join the two causes. In reality, feminism had become submerged to the point that it was but an empty phrase. Fearful of its bourgeois rivals, the French feminist socialist faction under Louise Saumoneau denied the existence of sex oppression and hesitated to raise women's issues for fear of "play[ing] into the hands" of bourgeois feminists.[7] Quite in contrast, German socialist feminists publicized hosts of women's topics in part to highlight what they saw as the bankruptcy of bourgeois feminism.

What made the German experience so unique? The answer is necessarily speculative. Socialist leaders had deliberately enclosed feminism in a tight class framework that made it more readily compatible with socialist objectives than elsewhere on the continent. Quite simply, it appeared less threatening. The German socialist feminists saw themselves as female proletarians (irrespective of their actual social background) and exerted social pressure on behalf of working-class women. If the leaders spoke of "the female sex," the category was abstract and projected into the distant future when the revolution would abolish class differences and liberate all women. A feminism cutting across class lines such as Lily Braun's was foreign to most German socialist feminists, whatever their ideological stance within Social Democracy. Thus when Braun appealed to their sex and neglected their class, her words fell on unreceptive ears. The identity of class created an amazingly strong bond, as seen in the debate over birth control. Zetkin and other radical socialists who, by 1913, had gone into strong opposition against the Party's reformist evolution, without hesitation joined the leadership in the effort to squelch those advocating a birth-control strike. In determining political choices, class interest immediately took precedence over considerations of individual family problems. This reflected an important consensus among leaders on feminist issues and an intuitive willingness to stop feminist pressure before it disrupted proletarian unity. What has been termed *reluctant feminism* in this book, then, was the implicit condition for effective participation in the socialist world.

The feminist pressure, however, was greater in Germany than in other cases and this requires further explanation. Perhaps the very strength of the socialist subculture permitted it to accommodate more diverse elements than socialist parties elsewhere felt able to do. The subculture was a product of the social ostracism and political impotence of the labor movement and its strength derived from its ability to serve crucial psychological, recreational, and educational needs in a stratum only marginally integrated into the body politic. Ironically, organized workers' "negative integration" contributed to the ultimate failure of socialism in Germany and thus to the defeat of the feminism that had been linked to a radical transformation of society. At the same time, through the subculture, it permitted the emergence of a novel experiment in social and sexual reform.

The historic experiment hinged on the results of three interrelated issues. The first involved the need to define feminism and to fashion appropriate strategies to realize the goals. The second concerned the extent of socialist and bourgeois contact on feminist matters. And the third was the question of whether socialist women would be bound by their ideological fathers—Marx, Engels, and Bebel—in orienting their movement. While German socialist feminism was conditioned by socialist theory, it was also a product of the experiences of women leaders operating in the political arena of Imperial Germany. These three issues warrant closer investigation.

The socialist feminist experiment began in earnest in the 1880s. In trade associations and cooperatives, socialists pressed for higher wages, better work conditions, and financial support during strikes for their female members; they advocated education and training for the acquisition of needed skills. Pressed in by discriminatory laws that hindered organizational efforts, these pathfinders also turned to the political realm, recognizing the need for legislative reforms to further women's rights. Yet they were operating in an ideological twilight zone. While they put forth, although with minimal analysis, the critical proposition that the causes of sex oppression lay with capitalism rather than with men, they were committed to vague notions of formal equality as seen in the rejection of special protective labor laws for women. Their feminist vision at this time essentially rested with the achievement of equality between male and female workers. Feminism meant the "right to work" and employment under better conditions. The membership of these early craft and general associations was ill-defined: wives of male socialists comprised good numbers as did needleworkers, seamstresses, and coatmakers, but considerable attention was given the rural woman. Leaders such as Emma Ihrer sought to promote distinctions between associations for working women of the lower classes and ladies' clubs, but perception of class differences was dim. It was in this context that socialist leaders sought to promote class identity by distributing Zetkin's writings from Paris. She had formulated, precisely, an equation the leaders clearly welcomed: the fate of the modern woman and the modern wage earner was one, and the modern women's and workers' questions were both children of the machine and industrial technology. Her analysis, however, stressed the division of the female sex by class.

The decade of the 1880s was the period of the anti-Socialist laws that saw the crystallization of deep-seated and long-lasting class hostilities and fears in Germany. This milieu worked to deter a coalition of bourgeois and socialist feminists that might have formed around such common aspirations as the "right to work" and improved educational and training opportunities for women, although each group, of course, understood the slogans differently. Such an alliance even then would have faced the litmus tests of the culpability of men for women's oppression and the organizational ties to political parties. Bourgeois women conceived of themselves as politically neutral and looked askance at working-class women's affiliations with the labor movement.

With hindsight, it is clear that not much chance existed for a productive alliance between bourgeois and socialist feminists in Imperial Germany. Class loyalty was instinctual on both sides. Perhaps, as one historian argues, the revolutionary tradition as well as the presence of mass parties committed to radical change intensified the perception of social divisions and fragmented society by class to a greater extent on the continent than in England or America. This helped account, then, for continental women's political orientation by class.[8] However, the Anglo-American feminist experience is not without examples of choices reflecting a class bias. The explanation must lie as well in the social turmoil accompanying industrial development. In the nineteenth and early twentieth centuries, social categories were being transformed; yet not all women experienced the change in the same way. Thus, real needs differed and were expressed in feminist organizations appropriate to the interests of various social strata. Apparently ongoing industrialization, with the trend toward service rather than primary manufacture, has provided a basis for a new feminist experiment in the second half of the twentieth century that deliberately seeks to overcome the class and race barriers dividing the female sex. This modern effort appears more self-consciously feminist in part because it has learned from the successes and the failures of the historic experiment.

Yet throughout the Imperial period, everything spoke for working-class women turning to the socialist subculture. Mainstream bourgeois feminism was timid, divided, and isolated, with a vision limited to welfare, charity, and enlarged professional opportunities in the 1870s and 1880s. While by the mid-1890s, its left wing had shed the timidity and pushed the middle class forward, the so-called radicalization of German feminism between 1894 and 1908 was "superficial and short-lived."[9] Bourgeois feminism eventually came to embrace the most moderate and nondisruptive demands. A lack of agreement on fundamental issues such as the extent of women's suffrage (restricted or universal) and the failure to win allies in parliament (the left-liberal parties equivocated on women's issues) made middle-class feminism a poor associate for socialists. Socialist women rightly took great pride in their movement as the most consistent advocate of feminist goals in Imperial Germany, a stand that might have been sacrificed for an alliance of dubious benefit to working-class women.

Any basis for bourgeois and socialist coalition on women's issues was undercut, in fact, when a new strategy for feminism emerged in the socialist context after 1893. That year, at the International workers' congress in Zurich, socialists adopted the principle of special protective labor laws for women. In the name of equality, bourgeois feminists rejected it while German socialists argued that since the social position of working-class women and men was not equal, women needed special rights to gain equality.

The new awareness that formal equality might perpetuate real social inequalities was the basis for socialist feminism in the two decades before World War I. It influenced the nature of the feminist platform as well as the socialist feminists' ties to both the Party and the Free Trade Unions. Their feminist proposals now were designed not to equalize the burdens of men and women workers under capitalism, but rather to help the working-class woman withstand capitalist exploitation better, since it fell on her doubly, even triply hard—as worker, wife, and mother. Rather than to abolish these roles, German socialist feminists sought to bring them into new harmony by transforming both social and family life and by instilling values of self-worth and dignity. What was a female human being, they asked? Proud of being women, they looked to apparent sex differences and envisioned a world changed qualitatively by the admittance of women into full partnership. The older generation leaders prescribed no paths for the woman but urged her to follow her talents and inclinations; the younger leaders, in contrast, took the same notion of difference and defined spheres of public activity most compatible with women's side. By this pursuit, they came to resemble social not socialist feminists.

The view of women as distinct human beings distanced German socialist feminists from the position of Marx and Engels, which, it must be said in fairness, had not been developed in any detail. The feminists saw that sex had "social validity" in the marketplace, the *Manifesto* notwithstanding, and they felt emancipation would require not only women's full integration into gainful labor but, equally important, labor's full reconciliation with motherhood. Thus, their reforms included proposals for municipal services such as day-care centers and communal laundries as well as extensive maternity insurance. These changes were seen as benefiting women primarily, because the socialists never really proposed, with any degree of insistence, that men perform domestic roles and tasks. At times, traditional norms filtered through socialist views.

If Marx and Engels provided inspiration but limited guidance, the role of Bebel's *Women under Socialism* on the formation of feminist conceptions is more difficult to judge. On a personal level the work crystallized felt sentiments at crucial times in some women's lives, and it certainly provided the activists with emotive myths so crucial in mobilizing and sustaining social groups. During controversies, adversaries used the book to gain political advantage and discredit opponents, but one notes its absence from the formulations of the 1896 political guidelines as well as from the reformulations of the women's question in 1917. Furthermore, harsh experience not Bebel was the source of the skepticism of formal equality. No direct correlation can be drawn between the book's great popularity (it went through five dozen editions between 1879 and 1914) and feminist awakening; it was read, in part, because it simply made good reading with its comparative, historical, and anthropological materials on subjects not often found in print. Besides, it offered as much an exposé of the evils of capitalism and an uncomplicated presentation of the socialist world view as an analysis of the women's question and women's role in social liberation.

The women's movement targeted a constituency that went beyond the key revolutionary group in socialist theory, the industrial working woman. Lenin, in his famous conversations with Clara Zetkin after the Russian Revolution, labeled as "deviation" all attention given to the needs of nonindustrial wage earners.[10] Yet experience had taught German socialists that the industrial working woman was a minority among the gainfully employed females in Germany. Observation turned the organization to those in home industry and domestic service as well as to the nonworking wives and mothers in the lower classes. The educational clubs, for example, had been designed originally to reach nonworking women barred from political activity. Thus, socialist propaganda appealed to

women in the variety of social roles they actually were performing.

The institutional arrangement for women in German Social
Democracy reflected the feminists' mistrust of formal equality. After much soul-searching and experimentation, the leaders had concluded reluctantly in the mid-1890s that their survival required special rights. They began to insist on their own
tactics and on quasi-independence within the Party and they
set up separate educational institutions. The "specter of
feminist separatism" that many first had viewed with misgivings appeared less inconsistent in light of legal discrimination,
male chauvinism, and low self-esteem among their constituency. Quasi-independence, it was maintained, encouraged
and supported female membership and thus promoted the
larger goal of bringing men and women together in a joint
struggle against capitalism. Yet as good socialists, women welcomed integration into the SPD in 1908 when it became legally possible, and, although they sought to maintain some
freedom and autonomy, changes were felt immediately. Prior
to integration, they had been able to act almost at will. Now
their activities had to be adjusted to other criteria and needs,
not always in the best interest of women though perhaps of
benefit to the Party. After 1908, division of labor meant that
women carried the main responsibility for such matters as
child care and municipal welfare work, a shift with implications for the formation of consciousness among the younger
members. Emphasis in the educational sessions on training in
practical matters reinforced this orientation, and, as a result,
the perspective of the new SPD leaders was decidedly more
limited in its understanding of the whole women's question.

Should socialist feminists have pushed more forcefully for
separatism within German Social Democracy? Once working-class women had entered the organized labor movement
as political allies, they could have sought greater independence and autonomy. Ironically, they never learned fully the
lesson of Gertrud Hanna's career. She emerged out of a special but imitable context. Her local Printers' Aids Union had

been self-consciously female, rejecting amalgamation with men and conducting business independently and highly successfully. The central union itself was run by women and this milieu of visible, active, and impressive role models had produced a group of talented females who had overcome the debilitating experience of female socialization: the lack of self-confidence, shyness, and diffidence. Too often, experience in the labor organizations reinforced a woman's negative self-image. Men monopolized the positions of power and made the crucial decisions on wage demands, strike funds, and job promotion. The labor movement, in turn, mirrored a work experience that also reinforced male prerogatives. The social stratification of the labor force, reflected most clearly in large enterprises, included a strong element of division by sex; women typically performed the lowest, least skilled, nonchallenging jobs for, or under the supervision of, men. Also, work itself rarely encouraged the adoption of less traditional consciousness as socialist theory had predicted. A greater degree of separatism would have offered a needed antidote to the cycle of negative reinforcement and provided women with challenging functions and more positive images of their own potentials and achievements. Yet separatism alone without a shift in priorities would not necessarily have promoted the feminist cause more effectively. If socialism still took precedence over feminism, even the most autonomous institution would not have acted more forcefully in championing women's issues. Whether or not separatism in and of itself—which implies power and strength in a shared identity—eventually could have encouraged a higher valuation of feminism remains an intriguing but unanswerable question.

Socialist feminists in Germany lacked a truly independent power base and upon integration they found their various difficulties magnified in the labor movement. Party women were in a political structure that was not, despite its professed principles, fully democratic. The institution itself was not sufficiently flexible to permit the existence of quasi-independent groups bent on self-determination in any significant degree. Concepts of unity and discipline, which served the needs of whatever wing dominated at a particular time, tended to impose consensus. Although socialist feminists had developed a distinctive strategy, the potentials for success were severely curtailed by a complex combination of antifeminism and ideological and jurisdictional conflicts.

Antifeminism was a fact of life, cutting across social classes, and the discrepancies between public and private postures of male SPD and union members frustrated socialist women's efforts to promote sex equality. Latent antifeminism, furthermore, transcended ideological differences among male colleagues. Women complained of lack of support from males in radical Berlin as well as in reformist Bavaria and from male members of the local union cartels everywhere. The choice made by women to serve the socialist movement required a reciprocity from men that too often was not forthcoming. Male socialists were ambivalent toward women in public life generally and in the socialist movement specifically. Women's liberation was part of socialist ideology, but it rarely comprised the actual belief systems of male socialists. In times of economic, political, or even ideological crises, the ideals proved unable to modify hostile behavior. With few exceptions, male socialists shared the assumptions of their era and culture, even if they did not adopt the attitude of the average German philistine clinging doggedly to his belief in women's intellectual and social inferiority.

Tensions between the Party and the unions served to aggravate the women's problems. Socialist feminists shared a constituency but not a view as to where it should be housed. The existence of two wings forced artificial distinctions, as, for example, between preparatory and actual unionization efforts, that created confusion not clarification. Women loyal to the unions, as seen in the careers of Grünberg and Hanna, looked critically at Party women's efforts on behalf of the economic struggle. The feminist tactic fell victim to leadership and jurisdictional controversies. Ideological antagonism also played a role. Although the women's movement embraced the whole range of socialist principles and programs, its radical wing in the years before World War I was articulate and evoked misgivings of Party and especially of union leaders. *Gleichheit* was an effective organ of radical socialism and the unions as well as more moderate women in the Party sought, with some success, to curb its autonomy. Also, efforts were made to end the women's conferences and thereby limit the spread of radical socialist ideas. Socialist feminists were not only divided internally, but under suspicion by powerful forces within the organizational superstructure.

As a group within Social Democracy, these feminists had put their faith in socialism to redress sex inequalities. To achieve this goal, they accorded first priority to the struggle for a new society. Hence, they did not fight for feminism if the issue threatened the advancement of socialism. To have acted more vigorously in the pursuit of feminism would have required different priorities, perhaps even knowledge of the lessons of their own movement that have been revealed only by the passage of time. These socialists never had the will to secure their own bailiwick; ideological and personal divisions as well as divergent loyalties prevented them from acting as a united front. Their decision to join with the organized working class in Imperial Germany had favored their feminist aspirations but subordinated these to their service in the cause of socialism. As a result, they became reluctant feminists by circumstances as well as by intent.

APPENDIX

APPENDIX

SPD Women Elected to the Constituent National Assembly, 1919: A Biographical Sketch

	YEAR BORN	CLASS ORIGIN	SCHOOLING	MARI- TAL STATUS	CHIL- DREN	FIRST CONTACT WITH SOCIALIST IDEAS
Anna Blos	1866	upper	university	M	*	socialist literature husband
Klara Bohm- Schuch	1879	working	village, trade schools	M	1	socialist literature
Minna Bollmann	1876	working	—	M	*	family
Minna Eichler	1872	working	primary school; trade union school, Berlin	M	*	husband
Frieda Hauke	1890	—	—	M	*	husband
Else Höfs	1876	lower middle	—	M	*	family
Marie Juchacz	1879	lower middle	village school; women's educational club	D	2	brother
Wilhelmine Kähler	1864	working	village school; Party school, Berlin	M	*	anti-Socialist laws strike
Gertrud Lodahl	1878	working	union school	M	*	strike
Frieda Lührs	1868	working	—	—	—	family
Ernestine Lutze	1873	working	primary school; trade union school, Berlin	M	3	husband and Emma Ihrer
Antonie Pfülf	1877	upper	teachers' seminar	M	*	socialist literature
Johanna Reitze	1878	working	primary school; Party school, Berlin	M	*	lecture by Bebel
Elizabeth Röhl	1888	lower middle	primary school; women's educational club	D	1	sister Marie Juchacz
Elfriede Ryneck	1872	working	primary school; Party school, Berlin	M	1	family (mother Pauline Staegemann)
Minna Schilling	1877	working	—	M	6	socialist literature background
Louise Schröder	1887	working	middle/trade school	S	0	family

ROLE IN ORGANIZED WORKING CLASS	EARLIEST DATE OF ATTENDANCE WOMEN'S CON-FERENCE	SPD CONGRESS	ATTENDED 1919 WOMEN'S CONFERENCE
municipal politics; Stuttgart school board	—	—	X
writer; child-labor committee; youth committee	—	—	—
Party functionary (district executive Halberstadt)	1908	1908	X
trade union/Party functionary (executive committee Saxony-Altenburg and Bookbinders Union)	1911	1911	X
municipal politics	—	—	X
women's movement	—	—	X
Party functionary (executive committee Berlin/ Cologne); president, women's educational club; child-labor committee	1911	1911	X
trade union functionary (general commission, president Unskilled Factory Workers Union), editor	1900	1895	X
trade union functionary (secretary, Printer's Aids Union); Cooperative Movement	—	—	X
SPD member, municipal politics (World War I)	—	—	X
trade union functionary (executive committee Artificial Flower Workers Union)	—	1910	X
municipal politics (World War I)	—	—	X
Party functionary (executive committee Hamburg), municipal politics (World War I)	1908	1908	X
Party functionary (executive committee Cologne); child-labor committee	—	1912	X
child-labor committee; Party functionary (executive committee Teltow-Beeskow-Storkow-Charlottenburg)	—	1913	X
municipal politics	—	—	X
Party functionary (executive committee Altona, Ottensen)	—	—	X

SPD Women Elected to the Constituent
National Assembly, 1919: A Biographical Sketch

	YEAR BORN	CLASS ORIGIN	SCHOOLING	MARI-TAL STATUS	CHIL-DREN	FIRST CONTACT WITH SOCIALIST IDEAS
Anna Simon	1862	working	—	S	0	father
Johanna Tesch	1875	working	middle school	M	*	husband

* For those whose marital status was ascertained, no information on numbers of children.

SOURCE: Louise Schröder, "Unsere Frauen in der deutschen Nationalversammlung," *Gleichheit*, 28 February 1919; Hermann Hillger, *Hillgers Handbuch der Verfassunggebenden deutschen Nationalversammlung 1919*, Berlin, 1919; Franz Osterroth, *Biographisches Lexikon des Sozialismus*, Hanover, 1960, 1: 27, 32, 150-151, 239-240, 247-248, 271-273, 297, and 309; Marie Juchacz, *Sie Lebten für eine bessere Welt*, Berlin, 1955, pp. 96-112, 121-124, and 134-137.

ROLE IN ORGANIZED WORKING CLASS	EARLIEST DATE OF ATTENDANCE WOMEN'S CONFERENCE	SPD CONGRESS	ATTENDED 1919 WOMEN'S CONFERENCE
trade union/Party functionary (executive committee Textile Union; Brandenburg state SPD)	1911	1911	X
trade union functionary (Servants Union Frankfurt/M); president, women's educational club	—	—	—

NOTES

CHAPTER I   FEMINIST AWAKENING

1. ZStA, RMdI, Nr. 13689, Bl. 121-122: Police survey of socialist activity for 1906-1907.

2. Werner Thönnessen, *The Emancipation of Women: The Rise and Decline of the Women's Movement in German Social Democracy, 1863-1933*, trans. Joris de Bres, London, 1973, p. 116; *Frauen-Beilage der Leipziger Volkszeitung*, 19 October 1917. For the French movement see Charles Sowerwine, "Causes and Choices: French Working Women in the Face of Feminism and Socialism, 1899-1914," paper presented at the December 1975 American Historical Association meeting in Atlanta.

3. *Bericht der 1. Internationalen Frauenkonferenz Stuttgart, 17 August 1907*, Stuttgart, 1907.

4. This paragraph draws from Peter N. Stearns, "Adaptation to Industrialization: German Workers as a Test Case," *Central European History* 3, no. 3 (1970): 313-331.

5. As Guenther Roth has described it, the organized working class was "negatively integrated" into the German state. See his work, *The Social Democrats in Imperial Germany: A Study in Working-Class Isolation and National Integration*, Totowa, New Jersey, 1963.

6. As a result of its negative integration, some historians have posited that the socialist subculture failed to challenge fundamentally the dominant cultural and ethical norms of German society. The inability to quarantine itself from the dominant society led to increasing absorption of traditional ideals and hindered socialists from acting on their critique. See, for example, Dieter Groh, *Negative Integration und revolutionärer Attentismus: Die deutsche Sozialdemokratie am Vorabend des Ersten Weltkrieges*, Frankfurt/M, 1973, p. 59. While the analysis has merit, I argue here that German socialist women did offer a penetrating feminist critique of existing assumptions governing sex roles and relationships and provide alternative role models for women.

7. Hans-Josef Steinberg, *Sozialismus und Deutsche Sozialdemokratie: Zur Ideologie der Partei vor dem I. Weltkreig*, Hanover, 1967, p. 45.

8. George Lichtheim, *Marxism: An Historical and Critical Study*, New York, 1969, p. 238.

9. This theme is a common one in the literature of German Social Democracy, particularly as it affected the writing of Karl Kautsky, chief theoretician for the Party. See, among others, Steinberg, *Sozialismus und Deutsche Sozialdemokratie*, pp. 48ff; Groh, *Negative Integration*, p. 57; Carl E. Schorske, *German Social Democracy, 1907-1917: The Development of the Great Schism*, New York, 1955, pp. 114-115.

10. Steinberg, *Sozialismus und Deutsche Sozialdemokratie*, pp. 47-48.

11. This and the following quotation are found in *Gleichheit*, 14 February 1910. The issue honored Bebel for his role in the socialist movement. Throughout this work, the translations from the German are the author's.

12. Hilde Lion, *Zur Soziologie der Frauenbewegung*, Berlin, 1926, p. 37.

13. See two interesting essays that clarify well the impact of industrialization on women's work. Mary Lynn McDougall, "Working-Class Women During the Industrial Revolution, 1780-1914," and Theresa M. McBride, "The Long-Road Home: Women's Work and Industrialization," both in *Becoming Visible: Women in European History*, ed. Renate Bridenthal and Claudia Koonz, Boston, 1977, pp. 255-279 and 280-295 respectively.

14. Peter N. Stearns and Patricia Branca Uttrachi, "Modernization of Women in the Nineteenth Century," *Forums in History*, 1973, p. 2.

15. Ibid., p. 5. Also, Joan W. Scott and Louise Tilly, "Women's Work and the Family in Nineteenth Century Europe," *Comparative Studies in Society and History* 17, no. 1 (January 1975): 44, 63; Edward Shorter, "Female Emancipation, Birth Control and Fertility in European History," *American Historical Review* 78, no. 3 (June 1973): 622-623. Shorter argues that women's wages are a key force in producing a more equal balance of power in the family. The liberalizing effect of wages, however, occurs at a rather late stage of industrial development.

16. Gerd Hohorst, Jürgen Kocka, and Gerhard A. Ritter, *Sozialgeschichtliches Arbeitsbuch: Materialien zur Statistik des Kaiserreichs, 1870-1914*, Munich, 1975, p. 100.

17. The West held common assumptions of women's social, political and economic inferiority that assigned them one proper role: to

act as guardians of the family. Legal discrimination, poor education, low pay, and male fear of and resistance to change were the common byproducts. Thus, women's movements throughout Europe and America fought similar battles. For interesting reading, see *The Woman Question in Europe*, edited by Theodore Stanton, New York, 1884.

18. Agnes Gosche, "Die organisierte Frauenbewegung," *Quellenhefte zum Frauenleben in der Geschichte*, vol. 2, Berlin, n.d.; also, Amy Hackett, "The German Women's Movement and Suffrage, 1890-1914: A Study of National Feminism," in *Modern European Social History*, ed. Robert J. Bezucha, Massachusetts, 1972, pp. 354-379.

19. The categories are drawn from a study of American and English feminism, William O'Neill, *The Woman Movement: Feminism in the United States and England*, Chicago, 1969. As the reader will see, I have redefined the terms. O'Neill's implicit identification of feminism with the vote is too narrow a basis for analysis even in the Anglo-Saxon world. I argue, too, that female unionists who pressure as women within the organization and who champion legislation favorable to their interests as workers are feminists.

20. Katherine S. Anthony, *Feminism in Germany and Scandinavia*, New York, 1915, pp. 4-7, as well as 83ff.

21. *Statistik der Frauenorganisationen im Deutschen Reich*, Berlin, 1909, p. 19.

22. Florence Bartoshesky, "Sexual Social Structure: A Brief Review of the Literature in American History," January 1973. I wish to thank Laura Oren for making available this very interesting paper.

23. Sowerwine, "Causes and Choices," p. 5.

24. *Protokoll des SPD-Parteitages zu Görlitz 18-24 September 1921 mit Bericht der Reichsfrauenkonferenz*, Berlin, 1921, p. 45.

25. Luxemburg's attitude toward the women's movement is captured very well by Karen Honeycutt, "Clara Zetkin: A Left-Wing Socialist and Feminist in Wilhelmian Germany," Ph.D. diss., Columbia University, 1975, p. 251; also, J. P. Nettl, *Rosa Luxemburg*, abridged edition, Oxford, 1969, p. 88. Rosa Luxemburg was an anomaly in the Central European context; typically radical women were committed to both socialism and feminism. Thus, the question raised by Aileen Kelly in the *New York Review of Books*, 17 July 1975, is too simplistic. Why, she asks, were middle-class radical women in England and Western Europe feminists while their counterparts from Russia or western Poland (Rosa Luxemburg, for exam-

ple) "passionately" socialists? Reality involved a constant interplay and tension between the women's loyalty to class and to sex.

26. Ritter, *Die Arbeiterbewegung im Wilhelminischen Reich*, Berlin, 1959, p. 220; Thönnessen, *The Emancipation of Women*, p. 71; also reflected in Schorske, *German Social Democracy*, p. 111, and most recently, Honeycutt, "Clara Zetkin," pp. 316 and 329. The assessment derives from two major sources. First, an emphasis on *Gleichheit*, the main women's paper that was clearly in the radical socialist camp, and second, stress on the national leadership, a good proportion of whom were radicals.

27. For the standard division of German Social Democracy into radical, center, and reform see Schorske, *German Social Democracy*. Recently, efforts have been made to refine the traditional categories. See, particularly, Groh, *Negative Integration*. The new definitions include left and center radical, reform activists, and the pragmatists who, after 1910, solidified into the center. In the new definition, most of the Party leaders were centrists, as was the trade union hierarchy, no longer the main fount of reformism in the German socialist movement. Whether old or new analyses, the works neglect the women's movement's peculiar ideological blend of socialism and feminism as well as the movement's contributions to the formulation of political ideology.

28. Mitchell, *Woman's Estate*, New York, 1973, pp. 76ff.; Rowbotham, *Women, Resistance and Revolution*, New York, 1974, pp. 60ff.

29. See the review of Werner Thönnessen's work by Richard J. Evans, *Newsletter*, European Labor and Working Class History, no. 8 (November 1975): 43-45. Evans rejects a "false symmetry of 'revisionism and antifeminism' versus 'revolutionary socialism and the emancipation of women.' "

30. *Protokoll des SPD-Parteitages zu Jena, 14-20 September 1913*, Berlin, 1913, pp. 337-338 and 515-516.

31. The distinction is E. J. Hobsbawm's. See "Labor History and Ideology," *Journal of Social History* 7, no. 4 (Summer 1974): 371-381.

CHAPTER II "WORK HORSE, BABY MACHINE"

1. Jürgen Kuczynski, *Die Geschichte der Lage der Arbeiter unter dem Kapitalismus*, vol. 4, Berlin, 1967, pp. 153-154; for the difficulties of bridging the intellectual, emotional, and political gap be-

tween members of the SPD and writers of the Naturalist school, see Vernon L. Lidtke, "Naturalism and Socialism in Germany," *American Historical Review* 79, no. 1 (February 1974): 14-37. The quotation in the chapter title is from Luise Zietz, 1913.

2. Dieter Groh, *Negative Integration*, pp. 274, 278-286, 472; also, Carl E. Schorske, *German Social Democracy*, p. 234.

3. StAP, Pr. Br. Rep. 30, Berlin C. Tit. 95, Sek. 7, Nr. 15852, Bl. 168-169: Police survey of socialist women's activities, 1913; Nr. 15850/1, Bl. 227-228: Clipping of *Vorwärts*, 11 November 1913.

4. Robert Michels, "Die deutsche Sozialdemokratie: Parteimitgliederschaft und soziale Zusammensetzung," *Archiv für Sozialwissenschaft und Sozialpolitik* 23 (1906): 534-536.

5. StAP, Pr. Br. Rep. 30, Berlin C, Tit. 95, Sek. 5, Nr. 14966, Bl. 22, 26, 45, 48-49: Police records of working women's associations for Hamburg, Nuremberg, and Frankfurt/M, 1885-1886; see also Ralf Lützenkirchen, *Der sozialdemokratische Verein für den Reichstagswahlkreis Dortmund-Hörde*, Dortmund, 1970, p. 115; membership lists of working women's clubs in Frankfurt/M in the 1890s: HHStA, Abt. 407, Nr. 163, Bl. 55-56, 57, 65, 109-110 and 257.

6. Kurt Heinig, "Vier Jahre Frauenleseabende," *Gleichheit*, 14 August 1911.

7. Kuczynski, *Der Lage der Arbeiter*, vol. 3, Berlin, 1962, p. 336.

8. StAN, 2923: Clippings of *Fränkische Tagespost*, 7 September 1908 and 22 August 1908.

9. Heinig, "Vier Jahre Frauenleseabende," no. 1; *Protokoll des SPD-Parteitages zu Jena, 10-16 September 1911 mit Bericht der 6. Frauenkonferenz*, Berlin, 1911, pp. 69-80, for membership statistics.

10. A similar occupational profile was true for the Working-Class Women and Girls' Educational Club for Frankfurt/M and Surroundings around 1902. See HHStA, Abt. 407, No. 164, Bl. 1. A writer and composer were found among its ranks.

11. *Gleichheit*, 10 June 1911; StAP, Pr. Br. Rep. 30, Berlin C, Tit. 95, Sek. 7, Nr. 15856, Bl. 7-8: Clipping of *Vorwärts*, 24 August 1913; Peter N. Stearns, "Adaptation to Industrialization," p. 326.

12. *Gleichheit*, 10 June 1911, for the breakdown of husbands' occupations; StAP, Nr. 15852, Bl. 153-154, 159: Police reports of the Social Democratic women's educational sessions and lectures for the fifth Berlin district and the third Berlin district, January 1913.

13. ZStA, RT, Nr. 124, Bl. 274-276: Parliamentary inquiry on the factory employment of working women and adolescent girls, January 1901; Kuczynski, *Der Lage der Arbeiter*, vol. 4, p. 311.

14. ZStA, RT, Nr. 3345, Bl. 49-51: Parliamentary debate on removing restrictions to women's rights of assembly, March 1906.

15. Karl Haase, *Der Weibliche Typus als Problem der Psychologie und Pädegogik*, Leipzig, 1915, p. 24.

16. As a Conservative Deputy Schall expressed it. ZStA, RT, Nr. 124, Bl. 23-27.

17. ZStA, RT, Nr. 3328, Bl. 184: Parliamentary debate on the question of extending the economic and political rights of the female sex, admitting them to university study and to the apprenticeship examinations, February 1913.

18. ZStA, RT, Nr. 126, Bl. 174: The remarks on women's immaturity were made by a Conservative Deputy Dr. Oertel during a debate in parliament on women's labor, March 1912; also, RT, Nr. 3328, Bl. 184: Parliamentary debate on the extension of political rights to women, February 1913; RMdI, Nr. 13578, Bl. 7-10: Literature on fighting Social Democracy; pamphlet by Walther Caron, "Die Gleichberechtigung der Frau in der Ehe und die Sozialdemokratie," Düsseldorf, 1899.

19. *Labour Laws for Women in Germany*, Strand, 1907, pp. 6-14; Gertrud Bäumer, *Die Frau in Volkswirtschaft und Staatsleben der Gegenwart*, Stuttgart, 1914, pp. 224-228.

20. Fr. Kleeis, "Das Wahlrecht der Frauen in den Krankenkassen," *Correspondenzblatt*, 4 January 1908.

21. FES, NL Gerda Weyl, TR 41/21; Klara Weyl, "Erinnerungen."

22. ZStA, RT, Nr. 3345, Bl. 106.

23. *Reichs-Arbeitsblatt* 9, no. 2 (21 February 1911): 133, 141; Helene Lange and Gertrud Bäumer, *Handbuch der Frauenbewegung*, Berlin, 1910, 5: 30; also, Richard J. Evans, *The Feminist Movement in Germany, 1894-1933*, London, 1976, pp. 17-22, for a discussion of the educational structure and reform.

24. See the following two issues of *Correspondenzblatt*: 3 April 1909, pp. 207-208, and 18 April 1914, pp. 238-239. Also, StAH, 20484: Clipping of *Arbeiter Jugend*, 21 October 1916.

25. *Statistik Frauenorganisationen im Deutschen Reiche*, Berlin, 1909, pp. 6-8; Karen Honeycutt, "Clara Zetkin," p. 33.

26. Wolfgang Plat, "Die Stellung der deutschen Sozialdemokratie zum Grundsatz der Gleichberechtigung der Frau auf dem Gebiet des Familienrechts bei der Schaffung des Bürgerlichen Gesetzbuches des Deutschen Reiches," diss. Humboldt University, Berlin, 1966; also a series of articles by Ernst Oberholzer in *Gleichheit*, 25 October 1909, 4 July 1909, 10 October 1910, and 27 February 1911.

27. August Bebel, *Women and Socialism*, trans. Meta A. Stern, New York, 1910, p. 212. The census dates vary: U.S. and Austria, 1900; France and Great Britain, 1901; Germany, 1907; also, Bäumer, *Die Frau in Volkswirtschaft*, p. 194.

28. Walter G. Hoffmann, "The Take-Off in Germany," in *The Economic Development of Western Europe: The Eighteenth and Early Nineteenth Centuries*, ed. Warren C. Scoville and J. Clayburn LaForce, Massachusetts, 1969, pp. 75-96.

29. "Aus meinem Leben," *Für unsere Kinder*: Beilage Zur *Kämpferin*, 15 April 1919. For general information on the growth of female labor see Jürgen Kuczynski, *A Short History of Labor Conditions under Industrial Capitalism: Germany, 1800 to the Present Day*, London, 1945, 3: 24-26; Franz F. Wurm, *Wirtschaft und Gesellschaft in Deutschland, 1848-1948*, Opladen, 1969, p. 40.

30. Hans Rosenberg, *Grosse Depression und Bismarckzeit*, Berlin, 1967; also, Helmut Böhme, "Big-Business Pressure Groups and Bismarck's Turn to Protectionism, 1873-79," *Historical Journal* 10, no. 2 (1967): 218-236.

31. Groh, *Negative Integration*, pp. 47-49.

32. W. F. Bruck, *Social and Economic History of Germany from William II to Hitler, 1888-1938*, New York, 1962, p. 100. For the debate in America on cartelization and the shifting historical interpretation see Gabriel Kolko, *The Triumph of Conservatism: A Reinterpretation of American History, 1900-1916*, London, 1963.

33. Groh, *Negative Integration*, pp. 93-94.

34. The question of fluctuations in real income, particularly after 1895, is a subject of some disagreement. See Groh, *Negative Integration*, pp. 39-40 and 85. Groh writes that real wages stagnated or rose only slightly after the turn of the century. Gerd Hohorst, Jürgen Kocka, and Gerhard A. Ritter, *Sozialgeschichtliches Arbeitsbuch*, pp. 94-95 and 107-108. In contrast, the authors estimate a 25 percent real wage gain between 1895 and 1913.

35. 1911 was an exception; consumption rose slightly. Hohorst, Kocka, and Ritter, *Sozialgeschichtliches Arbeitsbuch*, p. 120.

36. Kuczynski, *Der Lage der Arbeiter*, vol. 4, p. 338.

37. Hohorst, Kocka, and Ritter, *Sozialgeschichtliches Arbeitsbuch*, p. 106.

38. Therese Blase concluded in 1911 that the high cost of living was encouraging working-class women to join the socialist women's movement: *Pr. Jena, 1911, Frauenkonferenz*, p. 424. For efforts to capitalize on the rising costs of living see, among others, Lützenkirchen, *Der sozialdemokratische Verein*, pp. 115, 118-119; StAM,

RM, VII, Nr. 62v, 2342, Abt. 6, Nr. 160, 124; Nr. 160, 1578: SPD
meetings that dealt with the question of rising prices.

39. The overall rise partially reflects the incorporation of "supplementary" labor in agriculture into the full-time employment statistics
and thus is exaggerated. See Hohorst, Kocka, and Ritter, *Sozialgeschichtliches Arbeitsbuch*, pp. 60, 68-69. The authors cite the findings of Hoffmann, *Das Wachstum der deutschen Wirtschaft*, who argues that pre-1907 statistics generally do not include supplementary
labor and that if the same criteria were used for earlier censuses, the
proportion of women employed to total working population would be
revised as follows: 1882, 35.91 percent; 1895, 34.86 percent; and
1907, 34.88 percent. This would reflect definitional changes in both
agriculture and commerce. His findings are not inconsistent with the
works of other labor historians who document the fluctuations of
female labor with industrialization. See, for example, Joan W. Scott
and Louise Tilly, "Women's Work and the Family," pp. 36-64.

40. Groh, *Negative Integration*, p. 100; Rose Otto, *Über Fabrikarbeit verheirateter Frauen*, Stuttgart, 1910, p. 100; HStAS, E
150, Nr. 640, Bl. 303: Clipping of *Tägliche Rundschau*, 21 May 1903,
containing a special report on female labor for 1902, a recession year.

41. The figures in table 3 are considerably lower than contemporary analyses indicated. See, for example, Gertrud Hanna, "Die
Frauenerwerbsarbeit im Deutschen Reiche nach den Ergebnissen
der Berufszählungen von 1882-1907," *Statistische-Beilage des Correspondenzblatt*, 27 April 1912, p. 63. Her figures are as follows:

FEMALE WORKERS PER 100 MALE WORKERS

Year	Agriculture	Industry	Commerce
1882	62.0	15.3	24.8
1895	73.7	20.0	42.1
1907	140.5	22.2	44.7

The differences are partially definitional; those whom Hanna included in the "worker" category (*Arbeiter*) are now considered
"employees," (*Angestellten*), as for example, salesclerks.

42. Kuczynski, *Der Lage der Arbeiter*, vol. 3, p. 350; Otto, *Über
Fabrikarbeit*, p. 97.

43. ZStA, RMdI, Nr. 6460, Bl. 94: Chamber of Commerce report,
M. Gladbach.

44. "Die Arbeiterinnen in der Gewerkschaftsbewegung," *Correspondenzblatt*, 18 March 1905.

45. Lisbeth Franzen-Hellersberg, *Die Jugendliche Arbeiterin: Ihre Arbeitsweise und Lebensform*, Tübingen, 1932, pp. 40, 47; Scott and Tilly, "Women's Work and the Family," pp. 44, 54, for the use made of working women's wages; also, HStAS, E 150, Nr. 640, Bl. 303: Factory inspectors' reports.

46. Hanna, "Die Frauenerwerbsarbeit," p. 78.

47. Kuczynski, *Der Lage der Arbeiter*, vol. 3, p. 338.

48. StAH, S 1909: Clipping of *Fachzeitung für Schneider*, 29 April 1899.

49. ZStA, RMdI, Nr. 6456, Bl. 177-183: Report of the Ministry of Commerce and Industry, November 1884.

50. Käthe Duncker, "Über die Betheiligung der weiblichen Geschlechte an der Erwerbsthätigkeit," *Correspondenzblatt*, 28 August 1899.

51. Duncker, "Über die Betheiligung," and Hanna, "Die Frauenerwerbsarbeit," p. 64.

52. From Sombart to Stearns, the tendency has been to dismiss domestic industry as increasingly insignificant: Werner Sombart, *Die deutsche Volkswirtschaft im neunzehnten Jahrhundert*, Berlin, 1913, pp. 306-307, 512-513; Peter N. Stearns, *Lives of Labor: Work in a Maturing Industrial Society*, New York, 1975, p. 33. Although more research is needed, domestic industry continued to be an extremely important part of women's work well into the 1920s.

53. "Aus unserer Bewegung: Ernestine Lutze," *Gleichheit*, 15 July 1923.

54. ZStA, RT, Nr. 132, Bl. 3-7, and 127: Parliamentary debates on domestic industry, 1901 and 1903; RMdI, Nr. 6460, Bl. 35: On the dress and underclothing industries as reported during a debate in parliament, February 1903; Kuczynski, *Der Lage der Arbeiter*, vol. 3, pp. 347-348.

55. Hohorst, Kocka, and Ritter, *Sozialgeschichtliches Arbeitsbuch*, p. 67; Bäumer, *Die Frau in Volkswirtschaft*, pp. 122-135.

56. Otto, *Über Fabrikarbeit*, pp. 94, 100-101. According to contemporary analysis, between 1895 and 1905 employment of married women in agriculture rose 227.2 percent; in commerce, 103.6 percent; and in domestic service, 84.7 percent. See Hanna, "Die Frauenerwerbsarbeit," p. 92.

57. HStAS, E 150, Nr. 640: Clipping of *Soziale Praxis: Centralblatt für Sozialpolitik*, 20 September 1900; ZStA, RT, Nr. 125,

Bl. 5-11: Parliamentary discussion on the employment of women and adolescent girls, January 1902; RMdI, Nr. 6459, Bl. 145: Report of the director of the Imperial Office of Statistics containing information on divorcees and widows, 15 December 1900; Otto, *Über Fabrikarbeit*, pp. 116-118.

58. Otto, *Über Fabrikarbeit*, p. 118. For British attitudes toward married women's employment, see Peter N. Stearns, "Working-Class Women in Britain, 1890-1914," in *Suffer and Be Still: Women in the Victorian Age*, ed. Martha Vicinus, Bloomington, 1973, pp. 100-120; also, Stearns's article, "Adaptation to Industrialization," pp. 326-327. Whether German workers were less traditional in attitudes toward their wives's employment than their British counterparts remains open to question. The data are inconclusive.

59. Otto, *Über Fabrikarbeit*, pp. 95-97.

60. HStAS, E 150, Nr. 640: Clipping of *Soziale Praxis*; Otto, *Über Fabrikarbeit*, p. 107.

61. Zetkin, "Für die Befreiung der Frau," in *Clara Zetkin: Ausgewählte Reden und Schriften*, Berlin, 1957, 1: 4-5.

62. "Was wir gegenwärtig fordern," *Gleichheit*, 17 January 1900.

63. "Für die Befreiung der Frau," in *Clara Zetkin: Ausgewählte Reden*, 1: 10.

64. Zietz, *Zur Frage des Mutter-und Säuglingschutzes*, Leipzig, 1911; also, *Protokoll des SPD-Parteitages zu Dresden, 13-20 September 1903*, Berlin, 1903, pp. 125-126; *Protokoll des SPD-Parteitages zu München, 14-20 September 1902 mit Bericht uber die 2. Frauenkonferenz*, Berlin, 1902, pp. 296-298.

65. ZStA, RT, Nr. 124, Bl. 23-27, 40-49, and 86-103; Rt, Nr. 125, Bl. 5-11; RT, Nr. 126, Bl. 25: Parliamentary debates on women's labor, 1885, 1902, and 1908; Otto, *Über Fabrikarbeit*, p. 95. The number also reflects the higher wages men received in western Germany.

66. ZStA, RMdI, Nr. 6456, Bl. 131-141.

67. Ibid.

68. ZStA, RT, Nr. 124, Bl. 274-276; RT, Nr. 125, Bl. 5-11.

69. ZStA, RMdI, Nr. 6456, Bl. 131-141.

70. ZStA, RT, Nr. 124, Bl. 23-27; *Women's Work under Labor Law: A Survey of Protective Legislation*, Geneva, 1932, pp. 1-2, 95, 134, 153; *Labour Laws for Women in Germany*, pp. 2-5; Max Schippel, *Sozialdemokratisches Reichstag-Handbuch*, Berlin, n.d., pp. 452-453. Otto, *Über Fabrikarbeit*, p. 183.

71. ZStA, RT, Nr. 124, Bl. 2-3, 5, 20-22, 50, 108, 124.

72. ZStA, RMdI, Nr. 6462, Bl. 68-70, 125.

73. ZStA, RMdI, Nr. 6458, Bl. 252-253: Employment of women and girls in factories, September 1892.

74. FES, Personen-Sammlung, Marie Juchacz: Clipping of *Neuer Vorwärts*, 12 March 1954.

75. Richard Camp, "The 'Bourgeois' Campaign for Women's Rights in Post-Risorgimento Italy," and Claire Goldberg Moses, "French Feminism: 1848-1900," papers presented to the Annual Convention of the American Historical Association in Atlanta, December 1975.

76. Franzen-Hellersberg, *Die Jugendliche Arbeiterin*, p. 47.

77. Ibid., p. 21.

PART B   SOCIALIST FEMINISM IN

GERMAN SOCIAL DEMOCRACY: PERSONALITIES AND PERSPECTIVES

1. Ingrun Lafleur, "Adelheid Popp and the Feminist Education of Austrian Socialists," paper presented at the Second Berkshire Conference on the History of Women, October 1974.

CHAPTER III   EIGHT SOCIALIST FEMINISTS

1. Clara Zetkin, *Zur Geschichte der proletarischen Frauenbewegung Deutschlands*, 1928; reprint ed., Berlin, 1958, pp. 120-138; Hilde Lion, *Zur Soziologie der Frauenbewegung*, pp. 39-40.

2. StAP, Pr. Br. Rep. 30, Berlin C, Tit. 95, Sek. 5, Nr. 14966, Bl. 1-8: Police reports on Working Women's Associations, 1873-1874.

3. Emma Ihrer, "Mutter Staegemann," *Gleichheit*, 11 October 1909; *Vorwärts*, 10 January 1911, Second Supplement; Eduard Bernstein, *Die Geschichte der Berliner Arbeiter-Bewegung*, Berlin, 1907, 2: 27.

4. StAP, Nr. 14966, Bl. 126-127: Clipping of *Deutsche Manufakturarbeiter Zeitung*.

5. Emma Ihrer, *Die Arbeiterinnen im Klassenkampf*, Hamburg, 1898, pp. 9-10; FES, NL Marie Juchacz, D. 3, manuscript of "Sie Lebten für eine bessere Welt."

6. StAP, Nr. 14966, Bl. 14: 24 October 1885.

7. Ottilie Baader, *Ein steiniger Weg: Lebenserinnerungen*, Stuttgart, 1921, p. 21.

8. Ibid., p. 19.

9. Ibid., p. 15.

10. Ibid., p. 16.

11. Ibid., p. 20.

12. *Gleichheit*, 14 February 1910.

13. StAP, Pr. Br. Rep. 30, Berlin C. Tit. 95, Sek. 5, No. 14966, Bl. 135-137.

14. Ihrer, *Die Arbeiterinnen*, p. 50. For Baader's views, see *Gleichheit*, 20 April 1904.

15. As coined by Dieter Groh, *Negative Integration*, pp. 59ff.

16. Not much information exists on Grünberg's family background and early life. See FES, NL Juchacz, D. 1, materials for "Sie Lebten." The collection contains several letters from Grünberg's colleagues in Nuremberg.

17. *Der Abend*, 10 July 1928; *Fränkische Tagespost*, 9 July 1928; Verband der Schneider und Schneiderinnen: Filiale Berlin, *Jahresbericht der Ortsverwaltung über das Geschäftsjahr 1904/05*, Berlin, 1906, p. 26.

18. "Über den Stand der Nürnberger Arbeiterinnenbewegung 1909," *Gleichheit*, 15 August 1910. Part of the increase in numbers of working women between 1895 and 1907 reflected the incorporation of villages into Nuremberg proper. Erich Otremba, "Nürnberg, Die alte Reichsstadt in Franken auf dem Wege zur Industriestadt," *Forschung zur deutschen Landeskunde*, vol. 48, 1950, pp. 54-61.

19. *Gleichheit*, 20 February 1907.

20. Allan Mitchell, *Revolution in Bavaria, 1918-1919: The Eisner Regime and the Soviet Republic*, Princeton, 1965, pp. 17-21; Carl E. Schorske, *German Social Democracy*, pp. 7-8.

21. *Political Parties: A Sociological Study of the Oligarchical Tendencies of Modern Democracy*, trans. Eden and Cedar Paul, 1915; reprint ed., New York, 1966.

22. As it was called by the bourgeois feminist, Else Lüders, in *Correspondenzblatt*, 15 April 1905.

23. The statistics did not reveal the share of skilled and unskilled workers, although the overwhelming majority of women were workers' aids (*Hilfsarbeiterinnen*). *Protokoll vom Ersten Kongress der Buchdruckerei-Hilfsarbeiter-und Arbeiterinnen Deutschlands, Berlin 30-31 Mai-1 Juni 1898*, Berlin, 1898, pp. 7-11; Verband der Buchdruckerei-Hilfsarbeiter-und Arbeiterinnen Deutschlands, *Rechenschaftsbericht*, Berlin, 1899-1909.

24. In Lion, *Zur Soziologie der Frauenbewegung*, p. 100.

25. "Eine Gewerkschaftliche Frauenorganisation," *Gleichheit*, 10 May 1909; "Zur Geschichte einer gewerkschaftlichen Frauenorganisation," *Gleichheit*, 14 March 1910.

26. *Gleichheit*, 22 June 1908.

27. As she called herself during a debate on the orientation of *Gleichheit*. *Protokoll des SPD-Parteitages zu Jena, 17-23 September 1905*, Berlin, 1905, p. 281.

28. Simone de Beauvoir, *The Second Sex*, trans. and ed. H. M. Parshley, New York, 1964, pp. 267ff, section on "The Formative Years: Childhood."

29. Hanna Ilberg, *Aus dem Leben und Wirken einer grossen Sozialistin*, Berlin, 1956, p. 15; Luise Dornemann, *Clara Zetkin: Leben und Wirken*, 1957; reprint ed., Berlin, 1973, pp. 33-39.

30. G.G.L. Alexander, *Aus Clara Zetkins Leben und Werk*, Berlin, 1927, pp. 4-5; Luise Dornemann, *Clara Zetkin*, pp. 40-45.

31. IISH, NL Kautsky, KD 23, Nr. 303. Paris, 22 March 1886.

32. IISH, NL Kautsky, KD 23, Nr. 307. Paris, 28 August 1886.

33. Ibid.

34. StAP, Nr. 14966, Bl. 168: Clipping of *Neue Preussische Zeitung*, 26 May 1889.

35. "Abschied von der 'Gleichheit' " and "An die sozialistischen Frauen aller Länder!" in *Clara Zetkin: Ausgewählte Reden*, 1: 756, 763.

36. Karen Honeycutt, "Clara Zetkin," pp. 117-119.

37. FES, NL Dittmann, Tr, 01: Undated, photocopy.

38. *Protokoll des SPD-Parteitages zu Gotha, 11-16 Oktober 1896*, Berlin, 1896, pp. 160-168; Clara Zetkin, "Die Arbeiterinnen-und Frauenfrage der Gegenwart," in *Berliner Arbeiter-Bibliothek*, ed. Max Schippel, 1, no. 3, Berlin, 1894. Zetkin's analysis had become increasingly Marxist after reading Engels's work; her early account of women's oppression offered a bourgeois feminist analysis, locating the origin in men's physical supremacy. For an analysis of the change in Zetkin's views as a result of studying Engels, see Honeycutt, "Clara Zetkin," pp. 73-80.

39. IISH, Kleine Korrespondenz, D. German Socialists. Zetkin to Richard Fischer, Stuttgart, 1 October 1897.

40. *Women and Socialism*, sect. 1, "Women in the Past." For the opposite side of the coin, the negative impact of the idea of matriarchy, see Joan Bamberger, "The Myth of Matriarchy: Why Men Rule in Primitive Society," in *Women, Culture and Society*, ed. Michelle Zimbalist Rosaldo and Louise Lamphere, Stanford, 1974, pp. 263-280.

41. "Die Arbeiterinnen-und Frauenfrage," p. 6; *Pr. Gotha, 1896, SPD*, p. 160. This was too simplistic an assumption. Marxists recognize the persistence of sex-role differentiation in so-called socialist

countries today. Male and female role expectations have proven to be remarkably tenacious. See Harriet Holter, "Sex Roles and Social Change," in *Towards a Sociology of Women*, ed. Constantina Safilios-Rothschild, Massachusetts, 1972, pp. 331-343; Gerda Weber, "Um eine ganze Epoche voraus? 25 Jahre DFD," *Deutschland Archiv: Zeitschrift für Fragen der DDR und der Deutschlandspolitik* 5, no. 4 (April 1972): 410-416.

42. "Die Arbeiterinnen-und Frauenfrage," p. 14; *Pr. Gotha, 1896, SPD*, pp. 164-165.

43. *Gleichheit*, 8 February 1892; "Wir demonstrieren," *Gleichheit*, 6 February 1895.

44. "Arbeiterinnen, organisiert Euch," *Gleichheit*, 24 July 1895; "Die Parteitag der deutschen Sozialdemokratie zu Köln," *Gleichheit*, 15 November 1893.

45. "Die gewerkschaftlichen organisierten Arbeiterinnen in Deutschland," 16 October 1895; "Der zweite Kongress der zentralisierten Gewerkschaften Deutschlands," 27 May 1896.

46. *Protokoll des SPD-Parteitages zu Mainz, 17-21 September 1900 und der Frauenkonferenz*, Berlin, 1900, p. 248. Berlin women alone comprised a five-member commission to coordinate propaganda, prepare brochures and papers, and direct trade union activity. They chose a three-member revisions committee to execute decisions. The Mainz conference designated Berlin as the seat for the official national leader. Zetkin's proposal, however, that only Berliners elect the central representative was defeated. Election was given to the participants at the women's conferences.

47. Baader, *Lebenserinnerungen*, p. 19; also, IISH, NL von Vollmar, V 141. Baader to Georg von Vollmar, Berlin 21 July 1902; FES, NL Gerda Weyl, TR 41/5. Letter from Baader to Klara Haase Weyl, undated.

48. StAP, Pr. Br. Rep. 30, Berlin C, Tit. 94, Nr. 14128: Surveillance of Robert Wengels and his wife, Margarete, 1888-1904; Luise Dornemann, *Clara Zetkin*, p. 119; StAH, S 1909: Clipping of *Volkszeitung*, 26 October 1900.

49. FES, NL Gerda Weyl, TR 41/21, "Erinnerungen"; *Gleichheit*, 28 September 1898 and 29 August 1900; Franz Osterroth, *Biographisches Lexikon des Sozialismus*, Hanover, 1960, 1: 338-339; *Geschichte der deutschen Arbeiterbewegung: Biographisches Lexikon*, Berlin, 1970, pp. 493-494; "Aus der Bewegung" in *Gleichheit*, which carried the activities of these radical women. Immediately prior to World War I, Wulff was based in Breslau.

50. Jacqueline Strain, "Feminism and Political Radicalism in the German Social Democratic Movement, 1890-1914," Ph.D. diss., Berkeley, 1964, pp. 82ff.

51. "Brief an Heleen Ankersmit," in *Clara Zetkin: Ausgewählte Reden*, 1: 653. The Moroccan controversy involved the criticism by the leftwing of the failure of the executive committee to act decisively in the struggle against imperialism. For details see Schorske, *German Social Democracy*, pp. 197ff.

52. Marie Juchacz, *Sie Lebten für eine bessere Welt*, Berlin, 1955, p. 67.

53. "Die deutsche Sozialdemokratie," *Archiv für Sozialwissenschaft und Sozialpolitik* 23 (1906): 536 note; *Die Genossin*, January 1932; FES, NL Marie Juchacz, D. 4. "Vorkämpferinnen."

54. "Luise Zietz," *Gleichheit*, January 1952; FES, Personen-Sammlung. Manuscript of Dittmann's article.

55. StAH, S 5883: Clipping of *General Anzeiger*, 23 October 1902; for Zietz's complaints see *Gleichheit*, 18 April 1906; Anna Blos, *Die Frauenfrage im Lichte des Sozialismus*, Dresden, 1930, p. 143.

56. Despite various prewar divisions, German Social Democracy divided into two fundamental groups, those proposing reform and those advocating revolution. This is the interpretation of Groh, *Negative Integration*, and, earlier, of J. P. Nettl, *Rosa Luxemburg*, London, 1966, 2: 455.

57. Lily Braun, *Memoiren einer Sozialistin: Lehrjahre*, Munich, 1909, pp. 216ff; Lily Braun, *Kriegsbriefe aus den Jahren 1870-1871 von Hans von Kretschman*, Berlin, 1903, pp. ii-xxxviii; "Im Schatten der Titanen," in *Lily Braun: Gesammelte Werke*, Berlin, n.d., 1: 5, 106, 158, 199, 225, 244.

58. *Memoiren: Lehrjahre*, p. 430; also, *Kriegsbriefs*, p. liii.

59. *Kriegsbriefe*, p. liv; FES, Personen-Sammlung, Lily Braun: Clipping of *Süddeutsche Zeitung*, 26 June 1965.

60. Quoted in Julie Vogelstein, "Lily Braun: Ein Lebensbild," in *Lily Braun: Gesammelte Werke*, 1: xxxv-xxxvi.

61. *Frauenfrage und Sozialdemokratie: Reden anlässlich des Internationalen Frauenkongresses*, Berlin, 1896, p. 3. For information on the club "Frauenwohl," see Else Lüders, *Der "linke" Flugel: Ein Blatt aus der Geschichte der deutschen Frauenbewegung*, Berlin, n.d.

62. "Nach rechts und links," *Die Frauenbewegung*, 1 April 1895.

63. "Herrn Foerster zur Erwiderung," *Gleichheit*, 25 October 1899.

64. *Memoiren einer Sozialistin: Kampfjahre*, Munich, 1911, pp. 245-246.

65. Julie Vogelstein, *Ein Menschenleben: Heinrich Braun und Sein Schicksal*, Tübingen, 1932, pp. 92-94. For the purposes of clarity, I refer to Braun rather than to von Gizycki throughout this work even for her bourgeois feminist career from 1893 to 1895.

66. *Zur Beurteilung der Frauenbewegung in England und Deutschland*, Berlin, 1896, p. 25; Lily Braun, "Die Interessen der Arbeiterinnen und der Internationale Frauenkongress," *Correspondenzblatt*, 2 July 1904.

67. Fritzmichael Roehl, *Marie Juchacz und die Arbeiterwohlfahrt*, Hanover, 1961, p. 14.

68. Ibid., pp. 25-26; also, FES, Personen-Sammlung, Marie Juchacz: Clipping of *Neues Beginnen*; J. P. Nettl, *Rosa Luxemburg*, 1: 117.

69. FES, Personen-Sammlung, Marie Juchacz.

70. "Marie Juchacz erinnert sich," *Gleichheit*, December 1951.

71. "Wie es damals war," *Die Genossin*, November 1949.

72. Roehl, *Marie Juchacz*, p. 44; also, "Marie Juchacz erinnert sich."

73. *Gleichheit*, 25 December 1912 and 26 November 1913; Sozialdemokratischer Verein für die Wahlkreise Köln-Stadt und Köln-Land, *Bericht des Vorstandes und der Kommissionen über des Geschaftsjahr 1913-1914*, Cologne, 1914, pp. 13, 23-24.

CHAPTER IV   THE NEW WOMAN

1. "Sozialistische Stimmen über die Frauenfrage," *Neue Zeit* 15, no. 1 (1896): 786.

2. *Gleichheit*, 14 February 1910.

3. Steven R. Brown and John D. Ellithorp, "Emotional Experiences in Political Groups: The Case of the McCarthy Phenomenon," *American Political Science Review* 64, no. 2 (June 1970): 349-366; Cecil A. Gibb, "Leadership," in *International Encyclopedia of the Social Sciences*, ed. David L. Sills, New York, 1968, 9: 91-99.

4. Ottilie Baader, *Lebenserinnerungen*, p. 15; M. Kuhnert, "Ottilie Baader," *Gleichheit*, August 1950. For Marie Juchacz, see chap. 3 of this work; Lily Braun, *Memoiren einer Sozialisten: Lehrjahre*, pp. 545ff; Julie Vogelstein, "Lily Braun: Ein Lebensbild," in *Lily Braun: Gesammelte Werke*, 1: xxxii and xxxvii; FES, NL Marie Juchacz, D. 3, "Frauen ihrer-Jahrhunderts" (unpublished manuscript), for the direct quote.

5. Franz Osterroth, *Biographisches Lexikon des Sozialismus*, 1: 342; FES, NL Marie Juchacz, D. 3 manuscript of her book "Sie Lebten für eine bessere Welt."

6. *Lebenserinnerungen*, pp. 9-10.

7. "Unsere Vorkämpferinnen," *Gleichheit*, 1 April 1921.

8. *Lebenserinnerungen*, p. 19.

9. Vogelstein, "Lily Braun," p. xxxv.

10. *Lebenserinnerungen*, p. 25.

11. See the appendix of this book.

12. *Lehrjahre*, pp. 37, 41, 175, 179-180.

13. Ibid., p. 246.

14. Ibid., pp. 370-371.

15. Ibid., p. 374.

16. *20. Jahresbericht Arbeiter-Sekretariat Nürnberg: Geschäftsjahre 1914-1920*. Ortsausschuss Nürnberg des Allgemeinen Deutschen Gewerkschaftsbundes, Nürnberg, 1921, pp. 42, 44.

17. "Emma Ihrer," *Gleichheit*, 16 January 1911; for additional examples see "Genossin Baaders 70. Geburtstag," *Frauen-Beilage der Leipziger Volkszeitung*, 13 July 1917; *Vorwärts*, 28 January 1922, and *Freiheit*, 27 January 1922, for Zietz's obituaries.

18. "Die Frau in der Dichtung," *Neue Zeit* 14, no. 2 (1895-1896): 297.

19. Ibid., pp. 302-303.

20. "Nicht Haussklavin, Nicht Mannweib, weiblicher Vollmensch," *Gleichheit*, 19 January 1898.

21. "Die Frau in der Dichtung."

22. "Nicht Haussklavin."

23. "Die Arbeiterinnen-und Frauenfrage," pp. 29, 38. "Warum fordern wir Reformen im neuen Bürgerlichen Gesetzbuch?" *Gleichheit*, 7 August 1895.

24. StAH, S 1926: Versammlungsbericht, 6 September 1890.

25. StAN, 2923: Clipping of *Fränkische Tagespost*, 10 April 1909, for Grünberg's views; *Die Stellung der Frau in der Gegenwart*, Berlin, 1895, pp. 11-12, for Braun's position.

26. StAH, S 1909: Clipping of *Berliner Lokal Anzeiger*, 21 January 1899.

27. *Protokoll des SPD-Parteitages zu Mannheim, 23-29 September 1906 mit Bericht der 4. Frauenkonferenz*, Berlin, 1906, pp. 440-455. This includes both the resolution of the conference on suffrage written by Clara Zetkin and her speech.

28. See Richard J. Evans, *The Feminist Movement in Germany*, for the middle-class suffrage leagues.

29. Claire LaVigna, "The Marxist Ambivalence Toward Women: Between Socialism and Feminism in the Italian Socialist Party," and Marilyn J. Boxer, "Socialism Faces Feminism: The Failure of Synthesis in France, 1879-1914," in *Socialist Women: Case Studies in European Socialist Feminism in the Nineteenth and Early Twentieth Centuries*, ed. Marilyn J. Boxer and Jean H. Quataert, New York, 1978, pp. 159-161 and, for the French position, p. 102.

30. Boxer, "Socialism Faces Feminism," p. 94.

31. *Zur Frage des Frauenwahlrechts*, Berlin, 1907, p. 45.

32. Ingrun Lafleur, "Five Socialist Women: Traditionalist Conflicts and Socialist Visions in Austria, 1893-1934," in *Socialist Women*, ed. Boxer and Quataert, pp. 220, 232-234.

33. "Die Ehescheidung im Entwurf eines neuen Bürgerlichen Gesetzbuches und vor der Kommission zur Vorberathung desselben," *Gleichheit*, 10 June 1896. A belief in inevitable future change diverted the movement as a whole from a thorough analysis of the family in capitalist society and its place in perpetuating the subordination of women and sex-role divisions. This point is developed in more detail at the end of the chapter, and to some extent part C of this book is devoted to this issue.

34. For the position on divorce consult the following issues of *Gleichheit*: 7 August 1895, 24 June 1896, and 8 July 1896.

35. "Gebärzwang und Gebärstreik," *Gleichheit*, 10 June 1914.

36. *Lehrjahre*, p. 375.

37. "Mutterschaftsversicherung und Krankencassen," *Sozialistische Monatshefte* 9, no. 1 (April 1903): 271.

38. "Aus Meinem Briefwechsel," *Die Neue Gesellschaft*, 27 December 1905.

39. StAP, Pr. Br. Rep. 30, Berlin C, Tit. 95, Sek. 7, Nr. 15856, Bl. 33-45: As stated at a public meeting, 30 August 1913.

40. Hohorst, Kocka, and Ritter, *Sozialgeschichtliches Arbeitsbuch*, pp. 17-18, and 27-28.

41. StAN, 2923: Polizei-Bericht, October 1918. A similar debate surfaced toward the end of World War I: Vorstand der Sozialdemokratie Deutschland, *Material zur Geburtenfragen*, Berlin, 1918; StAH, S 20672: Clipping of *Vorwärts*, 22 October 1918; Luise Zietz, *Gegen den staatlichen Gebärzwang*, Hanover, 1914, pp. 18-23.

42. StAP, Nr. 15856, Bl. 1: Police records of the birth control controversy, 1913-1915.

43. StAP, Pr. Br. Rep. 30, Berlin C, Tit. 95, Sek. 7, Nr. 15850/1, Bl. 225-226; Nr. 15852, Bl. 178-179. For a study of fertility and family planning in Germany see John E. Knodel, *The Decline of Fertility in*

Germany, 1871-1939, Princeton, 1974. The author shows, for example, that metropolitan Berlin was among the first areas in which fertility declined.

44. StAP, Nr. 15856, Bl. 7-8, 11, 40-45, 55-56.

45. StAP, Nr. 15856, Bl. 7-8. Marx had not dealt with birth control per se; he had, however, related the question of population to the surplus labor problem and to wage levels. During this discussion neither side brought out these issues.

46. Ibid.

47. Potsdam archival materials help clarify several questions raised by R. P. Neuman, "The Sexual Question and Social Democracy in Imperial Germany," *Journal of Social History* 7 (Spring 1974): 278-281. The SPD leadership officially did not propagandize birth control because its assumptions were inimical to the Malthusian argument that population is the key variable in levels of living standards. This stance was its theoretical position on contraception.

48. *Zur Frage des Mutter-und Säuglingsschutzes*, p. 25; "Der Achtstundentag und die Gewerkschaftliche Agitation und Organization," *Gleichheit*, 20 April 1904; *Die Frau und der politische Kampf*, Berlin, 1912, p. 9.

49. "Notwendige Ergänzung," *Gleichheit*, 30 January 1901.

50. StAH, S 1926: Clipping of *Hamburger Echo*, 24 October 1899; S 20672, Abt. 4, Nr. 13817.

51. Clara Zetkin, "Nicht Schmutzkonkurrentin, Kampfesgefährtin, Arbeitsgenossin, *Gleichheit*, 11 August 1897.

52. "Neue Gründe zur Förderung der Agitation unter den Arbeiterinnen," *Correspondenzblatt*, 18 April 1914; "Die Vertretung der Arbeiterinneninteressen," *Sozialistische Monatshefte* 23, no. 1 (11 April 1917): 420; *Protokoll der Verhandlungen des 9. Kongresses der Gewerkschaften Deutschlands, München 22-27 Juni 1914*, Berlin, 1914, p. 197.

53. *Protokoll des SPD-Parteitages zu Bremen, 18-24 September 1904, mit Bericht der 3. Frauenkonferenz*, Berlin, 1904, pp. 360-370; StAH, S 1926: Clipping of *Reform*, 27 March 1890. For an interesting analysis of Clara Zetkin's pedagogical theories consult Karen Honeycutt, "Clara Zetkin."

54. Introduction to Adele Schreiber, *Mutterschaft: Ein Sammelwerk für die Probleme des Weibes als Mutter*, Munich, 1912, p. 3.

55. "Die Frauenfrage," *Sozialistische Monatshefte* 11, no. 3 (March 1905): 258-266. Fischer was not typical of the reform socialist stance.

56. Ibid., p. 258.

57. "Die Proletarische Frau und die Berufstätigkeit," *Sozialistische Monatshefte* 11, no. 1 (May 1905): 448.

58. Ibid., p. 446.

59. "Aus Krähwinkel," *Gleichheit*, 22 March 1905.

60. Ibid.

61. "Ehe und Sittlichkeit," 2 and 5, *Gleichheit*, 16 May 1906 and 8 August 1906.

62. "Aus Krähwinkel."

63. "Ehe und Sittlichkeit," 4, *Gleichheit*, 5 September 1906.

64. "Das Problem der Ehe," *Die Neue Gesellschaft*, 7 June 1905.

65. "Die Enthronung der Liebe," *Die Neue Gesellschaft*, 16 August 1905; "Die Ehe auf der Anklagebank," *Die Neue Gesellschaft*, 10 July 1907.

66. "Die Befreiung der Liebe," *Die Neue Gesellschaft*, 30 August 1905. For her position on maternity insurance see *Die Mutterschafts-Versicherung*, Berlin, 1906; also, *Pr. München, Frauenkonferenz, 1902*, p. 298.

67. "Die 'unterdruckte' Frau," *Die Neue Gesellschaft*, 18 July 1906.

68. "Sozialdemokratie und Volkserziehung," *Pr. Mannheim, 1906 Frauenkonferenz*, pp. 347-358; "Sozialistische Erziehung im Hause," *Protokoll des SPD-Parteitages zu Nürnberg, 13-19 September 1908 mit Bericht der 5. Frauenkonferenz*, Berlin, 1908, pp. 507-517.

69. Guenther Roth, *The Social Democrats in Imperial Germany*, pp. 315-316; R. P. Neuman, "The Sexual Question," p. 181.

70. Boxer, "Socialism Faces Feminism," p. 82.

CHAPTER V   CLARA ZETKIN, LILY BRAUN

1. "Proletarische und Bürgerliche Frauenbewegung," *Gleichheit*, 21 November 1900.

2. IISH, NL Kautsky, KD 23, Nr. 384, Stuttgart, 21 September 1901.

3. IISH, KD 23, Nr. 584, Berlin, 16 May 1895.

4. "Die Frauenrechtlerische Petition, das Vereins-und Versammlungsrecht des weiblichen Geschlechts betreffend," in *Clara Zetkin: Ausgewählte Reden*, 1:53-62; *Die Frauenbewegung*, 15 January 1894.

5. Section of a chapter on the relationship between socialist women and left-wing bourgeois feminist sent to the author by Richard J. Evans, University of East Anglia. Professor Evans is presently working on a book on the socialist women's movement in Imperial Germany, to be published by the Dietz Verlag.

6. Else Lüders, *Der "linke" Flügel*, pp. 15-27.

7. "Frauenrechtlerische Harmonieduselei," *Gleichheit*, 9 January 1895.

8. "Nach links und rechts," *Die Frauenbewegung*, 1 March 1895. For Zetkin's views see, "Frauenrechtlerische Harmonieduselei"; also, "Eine Antwort," *Gleichheit*, 3 April 1895, and "Kritik, keine Zustimmung; Mitleid, kein Vertrauen," *Gleichheit*, 17 April 1895.

9. Lüders, *Der "linke" Flügel*, p. 57. Lüders discusses the left-wing feminist position toward working women's organizations. Also, Helene Lange, *Lebenserinnerungen*, Berlin, 1921, pp. 221-223, for the official League position. Lange argues that the League did not admit socialist women's organizations because, under existing laws, they were illegal. She also maintains that the point was moot because socialist women were unwilling to join. For Braun's views see *Memoiren: Lehrjahre*, pp. 633-634.

10. Braun, *Memoiren: Lehrjahre*, p. 632.

11. *Gleichheit*, 29 August 1900 and 12 September 1900; *Pr. Mainz, 1900, Frauenkonferenz*, pp. 256-257; *Pr. München, 1902, Frauenkonferenz*, p. 294; "Die Frauenfrage auf dem Münchener Parteitag," *Sozialistische Monatshefte* 7, no. 2 (2 October 1902): 789; "Die Interessen der Arbeiterinnen und der Internationale Frauenkongress," *Correspondenzblatt*, 2 July 1904; *Die Frauenfrage: Ihre Geschichtliche Entwicklung und ihre wirtschaftliche Seite*, Leipzig, 1901, pp. 457-459.

12. *Pr. Mainz, 1900, Frauenkonferenz*, pp. 256-257.

13. "Wandlungen," *Gleichheit*, 5 December 1900. In this assessment, Braun was considerably ahead of her time. It has taken workers in the service sector until the post-1945 era in Europe and America to begin to see themselves as part of the working class rather than managerial group. Only in the 1950s and 1960s have, for example, clerks and teachers in large numbers taken a preliminary step and started forming unions for collective action.

14. "Die Wirtschaftsgenossenschaft: Eine Entgegnung," *Gleichheit*, 28 August 1901.

15. StAH, S 5883: Clipping of *Neue Hamburg Zeitung*, 21 March 1900; reports on Ihrer's activity in *Sozialistische Monatshefte* 7, no. 1 (March 1901): 235, and Anna Blos, *Die Frauenfrage im Lichte des Sozialismus*, p. 49.

16. BA, Kleine Erwerbungen, Nr. 129, Breslau, 1 November 1903.

17. FES, NL Gerda Weyl, TR 41/21, Klara Weyl, "Erinnerungen," p. 15.

18. Braun, *Memoiren: Kampfjahre*, p. 169.
19. IISH, KD 23, Nr. 313, 25 September 1896.
20. Ibid., and Braun, *Memoiren: Kampfjahre*, p. 171.
21. *Gleichheit*, 17 March 1897.
22. Ibid., "Die nächsten Aufgaben der deutschen Arbeiterinnen-bewegung."
23. "Kritische Bemerkungen zu Genossin Braun's Vorschlag," serialized over several issues of the paper, 17 March 1897, 31 March 1897, and 14 April 1897.
24. 31 March 1897.
25. 14 April 1897.
26. IISH, KD 23, Nr. 314, San Remo, 14 March 1897.
27. Ibid., Nr. 315, San Remo, 24 March 1897.
28. *Political Parties*, pp. 175-176.
29. Baader, *Lebenserinnerungen*, pp. 63-64; for her attitude toward "ladies" see, *Pr. München, 1902, Frauenkonferenz*, p. 293; consult, "Bahn Frei," *Gleichheit*, 20 April 1904; Klara Bohm-Schuch, "Unsere politische Werbearbeit," *Die Genossin*, February 1926; Marie Juchacz, *Sie Lebten für eine bessere Welt*, p. 57.
30. Braun, *Memoiren: Kampfjahre*, p. 546.
31. *Gleichheit*, 28 April 1897.
32. Ibid., 9 June 1897, 7 July 1897, and 21 July 1897.
33. "Die Frauenfrage auf dem Internationalen Kongress."
34. "Die Frauenfrage auf dem Münchener Parteitag," p. 789.
35. IISH, NL von Vollmar, Nr. 1006, Pankow, 8 September 1902. Ihrer's supporters were Martha Rohrlack, Berlin; Mathilde von Hofstellen; Lina Vogel, Gera; Helma Steinbach, Hamburg; and Auguste Bösse, Bremen. Also, *Pr. Munich 1902, Frauenkonferenz*, pp. 290-291.
36. "Die Frauen und das Organisationsstatut," *Die Neue Gesellschaft*, 20 September 1905; "Die Frauenfrage auf dem Münchener Parteitag," p. 791.
37. Julie Vogelstein, "Lily Braun: Ein Lebensbild," in *Lily Braun: Gesammelte Werke*, p. lxx; Clara Zetkin, "Der Parteitag zu Nürnberg," *Clara Zetkin: Ausgewählte Reden*, 1:454; *Pr. Nürnberg 1908, Frauenkonferenz*, p. 410, for Zietz's position.
38. *Memoiren: Kampfjahre*, p. 226.
39. Vogelstein, "Lily Braun," p. xvi; *Pr. Munich, 1902 SPD*, p. 298; Lily Braun, "Mutterschaftversicherung und Krankencassen," *Sozialistische Monatshefte* 9, no. 1 (April 1903): 265-277.
40. *Frauenfrage und Sozialdemokratie*, p. 14; "Die Ehe auf der Anklagebank," *Die Neue Gesellschaft*, 10 July 1907.

41. Braun, *Frauenarbeit und Hauswirtschaft*, Berlin, 1901, pp. 27, 30-31.

42. Braun, *Memoiren: Kampfjahre*, pp. 394-397; "Zur Frage der Wirtschaftsgenossenschaften," *Gleichheit*, 25 September 1901.

43. June 1901, pp. 469-471.

44. IISH, KD 23, Nr. 339, Stuttgart, 16 May 1901.

45. "Die Entgegnung zur Antwort," *Gleichheit*, 28 August 1901.

46. Consult the following issues of *Gleichheit*: 19 June 1901, 3 July 1901, 17 July 1901, and 31 July 1901.

47. *Gleichheit*, 28 August 1901.

48. *Zwischen Reformismus und Bolschewismus: Der Austromarxismus als Theorie und Praxis*, Vienna, 1968, p. 211.

49. Ibid., p. 208.

50. Ibid., pp. 103, 209; Carl E. Schorske, *German Social Democracy*, p. 114; Hans-Josef Steinberg, *Sozialismus und Deutsche Sozialdemokratie*. Steinberg explains the fatalistic or passive attitude by the intellectual marriage of Marxism and Darwinism. Also, Dieter Groh, *Negative Integration*.

51. By 1910, when the political divisions had crystallized, Zetkin was not in Kautsky's camp. In 1906, she had spoken out strongly against "fatalism" in her speech on "Volkserziehung," in *Pr Mannheim, 1906, Frauenkonferenz*, p. 356. Contrast Zetkin's response to the spontaneous outcry in 1910 over the German government's failure to institute suffrage reform, with Kautsky's. While Kautsky called for a policy of attrition, Zetkin and Luxemburg advocated action to "build up the revolutionary spirit" even if this sacrificed the organization. For these differences see Schorske, *German Social Democracy*, pp. 183-185. Furthermore, Zetkin never called "reform a revolutionary act"—which is characteristic of those whom Leser analyzes falling between bolshevism and reformism. He labels them generically "Austro-Marxists," but includes Kautsky in their ranks. See Leser, *Zwischen Reformismus*, p. 211. Also, Karen Honeycutt, "Clara Zetkin," who sees Zetkin as the embodiment of "revolutionary will." That Zetkin, sharing with radicals certain assumptions about the relationship between reform and revolution, adopted at times a fatalistic attitude is exemplified by her position on household cooperatives.

52. *Memoiren: Kampfjahre*, p. 230.

53. *Gewerkschaftliche Frauenzeitung*, 14 March 1917; *Gleichheit*, 14 February 1920.

54. August Bebel, "Zwei literarische Erzeugnisse über die

Frauenfrage," *Neue Zeit* 20, no. 2 (1902): 293, 301; Ledebour, "Die Frauenfrage," *Gleichheit*, 16 July 1902 and 30 July 1902.

55. Braun, *Memoiren: Kampfjahre*, pp. 233, 407.

56. FES, Briefe und Dokumente, TR 83/15, 25 May 1907; TR 83/16, 28 June 1907.

57. IISH, KD 23, Nr. 348, Stuttgart, 29 September 1901. Braun's work is a solid, factual analysis of the women's question stressing the economic and historical aspects of the problem, i.e., women's social position up to the nineteenth century, changes wrought by industrialization, and the distribution of women in the labor force in the late nineteenth century. This provides a context for a short discussion of both the middle-class and socialist women's movements. Braun consistently underplays the role of individuals—both socialist and bourgeois—and, in fact, does not credit Zetkin with the leading position in the socialist women's movement. Her book is not a propaganda tract, although she presents her particular interpretation of the orientation of the socialist women's movement. Her emphasis is not on the organized movement, but rather on the position of women in German society.

58. Ibid., Nr. 350, 9 December 1901.

59. Ibid., also, Nr. 349, 8 November 1901.

60. IISH, Kleine Korrespondenz, D, German Socialists, Zetkin to Richard Fischer, Stuttgart, 16 June 1900 and 9 November 1900.

61. Ibid., Braun to Fischer, Paris, 8 November 1900 and 16 November 1900; Berlin, 21 April 1901. IISH, NL August Bebel, B 71/1, Berlin, 2 March 1903.

62. NL Bebel, B 183/4, Stuttgart, 6 October 1903. NL Kautsky, KD 23, Nr. 366, Berlin, 21 August 1905 shows Zetkin's determination to prevent Braun's rehabilitation in the Party; she brought to Kautsky's attention the fact that a temporary replacement for the editor in Stuttgart published an article of Braun. Zetkin wanted Kautsky to use his influence to prevent such occurrences.

63. Joseph Joos, *Die sozialdemokratische Frauenbewegung in Deutschland*, M. Gladbach, 1912, pp. 21-26; Anna Blos, *Die Frauenfrage*, p. 37; Werner Thönnessen, *The Emancipation of Women*, London, 1973, p. 61. Also, Jacqueline Strain, "Feminism and Political Radicalism in the German Social Democratic Movement," pp. 143-144, states that Braun seriously challenged Zetkin's leadership; Honeycutt, "Clara Zetkin," pp. 311ff., devotes only a short section to the Zetkin-Braun controversy.

64. *Political Parties*, p. 176.

65. Ibid., pp. 174-175.

66. Ibid., pp. 178-179.

67. For Zetkin, *Protokoll des SPD-Parteitages zu Berlin, 14-21 November 1892*, Berlin, 1892, p. 277; for Braun, *Protokoll des SPD-Parteitages zu Hannover, 9-14 Oktober 1899*, Berlin, 1899, p. 283.

68. IISH, NL von Vollmar, V 2777, Stuttgart, 24 January 1894.

69. Ibid., Stuttgart, 25 January 1894.

70. *Memoiren: Kampfjahre*, pp. 326-327; "Abseits vom Wege," *Die Neue Gesellschaft*, 24 July 1907.

71. *Memoiren: Kampfjahre*, pp. 314-315.

72. Ibid., p. 507.

73. StAP, Pr. Br. Rep. 30, Berlin C, Tit. 95, Sek. 8, Nr. 16082, Bl. 68: Police record of Lily Braun, 17 November 1907; FES, Briefe und Dokumente, TR 83/14: Copy of a letter from Braun to the Executive Committee of the Charlottenburg Electoral District and to the Central Executive Committee of the Reichstag Electoral District of Teltow-Beeskow, 7 December 1907.

PART C   FEMINIST TACTICS IN GERMAN SOCIAL DEMOCRACY

1. Zetkin believed that the principle of equality did not imply that human beings would act similarly but only that each individual would have the same rights to fully develop to the best of his or her capacity. See "Das Prinzip der Gleichberechtigung der Frau und der gesetzliche Arbeiterinnenschutz," *Gleichheit*, 20 September 1893; *Zur Frage des Frauenwahlrechts*, Berlin, 1907, p. 11; her speech "Frauenstimmrecht," in *Pr. Mannheim, 1906, Frauenkonferenz*, p. 445. For Zietz's view see *Gewinnung und Schulung der Frau für die politische Betätigung*, Berlin, 1914, p. 19; "Die Sozialdemokratische Frauenbewegung Deutschlands," *Neue Zeit* 30, no. 2 (13 September 1912), p. 919.

CHAPTER VI   PARTY POLITICS

1. StAN, 2923: Clipping of *Fränkische Tagespost*, 29 December 1906.

2. *Pr. Mainz, 1900, SPD*, p. 143.

3. Sheila Rowbotham, *Women, Resistance and Revolution*, pp. 60-61; Juliet Mitchell, *Women's Estate*, pp. 76-81.

4. StAH, S 1909: Clipping of *Fachzeitung für Schneider*, 29 April 1899.

5. The analysis permeates socialist literature. See, for example,

Adolf Braun, *Die Arbeiterinnen und die Gewerkschaften*, Berlin, 1913, pp. 3-9; Lily Braun, "Probleme der Frauenarbeit," *Die Neue Gesellschaft*, 12 September 1906; also, *Correspondenzblatt*, 14 August 1898.

6. *Protokoll des SPD-Parteitages zu Halle, 12-18 Oktober 1890*, Berlin, 1890, pp. 114-115. The practice of admitting women delegates to socialist congresses goes back to the Gotha Congress of 1875.

7. *Pr. Berlin, 1892, SPD*, p. 146.

8. *Protokoll des SPD-Parteitages zu Frankfurt, 21-27 Oktober 1894*, Berlin, 1894, p. 174.

9. *Pr. Nürnberg, 1908, Frauenkonferenz*, p. 446

10. StAP, Pr. Br. Rep. 30, Berlin C, Tit. 95, Sek. 8, Nr. 16051, Bl. 54-55: In the police records of Ottilie Baader, August 1900.

11. *Pr. Mainz, 1900, Frauenkonferenz*, pp. 252-253.

12. *Pr. München, 1902, Frauenkonferenz*, pp. 292-294.

13. *Pr. Görlitz, 1921, SPD*, p. 68.

14. ZStA, RMdI, Nr. 13689, Bl. 13-14.

15. On the consumer boycotts see *Pr. Nürnberg, 1908, SPD*, p. 108.

16. StAP, Pr. Br. Rep. 30, Berlin C, Tit. 95, Sek. 8, Nr. 16051, Bl. 26; Tit. 95, Sek. 5, Nr. 14968, Bl. 452-456: Police survey of the women's movement of Social Democracy, December 1898.

17. Consult the following issues of *Gleichheit*; for Ihrer, 8 August 1894; Zietz, 25 April 1900 and 14 December 1904; Grünberg, 1 June 1904.

18. *Pr. Mannheim, 1906, Frauenkonferenz*, p. 408.

19. "Aus der Bewegung," *Gleichheit*, 8 July 1896, 14 April 1897, 28 March 1900, and 14 June 1907; for Zetkin's difficulties see StAL, F 201, Nr. 627, correspondence between Clara Zetkin and the Stuttgart police; also, StAH, S 1909, Die Polizeibehörde, Abt. 2, 1894, pp. 9-28, lengthy correspondence with Hamburg officials over the issue of using the name "Zetkin." Had Clara legally married Ossip, she would have lost her German citizenship since the law transferred citizenship of the husband onto the wife.

20. "Aus der Bewegung," *Gleichheit*, 1892, 1894, and 1899-1900.

21. For information on the committees see *Gleichheit*, 18 January 1899. The first committee, founded by Berlin women in May 1898, was comprised of Frauen Schneider, Rohrlach, Thiede, Lutz, Bauschke, Mesch, Frls. Baader and Haase, as well as Rud. Millarg, representing the trade union bureau. Ihrer joined later and wrote the annual report. StAP, Pr. Br. Rep. 30. Berlin C, Tit. 95, Sek. 5, Nr. 14968, Bl. 455. In 1902, women had set up similar committees in

Leipzig, Dresden, and Düsseldorf. See *Pr. München, 1902, SPD,* pp. 39-40.

22. Luise Zietz, *Kinderarbeit, Kinderschutz und die Kinderschutzkommissionen,* Berlin, 1912, pp. 36-53; "Kinderschutz und dessen Handhabung," *Neue Zeit* 22, no. 1 (1903-1904): 705-708; "Die Wirksamkeit des Kinderschutzgesetzes," *Neue Zeit* 24, no. 1 (1905-1906): 587-594; ZStA, RMdI, Nr. 13689, Bl. 283-284, 324-325: Yearly reports for 1910 and 1911 prepared by the police on the activity of the SPD.

23. ZStA, RMdI, Nr. 13689, Bl. 161-162: As contained in the 1908 yearly report on the SPD.

24. Ibid.

25. *Pr. Nürnberg, 1908, Frauenkonferenz,* pp. 501-502; StAP, Pr. Br. Rep. 30, Berlin C, Tit. 95, Sek. 7, Nr. 15850, Bl. 137: Police report, September 1911.

26. *Pr. Nürnberg, 1908, Frauenkonferenz,* p. 490; StAP, Pr. Br. Rep. 30, Berlin C, Tit. 95, Sek. 7, Nr. 15850, Bl. 135-36.

27. ZStA, RMdI, Nr. 13689, Bl. 161-162.

28. Ibid., Bl. 128, for the membership in 1907 and Bl. 324-325 for the 1911 figure. Police estimated that around 1907, there were 120,000 unionized females, 10,500 female members of political organizations, and 10,320 members of ninety-four educational clubs in those areas that forbade women's political participation.

29. *Pr. Jena, 1911, Frauenkonferenz,* p. 417.

30. StAP, Pr. Br. Rep. 30, Berlin C, Tit. 95, Sek. 7, Nr. 15850/1, Bl. 114, 131; Nr. 15852, Bl. 123-124: Meeting of female functionaries in the third electoral district of Berlin, September 1912.

31. Dieter Groh, *Negative Integration,* p. 144.

32. ZStA, RMdI, Nr. 13689, Bl. 410-411: Survey for 1912; StAP, Pr. Br. Rep. 30, Berlin C, Tit. 95, Sek. 7, Nr. 15850/1, Bl. 6-7, 66.

33. For more information on this evolution see chapter nine of this work, particularly the section on "Marie Juchacz and the Second Generation Female Leadership."

34. ZStA, RMdI, Nr. 13689, Bl. 247, 283-284, 324-325, 410-411, 467-468: Survey of socialist activity between 1909 and 1913.

35. Police reports clearly indicate that male comrades hesitated to accord women positions of authority, even though by 1912, 646 localities had women on the executive committees as was required by statute. Ibid., particularly Bl. 247 and 410-411; also, *Protokoll des SPD-Parteitages zu Leipzig, 12-18 September 1909,* Berlin, 1909, p. 386.

36. *Gleichheit,* 31 January 1910.

37. Ibid., 14 March 1910.

38. Ibid., 11 April 1910.

39. Ibid.

40. Future advocates of majority socialism such as Elise Jensen supported Clara Zetkin. See the following issues: 25 April, 9 and 23 May, and 6 June 1910.

41. *August Bebels Briefwechsel mit Karl Kautsky*, ed. Karl Kautsky, Jr., Assen, 1971, pp. 227, 353, Nr. 168, 16 August 1910 and Nr. 301, 18 July 1913.

42. Zetkin's position is found in the following issues of *Gleichheit*, 11 April 1910, 9 May 1910, and 23 May 1910.

43. FES, NL Dittmann, TR 01/140, 5 July 1910.

44. *Die Frau und Die Gesellschaft*, Leipzig, 1974, pp. 11, 28. The term *Fabrikmensch* was applied derogatorily to women in factories around the mid-nineteenth century.

45. Werner Thönnessen, *The Emancipation of Women*, pp. 15-16.

46. Reinhold Jaeckel, *Die Stellung des Sozialismus zur Frauenfrage im 19. Jahrhundert*, Potsdam, 1904, pp. 136-137; Lion, *Zur Soziologie der Frauenbewegung*, Berlin, 1926, p. 18; Thönnessen, *The Emancipation of Women*, pp. 16-26, 28-29.

47. StAL, F 201, Nr. 638, Bl. 1: Police report 23 February 1886.

48. StAP, Pr. Br. Rep. 30, Berlin C, Tit. 95, Sek. 5, Nr. 14966, Bl. 16: Clipping of *Deutsche Hausfrauen-Zeitung*, 6 September 1885.

49. StAL, F 201, Nr. 638, Bl. 2: Meeting on 7 August 1889 of the Stuttgart Association for Working Women; StAP, Nr. 14966, Bl. 105.

50. ZStA, RMdI, Nr. 13687, Bl. 26-36. Women could attend political gatherings not directly sponsored by a political club.

51. "Jugend und Sozialismus," *Gleichheit*, 9 August 1905; StAH, S 5883: Clipping of supplement to *Vorwärts*, 14 December 1901; *Pr. Bremen, 1904, Frauenkonferenz*, p. 339.

52. StAP, Pr. Br. Rep. 30, Berlin C, Tit. 95, Sek. 7, Nr. 15852, Bl. 64-65, 168-169, 222.

53. ZStA, RMdI, Nr. 13689, Bl. 128: Police survey for 1906/07.

54. "Die deutsche Sozialdemokratie," pp. 534-535.

55. Guenther Roth, *The Social Democrats in Imperial Germany*, pp. 159-160, 315-316. The German socialist women's movement conforms to Roth's theoretical framework; it was part of a subculture, separate from yet connected to the dominant society. Thus, socialist women's feminism was a blend of radical ideas infused with traditional notions. Its world view and association with the socialist movement dampened the emergence of a direct critique of working-

class family life, and the movement did stress the importance of women's traditional roles as wives, mothers, and educators of children *for socialism*. These are important themes in women leaders' speeches, pamphlets, and papers. This should not detract, however, from its notable contribution to feminist thought nor obscure the fact that the movement symbolized significant changes in attitudes about women's proper functions.

56. *Aus Meinem Leben*, Stuttgart, 1914, 1: 186; also, Barbara Stolterfaht's review of Thönnessen, *Frauenemancipation*, in *Internationale wissenschaftliche Korrespondenz*, nos. 11/12 (April 1971), pp. 93-94.

57. "Julie Bebel," *Neue Zeit* 29, no. 1 (2 December 1910): 276-277.

58. Gertrud Bäumer, *Die Frau in Volkswirtschaft*, pp. 22-25. Perhaps socialist history can offer a corrective to social history. Shorter and Stearns leave the reader with an impression of the emergence of new family relationships, greater equality, as well as female emancipation around the end of the nineteenth century. See Edward Shorter, "Female Emancipation, Birth Control and Fertility in European History," pp. 605-640; Peter N. Stearns, "Adaptation to Industrialization," pp. 326-327. This assessment is overdrawn in light of the evidence that clearly documents the various constraints on girls' and women's development in working-class homes—whether politically organized or not.

59. *Pr. Görlitz, 1921, SPD*, p. 186. Working-class women tended to vote nonsocialist. See chapter nine of this work.

60. FES, Personen-Sammlung, Marie Juchacz, "Parteitag 1952."

CHAPTER VII   PARTY AND UNIONS

1. StAP, Pr. Br. Rep. 30, Berlin C, Tit. 95, Sek. 5, Nr. 14966, Bl. 131-134, 135-137, 146: 1886.

2. Paul Umbreit, *25 Jahre Deutscher Gewerkschaftsbewegung 1890-1915*, Berlin, 1915, pp. 2-26; Karl Zwing, *Geschichte der deutschen freien Gewerkschaften*, Jena, 1926, pp. 149-150; *Protokoll der Verhandlungen des ersten Kongresses der Gewerkschaften Deutschlands, Halberstadt 14-18 März 1892*, Berlin, 1892, p. 43; *Protokoll der Verhandlungen des zweiten Kongresses der Gewerkschaften Deutschlands, Berlin 4-8 Mai 1896*, Berlin, 1896, pp. 50, 121; *Gleichheit*, 6 April 1892.

3. G.G.L. Alexander, *Aus Clara Zetkins Leben und Werk*, p. 25;

Verhandlungen des vierten ordentlichen Verbandstages des Verbands der Schneider-und Schneiderinnen, Eisenach 15-18 Juli 1896, 1896, pp. 21-27; *Verhandlungen der zweiten Internationalen Schneider-Konferenz, London 3-4 August 1896,* 1896, p. 104; *Verhandlung der dritten Internationalen Schneider-Konferenz, Paris 20-23 September 1900,* 1900, p. 144; *Protokoll der Verhandlungen des vierten Kongresses der Gewerkschaften Deutschlands, Stuttgart 16-21, Juni 1902,* Berlin, 1902.

4. StAH, S 5883: Police reports on her activity in the *Zahlstelle* St. Georg; Verband der Fabrik-Land-Hülfsarbeiter-und Arbeiterinnen Deutschlands, *Protokoll des 8. ordentlichen Verbandstages in Leipzig, 5-11 August 1906,* Hanover, 1906, pp. 140, 144, 172; *Pr. Stuttgart, 1902, Gewerkschaften,* p. 111; *Gleichheit,* 1 February 1909; Wilhelmine Kähler, "Der Fabrikarbeiterverband," *Gleichheit,* 15 August 1910.

5. *Protokoll der Verhandlungen des fünften Kongresses der Gewerkschaften Deutschlands, Köln 22-27 Mai 1905,* Berlin, 1905, p. 127, emphasis added; "Bahn Frei," *Gleichheit,* 20 April 1904.

6. "Aus der Bewegung," *Gleichheit,* 7 May 1902, 27 August 1902, 1 January 1903, and 11 March 1903. Dieter Groh, *Negative Integration,* p. 71, raises the general problem of the "depoliticizing" (*Entpolitisierung*) of the trade unions and the "unionizing" (*Vergewerkschaftung*) of the Social Democratic Party.

7. *Pr. Mannheim, 1906, Frauenkonferenz,* pp. 414-430; *Pr. Gotha, 1896, SPD,* p. 161. For Social Democracy's ambivalance toward the peasantry and for Kautsky's views see Peter Gay, *The Dilemma of Democratic Socialism,* 1952; reprint ed., New York, 1962, pp. 198-204.

8. "Die Landarbeiterfrage," *Pr. Leipzig, 1906, Fabrik-Landarbeiter,* pp. 173-178; Verband der Fabrik-Land-Hülfsarbeiter-und Arbeiterinnen Deutschlands, *Protokoll des 9. ordentlichen Verbandstages in München, 2-8 August 1908,* Hanover, 1908, p. 131.

9. Ernst Friedrich Goldschmidt, *Heimarbeit: Ihre Entstehung und Ausartung,* Munich, 1913, pp. 6-21; "Hausindustrie und Heimarbeiterschutz: Die Wirtschaftliche Entwicklung der Heimarbeit," *Correspondenzblatt,* 20 February 1904; Oda Olberg, *Das Elend in der Hausindustrie der Konfektion,* Leipzig, 1896, p. 22.

10. *Gleichheit,* 19 October 1892; *Protokoll des SPD-Parteitages zu Berlin, 14-21 November 1892,* Berlin, 1892, p. 24.

11. *Vorwärts,* 9 January 1896 and 28 February 1896; Ottilie Baader, *Lebenserinnerungen,* p. 58.

12. *Vorwärts*, 23 January 1896; *Pr. Eisenach, 1896, Schneider-Kongress*, pp. 6-7; *Correspondenzblatt*, 9 December 1895.

13. *Protokoll der Verhandlungen des ersten Allgemeinen Heimarbeiterschutz-Kongresses, Berlin 7-9 März 1904*, Berlin, 1904, p. 26.

14. *Vorwärts*, 22 January 1896, 14 February 1896, and 20 February 1896.

15. *Vorwärts*, 23 February 1896; *Pr. Eisenach, 1896 Schneider-Kongress*, p. 7; *Verhandlungen des zweiten Internationalen Schneider-Konferenz*, pp. 98-100.

16. *Verhandlungen des 5. ordentlichen Verbandstages des Verbands der Schneider-und Schneiderinnen, Mannheim 24-27 August 1898*, 1898, p. 41.

17. *Das Arbeiter-Elend in der Konfektions-Industrie vor dem Deutschen Reichstag: Stenographischer Bericht über die Verhandlungen vom 12 February 1896*, Berlin, 1896, pp. 1-5, 47-48.

18. Max Schippel, *Sozialdemokratisches Reichstags-Handbuch*, Berlin, n.d., pp. 594–598.

19. *Vorwärts*, 13 February 1896 and 18 February 1896.

20. *Pr. Mannheim, 1898, Schneider-Verbandstag*, pp. 5-7.

21. *Gleichheit*, 24 February 1904.

22. StAH, S 5883: Clipping of *Der Konfektionsarbeiter*, 18 August 1901; Emma Ihrer, "Die Aufgabe der Frau im Kampf gegen die Heimarbeit," *Sozialistische Monatshefte* 10, no. 1 (March 1904): 194-199.

23. *Pr. Heimarbeiterschutz-Kongress*, pp. 1, 41.

24. "Der allgemeine deutsche Heimarbeiterschutz-Kongress," *Correspondenzblatt*, 19 March 1904; Else Lüders, "Arbeiterinnenorganisation und Frauenbewegung," *Sozialer Fortschrift*, no. 30, Leipzig, 1904, p. 9; *Gleichheit*, 24 February 1904 and 23 March 1904.

25. *Correspondenzblatt*, 11 March 1905, 20 January 1906, 28 April 1906, and 2 April 1910; Gertrud Hanna, "Warum müssen die Arbeiterinnen Sozialistinnen sein," *Die Genossin*, May 1930.

26. *Pr. Heimarbeiterschutz-Kongress*, p. 23; *Illustriertes Konversations-Lexikon der Frau*, Berlin, 1900, 1: 160.

27. Emma Ihrer, "Zur Lage der Arbeiterinnen in der Berliner Blumen-Blätter-und Putzfederindustrie," *Gleichheit*, 5 June 1901; "Hausindustrie und Heimarbeit bei der Fabrikation künstlicher Blumen und Federn," in *Pr. Heimarbeiterschutz-Kongress*, pp. 186-189; *Illustriertes Konversations-Lexikon der Frau*, p. 160.

28. "Die Hungerpeitsche der Blumenarbeiterinnen," *Gleichheit*, 8 March 1905; Luise Zietz, "Zur Geschichte der Blumen-und Blattfabrikation in Sebnitz," *Gleichheit*, 16 November 1904; Emma Ihrer, "Fachschule und obligatorische Fortbildungsschule," *Correspondenzblatt*, 3 April 1909.

29. Zentralverband der in der Blumen, Blätter, Palmen und Putzfederfabrikation beschäftigten Arbeiter und Arbeiterinnen, *Protokoll des vierten Verbandstages, Berlin 25-27 Mai 1911*, 1911, p. 1; Emma Ihrer, "Zur Organisation der Arbeiter in der Federn-Blumen-und Blätter Industrie," *Correspondenzblatt*, 10 June 1901; "Konferenz der Blumen-Blätter-Federarbeiterinnen Deutschlands," *Correspondenzblatt*, 2 December 1901. Impetus for the founding of the union arose because the workers had been organized in the Transport Union, which, by the turn of the century, was no longer willing to assist the leaf workers.

30. *Correspondenzblatt*, 4 June 1904.

31. "Der Bezug künstlicher Blumen für Maifeste und andere Veranstaltungen," *Correspondenzblatt*, 1 March 1913.

32. Zentralverein für alle in der Hut und Filzwarenindustrie beschäftigten Arbeiter-und Arbeiterinnen, *Protokoll der Zehnten ordentlichen Generalversammlung, Altenburg 6-11 Juni 1910*, 1910, pp. 13, 24, 52-53, 62-64.

33. ZStA, RMdI, Nr. 15690, Bl. 15-22.

34. "Zur Frauenkonferenz," 12 September 1900.

35. HHStA, Abt. 407, Nr. 163, Bl. 274. "Cartels" were umbrella organizations coordinating the activity of various unions in one locality.

36. *Pr. Bremen, 1904, Frauenkonferenz*, p. 342.

37. "Dringende Aufgaben," in *Clara Zetkin: Ausgewählte Reden*, 1: 272-279.

38. *Pr. Jena, 1911, Frauenkonferenz*, p. 431.

39. *Pr. München, 1902, Frauenkonferenz*, pp. 297, 299; "Die Frauenkonferenz zu München," *Gleichheit*, 24 September 1902; "Die Thätigkeit der Berliner Mittelspersonen zwischen Arbeiterinnen und Fabrikinspection," *Gleichheit*, 18 January 1899.

40. *Pr. Jena, 1911, Frauenkonferenz*, pp. 431-432.

41. "Die Frauenkonferenz zu Mainz," *Gleichheit*, 26 September 1900.

42. The *Gesindeordnung* forbade strikes or collective bargaining, required that servants accord masters "respect and diffidence" and accept patriarchal discipline, governed work hours, conditions of

employment, notice, and prescribed mandatory service records. Protective legislation, including those governing child labor, excluded servants. Helene Grünberg, "Agitation unter den Dienstboten," *Protokoll der Verhandlungen des 6. Kongresses der Gewerkschaften Deutschlands, Hamburg, 22-27 Juni 1908*, Berlin, 1908, pp. 165-174; Helene Grünberg, "Die Dienstbotenbewegung," *Pr. Mannheim, 1906, Frauenkonferenz*, pp. 430-433; Max Schippel, *Handbuch*, pp. 494-502.

43. Emma Ihrer, "Unsere Hausangestellten," *Sozialistische Monatshefte* 14, no. 2 (20 August 1908): 1074; Helene Grünberg, "Fortbildung, Unterhaltung, Geselligkeit," *Protokoll der Verhandlung des ersten Verbandstages des Zentralverbandes der Hausangestellten Deutschlands, Berlin 14-16 April 1912*, Berlin, 1912, pp. 70-71.

44. Louise Kähler, "25 Jahre Hausangestelltenbewegung," *Die Genossin*, April 1931; Helene Grünberg, "Zur Frage der Dienstbotenbewegung," *Correspondenzblatt*, 17 November 1906. Since servants could not strike or engage in collective bargaining, the employment agency became the lifeblood of the new union. It brought girls and employers together and imposed better work conditions such as higher wages, warm sanitary rooms, adequate food, and free Sunday afternoons. Grünberg took employers to court if they failed to fulfill their obligations.

45. "Eine Dienstbotenbewegung in Nürnberg," *Gleichheit*, 1 January 1904.

46. *Pr. Mannheim, 1906, Frauenkonferenz*, pp. 430-434.

47. Consult the following issues of *Gleichheit*: Fürth: 16 May 1906; Munich: 30 May 1906; Cologne: 25 July 1906; Bremen: 20 February 1907; Hamburg: 14 November 1906; Kiel: 21 December 1908; Mannheim: 27 May 1907, 2 March 1908 and 11 May 1908; Wiesbaden: 17 February 1908; also, ZStA, RMdI, Nr. 13689, Bl. 161-162: Survey of socialist activity for 1908; *19. Jahres-und Kassen-Bericht der Berliner Gewekschafts-Kommission und Bericht des Sekretariats Berlin pro 1907*, Berlin, 1908, p. 15.

48. The contract was reprinted in *Correspondenzblatt*, 17 November 1906.

49. "Zur Frage der Dienstbotenbewegung," *Correspondenzblatt*, 17 November 1907; *Gleichheit*, 28 November 1906.

50. *Gleichheit*, 14 November 1906 and 12 December 1906.

51. *Gleichheit*, 12 December 1906; *Correspondenzblatt*, 17 November 1906.

52. Hamburg and Jena: *Gleichheit* 3 April 1907; for the response of, for example, Frankfurt: 1 May 1907; Munich: 20 February 1907; and Berlin: 23 January 1907.

53. "Die Dienstbotenkonferenz," *Correspondenzblatt*, 9 November 1907; *13. Jahresbericht des Arbeiter-Sekretariats Nürnberg für das Jahr 1907*, Nuremberg, 1908, p. 76.

54. *Gleichheit*, 11 November 1907.

55. Luise Zietz, "Die Berliner Frauenkonferenz," *Gleichheit*, 9 December 1907; *Pr. Nürnberg, 1908, SPD*, pp. 102-103.

56. Seymour M. Lipset, *Political Man: The Social Bases of Politics*, New York, 1960, p. 215.

57. "Zehn Jahre Freie Dienstbotenbewegung," *Gleichheit*, 14 April 1916; *Pr. Berlin, Hausangestellte, 1912*, pp. 10-14.

58. *Pr. München, 1914, Gewerkschaften*, pp. 198-199.

59. *Pr. Nürnberg, 1908, Frauenkonferenz*, pp. 504-505.

60. "Zur sozialdemokratischen Frauenkonferenz in Bremen," *Sozialistische Monatshefte* 10, no. 2 (September 1904): 763-765.

61. "Einrichtung und Ausgestaltung der Sozialdemokratischen Frauenkonferenz," *Sozialistische Monatshefte* 17, no. 3 (7 September 1911): 1248-1250.

62. FES, NL Gerda Weyl, Tr 41/5.

63. *Correspondenzblatt*, 27 June 1908; *Gleichheit*, 25 May 1908.

64. *Correspondenzblatt*, 1 August 1898 and 28 November 1914.

65. Norbert Soldon, "British Women's Trade Unionism, 1874-1931," paper presented to the December 1977 meeting of the American Historical Association in Dallas, p. 2; William L. O'Neill, *The Woman Movement*, Chicago, 1969, pp. 66-67.

66. *Correspondenzblatt*, 28 November 1914; also Gertrud Hanna, "Die Arbeiterin in der Gewerkschaftsbewegung," *Sozialistische Monatshefte* 19, no. 3 (30 October 1913): 1332-1338.

67. *Correspondenzblatt*, 15 August 1903.

68. *Correspondenzblatt*, 28 November 1914; Gertrud Hanna, "Die Frauenerwerbsarbeit im Deutschen Reiche nach den Ergebnissen der Berufszählungen von 1882-1907," *Statistische Beilage des Correspondenzblatt*, 27 April 1912, pp. 61-100.

CHAPTER VIII   WOMEN'S SOCIALIST EDUCATION

1. *Gleichheit*, 6 April 1892.

2. Ibid.

3. *Gleichheit*, 1 February 1899; Anna Blos, *Die Frauenfrage*, p. 41.

4. *Pr. Mainz, 1900, Frauenkonferenz*, pp. 255-256.

5. "Die Frauenkonferenz in Mainz," *Gleichheit*, 12 September 1900.

6. *Jahres-Bericht der vereinigten Vorstände der drei Sozialdemokratischen Vereine und Einzelberichte: Geschäftsjahr 1908-09*, Hamburg, 1909, p. 24; Zietz's pamphlet, *Gewinnung und Schulung der Frau für die politische Betätigung*, Berlin, 1914, pp. 14-15; Sozialdemokratischer Kreisverein des 1. Württemberg Reichstagswahlkreis, *Tätigkeitsbericht für die Zeit 1 Juli 1911-30 Juni 1912*, Stuttgart, 1912, p. 17; for Baader's activity in the educational movement, *Frauen-Beilage der Leipziger Volkszeitung*, 13 July 1917.

7. *Dreizehnter Jahresbericht des Arbeiter-Sekretariats Nürnberg für das Jahr 1907*, Nuremberg, 1908, pp. 63-64; *Vierzehnter Jahresbericht des Arbeiter-Sekretariats Nürnberg für das Geschäftsjahr 1908*, Nuremberg, 1909, pp. 64-65; *Gleichheit*, 2 September 1907, 25 November 1907, 6 December 1909, and 19 December 1910; *Sechszehnter Jahresbericht vom Arbeiter-Sekretariat in Nürnberg für 1910*, Nuremberg, 1911, p. 59.

8. Marie Juchacz, "Einst und Jetzt," *Gleichheit*, 9 October 1920; *Gleichheit*, 7 December 1908, for the composition of the child-labor committee; also, StAP, Pr. Br. Rep. 30, Berlin C, Tit. 95, Sek. 7, Nr. 15852, Bl. 24, 139-140.

9. *Pr. Nürnberg, 1908, Frauenkonferenz*, p. 485.

10. Ibid., p. 487; also, "Frauenbildungsvereine," *Gleichheit*, 17 August 1908.

11. After the anti-Socialist laws lapsed, Baader, as seen, had been elected to the executive committee of the Berlin Workers' Educational School (*Arbeiterbildungsschule*) and throughout the 1890s encouraged women to participate in its program. See Emma Ihrer, *Die Organisation der Arbeiterinnen Deutschlands*, pp. 8-11; *Gleichheit*, 1 April 1921.

12. *Protokoll des SPD-Parteitages zu Magdeburg, 18-24 September 1910*, Berlin, 1910, p. 49.

13. StAP, Pr. Br. Rep. 30, Berlin C, Tit. 95, Sek. 5, Nr. 14968, Bl. 94.

14. StAP, Pr. Br. Rep. 30, Berlin C, Tit. 95, Sek. 7, Nr. 15852, Bl. 1-3: Notes 14-20 are from police records of the Social Democratic Women's and Girls' Educational Sessions in Greater Berlin, 1904-1915.

15. Ibid., Bl. 5, 25–26.

16. Ibid., Bl. 32-33, 75-76, 109-110.

17. Ibid., Bl. 25-26: Clipping of *Vorwärts*, 12 September 1907; also, 39-40.

18. Ibid., Bl. 48, 146 for the male leadership; on attendance, 7-8, 32-33, 37-38, 137-138, 109-110, 168-69.

19. Ibid., Bl. 30, 35-36.

20. Ibid., Bl. 56-57.

21. *Pr. Görlitz, 1921, SPD*, pp. 48-49.

22. StAP, Pr. Br. Rep. 30, Berlin C, Tit. 95, Sek. 7, Nr. 15850/1 Bl. 234.

23. StAP, Nr. 15852, Bl. 48: Clipping of *Mitteilungsblatt*, 11 May 1910.

24. For an assessment of the Frankfurt educational club, see HHStA, Abt. 407, Nr. 164, Bl. 5: Clipping of *Volksstimme*, 17 October 1902; for Dortmund, consult Ralf Lützenkirchen, *Der sozialdemokratische Verein*, p. 117.

25. StAP, Pr. Br. Rep. 30, Berlin C, Tit. 95, Sek. 7, Nr. 15852, Bl. 61-62, 75-76.

26. Ibid., Bl. 71, 137-138, 202-203.

27. ZStA, RMdI, Nr. 13689, Bl. 283-284: Survey of socialist activity for 1910.

28. StAP, Nr. 15852, Bl. 137-138. In the years immediately preceding the outbreak of World War I, there was a "general sense of sickness" and indifference in the socialist subculture, which these figures reflect. See Carl E. Schorske, *German Social Democracy*, pp. 257ff; also Dieter Groh, *Negative Integration*, pp. 202-203, 472.

29. StAP, Nr. 15852, Bl. 191-192.

30. Friedrich Stampfer in the introduction to her book, *Sie Lebten für eine bessere Welt*.

31. StAP, Nr. 15852, Bl. 215-216: Opinion of both the observing officials and the Social Democratic leadership.

32. ZStA, RMdI, Nr. 13689, Bl. 247: Survey of socialist activity for 1909.

33. StAP, Nr. 15852, Bl. 177.

34. Ibid., Bl. 202-203.

35. *Pr. Magdeburg, 1910, SPD*, p. 51; *Pr. Jena, 1911, SPD*, p. 78; *Pr. Leipzig, 1909, SPD*, p. 51.

36. Hertha Siemering, *Arbeiterbildungswesen in Wien und Berlin: Eine kritische Untersuchung*, Karlsruhe, 1911, pp. 166-167.

37. *Protokoll des SPD-Parteitages zu Chemnitz, 15-21 September 1912*, Berlin, 1912, p. 53.

38. In 1910 and 1912, see *Pr. Magdeburg, 1910, SPD*, p. 51; *Pr. Jena, 1913, SPD*, p. 38.

39. Siemering, *Arbeiterbildungswesen*, p. 168; Gertrud Hanna, "Was sollen die Arbeiterinnen lesen?" *Literatur-Beilage des Correspondenzblatt*, 18 January 1913, pp. 1-3.

40. Siemering, *Arbeiterbildungswesen*, pp. 130-158, 161-173.

41. *Pr. Jena, 1911, Frauenkonferenz*, p. 433; *Pr. Bremen, 1904, Frauenkonferenz*, p. 342.

42. *Pr. Jena, 1911, Frauenkonferenz*, pp. 433, 435.

43. *Pr. München, 1902, Frauenkonferenz*, p. 307.

44. *Pr. Chemnitz, 1912, SPD*, pp. 257-258.

45. "Die Frauenkonferenz in Mainz," *Gleichheit*, 12 September 1900.

46. *Pr. Jena, 1911, Frauenkonferenz*, p. 428; for the debate over *Gleichheit* see pp. 422-429.

47. Karen Honeycutt, "Clara Zetkin," pp. 297-298.

48. Guenther Roth, *The Social Democrats in Imperial Germany*, p. 160. For the difficulties in generating interest in books and education see pp. 232ff. Also, Hans U. Wehler, *Sozialdemokratie und Nationalstaat: die deutsche Sozialdemokratie und die Nationalitätenfragen in Deutschland von Karl Marx bis zum Ausbruch des Ersten Weltkrieges*, Würzburg, 1962. Wehler reaches a similar conclusion with respect to the spread of nationalistic values among the organized working class.

CHAPTER IX   WARTIME DIVISIONS

1. Dieter Groh, *Negative Integration*, pp. 718ff.

2. Gertrud Hanna, "Die Arbeiterinnen und der Krieg," in *Kriegs-Probleme der Arbeiterklasse*, Berlin, 1916, 20: 7-11; Gertrud Hanna, "Die Förderung der Frauenerwerbsarbeit durch den Krieg," *Sozialistische Monatshefte* 21, no. 2 (9 September 1915): 874; Renate Bridenthal, "Beyond *Kinder, Küche, Kirche*: Weimar Women at Work," *Central European History* 6, no. 2 (June 1973): 155-156.

3. *The Emancipation of Women*, p. 89.

4. Gerald D. Feldman, *Army, Industry, and Labor in Germany, 1914-1918*, Princeton, 1966, p. 117.

5. Ibid., pp. 108ff.

6. ZStA, RMdI, Nr. 13580, Bl. 177-179; StAP, Pr. Br. Rep. 30, Berlin C, Tit. 95, Sek. 7, Nr. 15852, Bl. 256-259; Nr. 15853, Bl. 14-15; HStAS, E 150, Nr. 2051, Bl. 227-228.

7. "Unsere Aufgaben in der Organisation," *Gleichheit*, 2 October 1914; Luise Zietz, *Die sozialdemokratischen Frauen und der Krieg*, Berlin, 1915, pp. 2-21.

8. StAH, S 5883: Clipping of *Berliner Volkszeitung*, 4 August 1914; Zietz, *Die sozialdemokratischen Frauen*, pp. 6-7.

9. FES, Personen-Sammlung, Marie Juchacz: Clipping of *Neuer Vorwärts*, 12 March 1954; *Gleichheit*, 4 September 1914; Zietz, *Die sozialdemokratischen Frauen*, p. 5.

10. *20. Jahresbericht des Arbeiter-Sekretariats Nürnberg: Geschäftsjahre 1914-1920*, Nuremberg, 1921, pp. 40-44.

11. "Brief an Heleen Ankersmit," in *Clara Zetkin: Ausgewählte Reden*, 1: 655-656.

12. StAP, Pr. Br. Rep. 30, Berlin C, Tit. 95, Sek. 7, Nr. 15851, Bl. 40-41, 64.

13. HStAS, E 150, Nr. 2051, Bl. 169.

14. Ibid., Bl. 255-256, 272; StAP, Nr. 15853, Bl. 24-25.

15. Werner Thönnessen, *The Emancipation of Women*, pp. 75-83; also, for example, Luise Dornemann, *Clara Zetkin: Leben und Wirken*, p. 304, who writes that most female functionaries joined the USPD.

16. *Frauen-Beilage der Leipziger Volkszeitung*, 13 July 1917; *Gleichheit*, 26 May 1916 and 23 June 1916; StAP, Nr. 15851, Bl. 97-98.

17. HStAS, E 46-48, Nr. 309a, 15233.

18. *Sonderbeilage der Gleichheit*, 20 July 1917.

19. *Protokoll des SPD-Parteitages zu Weimer 10-15 Juni 1919 mit Bericht der 7. Frauenkonferenz*, Berlin, 1919, pp. 463, 471, 484; FES, NL Gerda Weyl, TR 41/33-37: Clipping of *Freiheit*, 24 September 1922.

20. *Protokoll der Verhandlungen des zehnten Kongresses der Gewerkschaften Deutschlands, Nürnberg 30 Juni-5 Juli 1919*, Berlin, 1919, pp. 421-425; HStAS, E 150, Nr. 2051, Bl. 257-258, 322-325: Wartime surveys of socialist activity prepared for the war ministry by the "Bureau für Sozialpolitik," 10 January 1916, 14 August 1916.

21. StAP, Nr. 15838/1, Bl. 479-480.

22. *Gleichheit*, 11 May 1917.

23. StAH, S 5883: Clipping of *Leipziger Volkszeitung*, 3 March 1917; also, "Die Auseinandersetzung in der Sozialdemokratie," *Gleichheit*, 16 March 1917; StAP, Nr. 15851, Bl. 132-136.

24. HStAS, E 150, Nr. 2051, Bl. 257-258: Survey of socialist activity 10 January 1916; StAP, Nr. 15851, Bl. 76.

25. *Gleichheit*, 11 May 1917; *Frauen-Beilage der Leipziger Volkszeitung*, 13 July 1917; Thönnessen, *The Emancipation of Women*, p. 78, makes a similar point.

26. *Die Arbeiterbewegung im Wilhelminischen Reich*, Berlin, 1959, p. 220.

27. See Groh, *Negative Integration*, p. 288, for the ways in which emphasis on the parliamentary tactic hindered the employment of alternative strategies.

28. Gabriele Bremme, *Die Politische Rolle der Frau in Deutschland*, Göttingen, 1956, pp. 63-73.

29. The demobilization order found in Thönnessen, *The Emancipation of Women*, p. 91.

30. "Zur Frage der Entlassungen von Arbeiterinnen," *Gewerkschaftliche Frauenzeitung*, 21 May 1919; *Pr. Nürnberg, 1919 Gewerkschaften*, p. 412; Unabhängige Sozialdemokratische Partei Deutschlands, *Protokoll der Reichskonferenz vom November 30- December 6 1919 zu Leipzig, mit Bericht der Reichs-Frauen-Konferenz*, Berlin, 1919.

31. Thönnessen, *The Emancipation of Women*, pp. 95-97; Gertrud Hanna, "Die Frauenarbeit nach dem Krieg," *Sozialistische Monatshefte* 29 (23 May 1923): 280-288. Hanna's assessment might have been too rosy. See Bridenthal, "Beyond *Kinder, Küche, Kirche*," pp. 159-161.

32. The priority is reflected in police reports that surveyed USPD wartime activity. They indicate that women played a vital role in the series of strikes and demonstrations that wracked Germany in late 1917 and 1918. StAP, Nr. 15851, Bl. 313-314: Report of 22 February 1918.

33. For the concept of generation as a tool to analyzing historical change, see Ortega Y. Gasset, *The Modern Theme*, trans. James Cleugh, New York, 1961; also, Carl Mannheim, "The Problem of Generations," *Essays on the Sociology of Knowledge*, ed. Paul Kecskemeti, 1952; reprint ed., London, 1968, pp. 276-320.

34. "Unsere Frauen in der deutschen Nationalversammlung," *Gleichheit*, 28 February 1919; Hermann Hillger, *Hillgers Handbuch der Verfassunggebenden deutschen Nationalversammlung 1919*, Berlin, 1919; Franz Osterroth, *Biographisches Lexikon des Sozialismus*, vol. 1; Marie Juchacz, *Sie Lebten für eine bessere Welt*.

35. James Joll, *The Second International*, New York, 1966, p. 145.

36. The comparison is inexact because I was unable to locate the actual minutes of the 1917 women's conference; *Gleichheit* reported on only twenty-two out of the fifty participants.

37. *Pr. Jena, 1911, Frauenkonferenz*, p. 414.

38. "Wie es damals war," *Die Genossin*, November 1949.

39. "Die ersten Frauen im Parlament," *Die Genossin*, May 1949.

40. *Sonderbeilage der Gleichheit*, 20 July 1917.

41. *Protokoll des SPD-Parteitages zu Würzburg, 14-20 Oktober 1917*, Berlin, 1917, p. 265.

42. "Berufsarbeit und Politisches Interesse der Frau," *Sozialistische Monatshefte* 23, no. 2 (1 August 1917): 833.

43. *Pr. Görlitz, 1921, SPD*, p. 11.

44. "Notwendige Ergänzung," *Gleichheit*, 30 January 1901.

45. "Die Sozialdemokratische Frauenbewegung Deutschlands," *Neue Zeit* 30, no. 2 (13 September 1912): 919.

46. *Gleichheit*, 14 August 1911; also, "Kommunale Mitarbeit der Frau in Bayern," *Gleichheit*, 14 May 1913; Sozialdemokratischer Verein Nürnberg-Altdorf, *Jahres-Bericht 1 Juli 1912-31 März 1913*, Nuremberg, 1913, p. 26; Anna Blos, *Die Frauenfrage*, pp. 80-81.

47. Interview with John Caspari, San Francisco, California, 4 August 1972.

48. Arbeiterwohlfahrt Library, Bonn, Germany, AW III, 13; Marie Juchacz, "Die Arbeiterwohlfahrt bis 1933," *Die Genossin*, December 1949; *Pr. Görlitz, 1921, SPD*, p. 18.

49. Marie Juchacz, *Die Arbeiterwohlfahrt: Voraussetzungen und Entwicklung*, Berlin, 1926, pp. 39-45; also, interview with John Caspari. He corraborated this by stating that the women's movement contributed the best workers for the "Arbeiterwohlfahrt," as did Walter Friedlander, whom I interviewed in Berkeley, California, on 25 July 1972.

50. Thönnessen, *The Emancipation of Women*, pp. 125ff; Bremme, *Die Politische Rolle der Frau*, p. 244.

51. The disintegration of the radical synthesis had opened the door to ideological change. Juchacz used liberal arguments in pressing for reform, claiming "we want the rights *we are born with*" [my emphasis]. "In eigener Sache," *Gleichheit*, 8 June 1917.

52. *Gleichheit*, 24 May 1918.

53. *Sonderbeilage der Gleichheit*, 20 July 1917.

54. *Praktische Winke für die sozialdemokratische Frauenbewegung*, Berlin, 1921, p. 22.

CHAPTER X   CONCLUSION

1. Charles Sowerwine, "The Organization of French Socialist Women, 1880-1914: A European Perspective for Women's Movements," *Historical Reflections* 3, no. 2 (Winter 1976): 3-23.

2. Beatrice Brodsky Farnsworth, "Bolshevism, the Woman Ques-

tion, and Aleksandra Kollontai," *American Historical Review* 81, no. 2 (April 1976): 293.

3. Ibid.

4. Claire LaVigna, "The Marxist Ambivalence toward Women," pp. 155-156.

5. Marilyn J. Boxer, "Socialism Faces Feminism," p. 77.

6. Ibid., p. 86.

7. Sowerwine, "The Organization of French Socialist Women," p. 10.

8. Ibid., pp. 22-23.

9. Richard J. Evans, *The Feminist Movement in Germany*, p. x.

10. Lenin, *The Emancipation of Women*, New York, 1975, p. 100.

BIBLIOGRAPHY

The bibliography covers the variety of sources for this work, but is not an exhaustive compilation. The secondary materials include only references found in the footnotes; specific articles from newspapers and periodicals of the time are not cited individually. The explanatory remarks are designed primarily to introduce the rich archival materials and the range of published primary sources on which this book is based. To date, these materials largely have been unexplored from the vantage point of the women's question.

I ARCHIVAL SOURCES

A. General Archives

Several archives contain materials that offer a national perspective on women and socialism. Two are the main repositories for documents on German Social Democracy. The International Institute for Social History in Amsterdam is the archive of the Second International and includes the main archives of the German Social Democratic Party, while the Friedrich Ebert Stiftung in Bonn-Bad Godesberg contains additional informative materials on the SPD.

At the International Institute, I dealt primarily with personal collections: the Karl Kautsky *Nachlass*, specifically Clara Zetkin's letters to Kautsky (KD 23); Zetkin's letters to Eduard Bernstein in his collection (D 855); Lily Braun's and Clara Zetkin's correspondence in the Bebel *Nachlass* (B/71 for Braun; B/183 for Zetkin); and various letters of Braun, Zetkin, Ottilie Baader, Helene Grünberg, and Emma Ihrer to Georg von Vollmar. The section in the *Kleine Korrespondenz* on German socialists contained letters from Braun, Zetkin, Luise Zietz. The Friedrich Ebert Stiftung, too, housed personal collections. Marie Juchacz's papers have been deposited at the Stiftung, including her correspondence as well as data she collected for her book *Sie Lebten für eine bessere Welt*. Wilhelm Dittmann's *Nachlass* as well as that of Alfred Henke contained letters from Zetkin, Baader, Braun, and Zietz. Klara Haase Weyl's short but informative memoir is contained in the Gerda Weyl collection, which also includes letters from Baader and materials on the Independent Social Democratic Party after World War I. Insights into the controversy between Zetkin and

Braun are found in the letters of both women in the *Briefe und Dokumente* collection. A rich source of biographical material and articles on various socialist personages is the *Personen-Sammlung*.

The Bundesarchiv in Koblenz contains the correspondence between Werner Sombart and Lily Braun (*Kleine Erwerbung* 129) at the period of her greatest difficulty with the SPD (1903-1907) as well as materials on middle-class feminism under *Partei u. Verbandsdrucksachen*. The main archives of the Imperial German government, located in Potsdam in the *Zentrales Staatsarchiv*, provide a range of documents on such topics as female labor, industrial conditions, branches of industry, official attitudes toward women's employment, as well as the socialists in German society. I consulted the following collections: *Reichstag* (RT); *Reichskanzlei* (RK); *Auswärtiges Amt* (AA); and *Reichsministerium des Innern* (RMdI).

B. Regional Archives

Prussian police records in the *Staatsarchiv* in Potsdam offer a wealth of information on the history of women's movements, women in Social Democracy, educational institutions and sessions, and the careers of selected individuals, as well as behind-the-scenes view of ideological and personal conflicts among the activists in the movement. One catalogue number (Pr. Br. Rep. 30, Berlin C, Tit. 95: Sek. 5) deals with women's club and associations (Nr. 14966), women's trade union groups in Berlin (Nr. 14967-14968), or, for example, special unions for female workers in the garment trades. Another section (Sek. 7), entitled Socialism, contains documents on the educational courses set up in Berlin for female members (Nr. 15852-15853) as well as on the divisive issue of birth control (Nr. 15856). The section entitled Anarchists and Socialists (Sek. 8) had police reports on Ottilie Baader (Nr. 16050) and Lily Braun (16082). The Potsdam *Staatsarchiv* also contains the police surveillance of Robert and Margarete Wengels between 1888 and 1904 (Tit. 94, Nr. 14128).

At the Hamburg *Staatsarchiv* I consulted police records on most of the key women of this work: Emma Ihrer (S 1926); Gertrud Hanna (S 20484); Ottilie Baader (S 6570); Marie Juchacz (S 20672); Clara Zetkin (S 1909); and Luise Zietz (S 5883). From the Nürnberg *Stadtarchiv* I obtained the collection "Sozialdemokratische Frauenagitation, 1906-1918" (2923), covering the career of Helene Grünberg. The *Hauptstaatsarchiv* Stuttgart documents helped analyze the split among Württemberg socialist women beginning in 1915 (E 46-48, *Ministerium der Auswärtigen Angelegenheiten*, section 3, 1850-1918,

Nr. 309a and E 150 *Ministerium des Innern—Vereine und Versammlungen*, Nr. 2051). They also contained collections on women workers in the state (E 33-34 *Geheimer Rat*, section 3, Nr. 584), and the yearly reports of the factory inspectors, 1893-1904 (E 150, Nr. 640). The *Staatsarchiv* Ludwigsburg, for materials primarily on the city of Stuttgart (F 201), had collections on Zetkin between 1892 and 1895 as well as on working women's trade associations during the anti-Socialist laws (Nr. 638).

Documents from three additional archives provided supplementary data: from the *Stadtarchiv* Dortmund, meetings of Social Democratic women (SB, 3/n 263), as well as those of the *Verein der Frauen und Mädchen der Arbeiterklasse zu Eving* (17/22 n 2); from the Hessische *Hauptstaatsarchiv*, Abt. 407, *Polizeipräsidium* Frankfurt, Nr. 163, *Verein zur Vertretung der Interessen der Arbeiterinnen*, 1891-1899, and Nr. 164, *Bildungsverein für Frauen und Mädchen der Arbeiterklasse für Frankfurt a.M. und Umgebung*, 1902-1907; and from the Münster *Staatsarchiv*, RM, 7, 620, v on "Sozialdemokratische Frauenbewegung."

II PRIMARY WORKS

A. *Works by the Eight Socialist Feminists of this Book*

Baader, Ottilie. *Ein steiniger Weg: Lebenserinnerungen*. Stuttgart, 1921.

Braun, Lily (von Gizycki). *Zur Beurteilung der Frauenbewegung in England und Deutschland*. Berlin, 1896.

———— (von Gizycki). *Die Bürgerpflicht der Frau: Vortrag gehalten in Dresden, Breslau und Berlin*. Berlin, 1895.

————. *Die Emanzipation der Kinder: Eine Rede an die Schuljugend*. Munich, 1911.

————. *Die Frau und die Politik*. Berlin, 1903.

————. *Die Frauen und der Krieg: Zwischen Krieg und Frieden*. Vol. 17. Leipzig, 1915.

————. *Frauenarbeit und Hauswirtschaft*. Berlin, 1901.

————. *Die Frauenfrage, ihre geschichtliche Entwicklung und wirtschaftliche Seite*. Leipzig, 1901.

————. *Frauenfrage und Sozialdemokratie: Reden anlässlich des Internationalen Frauenkongresses; Ansprache an den Internationalen Kongress für Frauenwerke und Frauenbestrebungen, 23 September 1896 zu Berlin*. Berlin, 1896.

————. *Lily Braun: Gesammelte Werke*. 5 vols. Berlin, n.d.

Braun, Lily (von Gizycki). *Kriegsbriefe aus den Jahren 1870-1871 von Hans von Kretschman*. Berlin, 1903.

———. *Memoiren einer Sozialistin*. 2 vols. Munich, 1909-1911.

———. *Die Mutterschafts-Versicherung: Ein Beitrag zur Frage der Fürsorge für Schwangere und Wöchnerinnen*. Berlin, 1906.

——— (von Gizycki). *Die Stellung der Frau in der Gegenwart: Vortrag gehalten in der Abteilung Berlin der deutschen Gesellschaft für ethische Kultur, in der Arbeiterbildungschule in Berlin, und in der Leipzig Gesellschaft für ethiche Kultur*. Berlin, 1895.

———. *Was Wir Wollen: Flugschrift des Vereins für Hauswirtschafts-Genossenschaften zu Berlin*, Berlin, 1902.

Hanna, Gertrud. "Die Arbeiterinnen und der Krieg." *Kriegs Probleme der Arbeiterklasse*. Vol. 20. Berlin, 1916.

———. *Frauenarbeit und Frauenorganisation*. Weimar, 1919.

———. *Frauenarbeit und Internationales Arbeitsamt*. Berlin, 1930.

Ihrer, Emma. *Die Arbeiterinnen im Klassenkampf: Anfänge der Arbeiterinnen-Bewegung, ihr Gegensatz zur bürgerlichen Frauenbewegung und ihre nächsten Aufgaben*. Hamburg, 1898.

———. *Die Organisationen der Arbeiterinnen Deutschlands, ihre Entstehung und Entwicklung*. Berlin, 1893.

Juchacz, Marie, et al. *Die Arbeiterwohlfahrt: Voraussetzungen und Entwicklung*. Berlin, 1926.

———. *Der kommende Friede*. Berlin, n.d.

———. *Sie Lebten für eine bessere Welt: Lebensbilder Führender Frauen des 19. und 20. Jahrhunderts*. Berlin, 1955.

———. *Praktische Winke für die sozialdemokratische Frauenbewegung*. Berlin, 1921.

Zetkin, Clara. "Die Arbeiterinnen-und Frauenfrage der Gegenwart." Max Schippel, *Berliner Arbeiter-Bibliothek*. Vol. 1. No. 3. Berlin, 1894.

———. *Bericht an die Zweite Internationale Konferenz sozialistischer Frauen zu Kopenhagen, 22-27 August 1910*. Stuttgart, n.d.

———. *Zur Frage des Frauenwahlrechts*. Berlin, 1907.

———. *Geistiges Proletariat, Frauenfrage und Sozialismus: Nach einem Vortrage gehalten in einer öffentlichen Studenten-Versammlung zu Berlin im Januar 1899*. Berlin, 1902.

———. *Zur Geschichte der proletarischen Frauenbewegung Deutschlands*. 1928. Reprint. Berlin, 1958.

———. *Rede gehalten auf dem USP Parteitag am 4 März 1919*. Berlin, 1919.

——. *Clara Zetkin: Ausgewählte Reden und Schriften; Auswahl aus den Jahren 1889 bis 1917*. Vol. 1. Berlin, 1957.

Zietz, Luise. *Bist Du eine der Unsrigen? Ein Mahnwort an die Frauen und Mädchen des arbeitenden Volkes*. Berlin, 1912.

——. *Zur Frage der Frauenerwerbsarbeit während des Krieges und Nachher*. Berlin, 1916.

——. *Zur Frage des Mutter-und Säuglingsschutzes*. Leipzig, 1911.

——. *Die Frauen und der politische Kampf*. Berlin, 1912.

——. *Die Frauen und die Reichstagwahlen: Politische Gespräche zwischen zwei Frauen*. Leipzig, 1911.

——. *Gewinnung und Schulung der Frau für die politische Betätigung*. Berlin, 1914.

——. *Kinderarbeit, Kinderschutz und die Kinderschutzkomissionen*. Berlin, 1912.

——. *Komm zu uns! Ein Wegruf an die junge Arbeiterin*. Berlin, 1913.

——. *Landarbeiter und Sozialdemokratie*. Berlin, 1907.

——. *Die sozialdemokratischen Frauen und der Krieg: Ergänzungsheft zur Neuen Zeit*, Berlin, 1915.

——. *Warum sind wir arm? Eine eindringliche Frage an alle Arbeiterinnen*. Berlin, n.d.

B. Additional Primary Works

Bebel, August. *Aus Meinem Leben*. Vol. 1. Stuttgart, 1914.

——. *August Bebel's Briefwechsel mit Karl Kautsky*. Edited by Karl Kautsky, Jr., Assen, 1971.

——. *Women and Socialism*. Translated by Meta A. Stern, New York, 1910.

Braun, Adolf, et al. *Ziele und Wege: Erläuterungen der Sozialdemokratischen Gegenwartsforderungen*. Berlin, 1911.

Deutsch, Regine. *Die politische Tat der Frau: Aus der Nationalversammlung*. Gotha, 1920.

Foerster, Wilhelm. *Lebenserinnerungen und Lebenshoffnungen*. Berlin, 1911.

Frauenstimmen aus der Nationalversammlung: Beiträge der sozialdemokratischen Volksvertreterinnen zu den Zeitfragen. Berlin, 1920.

Gegen den staatlichen Gebärzwang: Reden des Reichstagsabgeordneten Genossen August Bebel, des Genossen Dr. Silberstein und der Genossin Luise Zietz. Hanover, 1914.

Gewaltherrschaft und Spitzelpolitik der "sozialistischen" Regier-

*ungen: Amtlicher stenographischer Bericht der National-
versammlung über die Reden der Genossin Zietz, und der
Genossen Wilhelm Bock und Otto Brass.* Leipzig, 1919.
Illustriertes Konversations-Lexikon der Frau. Vol. 1. Berlin, 1900.
Lange, Helene. *Lebenserinnerungen.* Berlin, 1921.
Löbe, Paul. *Erinnerungen eines Reichstagpräsidenten.* Berlin, 1949.
Statistik der Frauenorganisation im Deutschen Reich. Berlin, 1909.
Vorstand der Sozialdemokratie Deutschlands. *Material zur Gebur-
tenfrage.* Berlin, 1918.

C. Minutes, Protocols, and Reports

Much of the information on organizational questions and union and
Party tactics for the female constituency as well as the careers of the
eight women was derived from minutes and protocols of national, regional, and local Party and union structures. I looked at the minutes
of the SPD congress that included reports of the women's conferences, *Protokoll über die Verhandlungen des Parteitages der Sozialdemokratischen Partei Deutschlands. . . .* Berlin, 1890-1925; those of
the trade unions between 1892 and 1922, *Protokoll der Verhandlungen des . . . Kongresses der Gewerkschaften Deutschlands.* Berlin, 1892-1922; protocols of the International socialist congresses from
1889 to 1912; and the reports of post-World War I USPD congresses
up to the Party's disintegration in 1922. I also worked with the yearly
reports of the SPD locals in Hamburg (1904-1909), Nuremberg
(1908-1914), Cologne (1912-1914), district SPD meetings in northern
Bavaria (1909-1913), and state reports from Württemberg, 1907,
1911, and 1913-1914.

The library of the Free Trade Unions (*Zentralbibliothek der
Gewerkschaften*) in the capital of the German Democratic Republic
contains invaluable materials for the union experience with women's
questions. The collection includes the records of obscure Free Trade
Unions concerned particularly with the extent of female labor. I consulted the minutes of national and local congresses of the following
unions: (1) *Deutscher Hutarbeiter-Verband* (Hatmakers), 1883-1901;
(2) *Zentralverband der Hausangestellten Deutschlands* (Domestic
Servants), 1912 (including a 1909 meeting prior to centralization); (3)
*Zentralverband der in der Blumen-, Blätter-, Palmen-und Putzfeder-
fabrikation beschäftigten Arbeiter und Arbeiterinnen Deutschlands*
(Artificial Flower Workers), 1911; (4) *Verband der Fabrik-, Land-
Hülfsarbeiter und-Arbeiterinnen Deutschlands* (Unskilled Factory
and Rural Workers), 1906-1908; (5) *Deutscher Schneider-und
Schneiderinnen-Verband* (Tailors and Seamstresses), 1888-1914, in-

cluding international meetings (variously entitled: 1892, *Verband deutscher Schneider und Schneiderinnen und verwandter Berufsgenossen*; 1894, *Verband der Schneider, Schneiderinnen und verwandter Berufsgenossen Deutschlands*; 1907, *Verband der Schneider, Schneiderinnen und Wäschearbeiter Deutschlands*); and (6) *Verband der in Buchdruckereien und verwandten Berufen beschäftigten Hilfsarbeiter und Arbeiterinnen Deutschlands* (Printers' Aids), 1898-1910 (as of 1902 called *Verband der Buch-und Steindruckerei-Hilfsarbeiter und-arbeiterinnen Deutschlands*).

I also looked at the reports of the *Berliner Gewerkschafts-Kommission* (Berlin Trade Union Commission), 1895-1914, those from the Nuremberg workers' secretariat between 1905 and 1920, and special reports such as those of the Berlin *Kinderschutz-Kommissionen* (child-labor committee) 1910-1912, and the *Heimarbeiterschutz-Kongress* (the 1904 Congress for the Protection of Domestic Industry Workers).

III   NEWSPAPERS AND PERIODICALS

Correspondenzblatt der Generalkommission der Gewerkschaften Deutschlands, Berlin, 1891-1914.
    Literatur-Beilage, 18 January 1913.
    Statistische Beilage, 27 April 1912.
Die Frauenbewegung: Revue für die Interessen der Frau. Berlin, January 1895-January 1896.
Frauen-Beilage der Leipziger Volkszeitung. Leipzig, 29 June 1917-9 August 1918; 9 September 1918-20 September 1918; 7 November 1918.
Freiheit. Berlin, 27 January 1922.
Die Genossin: Informationsblätter der Weiblichen Funktionäre der Sozialdemokratischen Partei Deutschlands. Berlin, 1924-1933.
———. *SPD Informationsblatt fur Funktionärinnen*. 1947-1949.
Gewerkschaftliche Frauenzeitung. Berlin, 1916-1920.
Die Gleichheit: Zeitschrift für Interessen der Arbeiterinnen. Stuttgart/Berlin, 1891-1923.
———. *Das Blatt der arbeitenden Frau*. 1950-1957.
Die Kämpferin: Zeitschrift fur Frauen und Mädchen des gesamten werktätigen Volkes. Leipzig, 1 April 1919-23 December 1920.
    Fur unsere Kinder: Beilage zur Kämpferin, 15 April 1919.
Leipziger Volkszeitung. Leipzig, 1914-1918. Various issues.
Die Neue Gesellschaft. Berlin, 5 April 1905-27 December 1905; 3 January 1906-26 September 1906; 3 April 1907-26 June 1907; 3

July 1907-31 October 1907. 1907 subtitled: *Sozialistische Wochenschrift.*

Die Neue Zeit: Revue des geistigen und öffentlichen Lebens. Wochenschrift der Deutschen Sozialdemokratie. Stuttgart, 1890-1922. Various issues.

Der sozialistische Akademiker: Organ der sozialistischen Studierenden und Studierten deutscher Zunge. Berlin, 1895-1896.

Sozialistische Monatshefte. Berlin, 1900-1923. Selected issues.

Vorwärts. Zentralorgan der Sozialdemokratischen Partei Deutschlands: Berliner Volksblatt. Berlin 1896 and various other issues.

IV SECONDARY WORKS

A. *Books*

Alexander, G. G. L. *Aus Clara Zetkins Leben und Werk.* Berlin, 1927.

Anthony, Katherine S. *Feminism in Germany and Scandinavia.* New York, 1915.

Bäumer, Gertrud. *Die Frau in Volkswirtschaft und Staatsleben der Gegenwart.* Stuttgart, 1914.

de Beauvoir, Simone. *The Second Sex.* Translated and edited by H. M. Parshley. 1949. Reprint. New York, 1964.

Beckmann, Emmy, and Kardel, Elisabeth. *Quellen zur Geschichte der Frauenbewegung.* Frankfurt am Main, 1955.

Bernstein, Eduard. *Die Geschichte der Berliner Arbeiter-Bewegung: Die Geschichte des Sozialistengesetzes in Berlin.* Vol. 2. Berlin, 1907.

Blos, Anna. *Die Frauenfrage im Lichte des Sozialismus.* Dresden, 1930.

Boxer, Marilyn J., and Quataert, Jean H., eds. *Socialist Women: European Socialist Feminism in the Nineteenth and Early Twentieth Centuries.* New York, 1978.

Braun, Adolf. *Die Arbeiterinnen und die Gewerkschaften.* Berlin, 1913.

Bremme, Gabriele. *Die Politische Rolle der Frau in Deutschland.* Schriftenreihe des UNESCO-Institutes für Sozialwissenschaften, Cologne, no. 4. Göttingen, 1956.

Bridenthal, Renate, and Koonz, Claudia, eds. *Becoming Visible: Women in European History.* Boston, 1977.

Bruck, W. F. *Social and Economic History of Germany from William II to Hitler, 1888-1938: A Comparative Study.* New York, 1962.

Dornemann, Luise. *Clara Zetkin: Leben und Wirken.* Berlin, 1973.

Eschbach, Walter. *Proletarisches Kinderelend*. Geleitwort von Luise Zietz. Berlin, n.d.

Evans, Richard J. *The Feminist Movement in Germany, 1894-1933*. London, 1976.

Feldman, Gerald D. *Army, Industry, and Labor in Germany, 1914-1918*. Princeton, 1966.,

Franzen-Hellersberg, Lisbeth. *Die Jugendliche Arbeiterin: Ihre Arbeitsweise und Lebensform*. Tübingen, 1932.

Die Frau und die Gesellschaft. Leipzig, 1974.

Gay, Peter. *The Dilemma of Democratic Socialism: Eduard Bernstein's Challenge to Marx*. 1952. Reprint. New York, 1962.

Geschichte der deutschen Arbeiterbewegung: Biographisches Lexikon. Berlin, 1970.

Goldschmidt, Ernst Friedrich. *Heimarbeit: Ihre Entstehung und Ausartung*. Munich, 1913.

Groh, Dieter. *Negative Integration und revolutionärer Attentismus: Die deutsche Sozialdemokratie am Vorabend des Ersten Weltkrieges*. Frankfurt am Main, 1973.

Haase, Karl. *Der weibliche Typus als Problem der Psychologie und Pädagogik*. Leipzig, 1915.

Hillger, Hermann. *Hillgers Handbuch der Verfassunggebenden deutschen Nationalversammlung 1919*. Berlin, 1919.

Hoffmann, Adolph. *Die zehn Gebote und die besitzende Klasse*. Mit einem Geleit-Brief von Frau Clara Zetkin. Berlin, 1904.

Hohorst, Gerd; Kocka, Jürgen; and Ritter, Gerhard A. *Sozialgeschichtliches Arbeitsbuch: Materialien zur Statistik des Kaiserreichs 1870-1914*. Munich, 1975.

Honeycutt, Karen. "Clara Zetkin: A Left-Wing Socialist and Feminist in Wilhelmian Germany." Ph.D. dissertation, Columbia University, 1975.

Ilberg, Hanna. *Clara Zetkin: Aus dem Leben und Wirken einer grossen Sozialistin*. Berlin, 1956.

International Labour Office: Studies and Reports, series 1, no. 2. *Women's Work under Labour Law: A Survey of Protective Legislation*. Geneva, 1932.

Jaeckel, Reinhold. *Die Stellung des Sozialismus zur Frauenfrage im 19. Jahrhundert*. Inaugural dissertation. Potsdam, 1904.

Joll, James. *The Second International, 1889-1914*. New York, 1966.

Joos, Joseph. *Die sozialdemokratische Frauenbewegung in Deutschland*. M. Gladbach, 1912.

Knodel, John E. *The Decline of Fertility in Germany, 1871-1939*. Princeton, 1974.

Kolko, Gabriel. *The Triumph of Conservatism: A Reinterpretation of American History, 1900-1916*. London, 1973.

Kuczynski, Jurgen. *Die Geschichte der Lage der Arbeiter unter dem Kapitalismus*. Vols. 3 and 4. Berlin, 1962 and 1967.

————. *A Short History of Labor Conditions under Industrial Capitalism: Germany, 1800 to the Present Day*. Vol. 3. London, 1945.

Labour Laws for Women in Germany. Translated from the German of Alice Salomon, Berlin. Strand: Women's Industrial Council, 1907.

Lange, Helene and Bäumer, Gertrud. *Handbuch der Frauenbewegung: Die Geschichte der Frauenbewegung in den Kulturländern*. Vol. 1. Berlin, 1901.

Lemke, Lotte. "Marie Juchacz: Gründerin der Arbeiterwohlfahrt, 1879-1956." Reprint from *Kampf ohne Waffen: Helfer den Menschen*, edited by Erich Grassel. Donauworth, n.d.

Leser, Norbert. *Zwischen Reformismus und Bolschewismus: Der Austromarxismus als Theorie und Praxis*, Vienna, 1968.

Lichey, Margarete. *Sozialismus und Frauenarbeit: Ein Beitrag zur Entwicklung des deutschen Sozialismus von 1869 bis 1921*. Breslau, n.d.

Lichtheim, George. *Marxism: An Historical and Critical Study*. New York, 1969.

Lion, Hilde. *Zur Soziologie der Frauenbewegung: Die Sozialistische und die Katholische Frauenbewegung*. Berlin, 1926.

Lipset, Seymour M. *Political Man: The Social Bases of Politics*. 1960. Reprint. New York, 1963.

Lüders, Else. "Arbeiterinnenorganisation und Frauenbewegung." *Sozialer Fortschritt: Hefte und Flugschriften für Volkswirtschaft und Sozialpolitik*, no. 30. Leipzig, 1904.

————. *Der "linke" Flügel: Ein Blatt aus der Geschichte der deutschen Frauenbewegung*. Berlin, n.d.

Lützenkirchen, Ralf. *Der sozialdemokratische Verein für den Reichstagswahlkreis Dortmund-Hörde*. Dortmund, 1970.

Michels, Robert. *Political Parties: A Sociological Study of the Oligarchical Tendencies of Modern Democracy*. Translated by Eden and Cedar Paul. 1911. Reprint. New York, 1962.

Mitchell, Allan. *Revolution in Bavaria, 1918-1919: The Eisner Regime and the Soviet Republic*. Princeton, 1965.

Mitchell, Juliet. *Woman's Estate*. New York, 1973.

Nettl, J. P. *Rosa Luxemburg*. 2 vols. London, 1966. (Abridged edition, London, 1969.)

Olberg, Oda. *Das Elend in der Hausindustrie der Konfektion*. Leipzig, 1896.

O'Neill, William. *The Woman Movement: Feminism in the United States and England*. Chicago, 1969.

Ortega y Gasset, José. *The Modern Theme*. Translated by James Cleugh. New York, 1961.

Osterroth, Franz. *Biographisches Lexikon des Sozialismus*. Vol. 1. Hanover, 1960.

Otto, Rose. *Über Fabrikarbeit verheirateter Frauen*. Stuttgart, 1910.

Plat, Wolfgang. "Die Stellung der deutschen Sozialdemokratie zum Grundsatz der Gleichberechtigung der Frau auf dem Gebiet des Familienrechts bei der Schaffung des Bürgerlichen Gesetzbuches des Deutschen Reiches." Dissertation, Humboldt University, Berlin, 1966.

Preuss, Traute. *Starkes schwaches Geschlecht: Weg und Leistung der Frau*. Hamm, 1956.

Ritter, Gerhard A. *Die Arbeiterbewegung im Wilhelminischen Reich*. Berlin, 1959.

Roehl, Fritzmichael. *Marie Juchacz und die Arbeiterwohlfahrt*. Hanover, 1961.

Rosenberg, Hans. *Grosse Depression und Bismarckzeit: Wirtschaftsablauf, Gesellschaft und Politik in Mitteleuropa*. Berlin, 1967.

Roth, Guenther. *The Social Democrats in Imperial Germany*. Totowa, New Jersey, 1963.

Rowbotham, Sheila. *Women, Resistance and Revolution: A History of Women and Revolution in the Modern World*. New York, 1974.

Schippel, Max. *Sozialdemokratisches Reichstags-Handbuch: Ein Führer durch die Zeit-und Streitfragen der Reichsgesetzgebung*. Berlin, n.d.

Schmidt-Beil, Ada, ed. *Die Kultur der Frau: Eine Lebenssymphonie der Frau des XX. Jahrhunderts*. Berlin, 1931.

Schorske, Carl E. *German Social Democracy, 1905-1917: The Development of the Great Schism*. 1955. Reprint. New York, 1965.

Schreiber, Adele. *Mutterschaft: Ein Sammelwerk für die Probleme des Weibes als Mutter*. Munich, 1912.

Siemering, Hertha. *Arbeiterbildungswesen in Wien und Berlin: Eine kritische Untersuchung*. Karlsruhe, 1911.

Sombart, Werner. *Die deutsche Volkswirtschaft im neuzehnten Jahrhundert*. Berlin, 1913.

Stanton, Theodore, ed. *The Woman Question in Europe*. New York, 1884.

Stearns, Peter N. *Lives of Labor: Work in a Maturing Industrial Society*. New York, 1975.

Steinberg, Hans-Josef. *Sozialismus und Deutsche Sozialdemokratie: Zur Ideologie der Partei vor dem I. Weltkrieg*. Hanover, 1967.

Strain, Jacqueline. "Feminism and Political Radicalism in the German Social Democratic Movement, 1890-1914." Ph.D. dissertation, University of California, Berkeley, 1964.

Thönnessen, Werner. *The Emancipation of Women: The Rise and Decline of the Women's Movement in German Social Democracy, 1863-1933*. Translated by Joris de Bres. 1969. Reprint. London, 1973.

Umbreit, Paul. *25 Jahre Deutscher Gewerkschaftsbewegung, 1890-1915*. Berlin, 1915.

Vogelstein, Julie. *Ein Menschenleben: Heinrich Braun und Sein Schicksal*. Tübingen, 1932.

Wehler, Hans U. *Sozialdemokratie und Nationalstaat: die deutsche Sozialdemokratie und die Nationalitätenfragen in Deutschland von Karl Marx bis zum Ausbruch des Ersten Weltkrieges*. Würzburg, 1962.

Wurm, Franz F. *Wirtschaft und Gesellschaft in Deutschland, 1848-1948*. Opladen, 1969.

Zepler, Wally. *Welchen Wert hat die Bildung für die Arbeiterin?* Berlin, 1910.

Zwing, Karl. *Geschichte der deutschen freien Gewerkschaften*. Jena, 1926.

B. *Articles, Essays, and Papers*

Bamberger, Joan. "The Myth of Matriarchy: Why Men Rule in Primitive Society." In *Women, Culture and Society*, edited by Michelle Zimbalist Rosaldo and Louise Lamphere, pp. 263-280. Stanford, 1974.

Bartoshesky, Florence. "Sexual Social Structure: A Brief Review of the Literature in American History." Paper. January 1973.

Böhme, Helmut. "Big-Business Pressure Groups and Bismarck's Turn to Protectionism, 1873-1879." *Historical Journal* 10, no. 2 (1967): 218-236.

Bridenthal, Renate. "Beyond *Kinder, Küche, Kirche*: Weimar Women at Work." *Central European History* 6, no. 2 (June 1973): 148-166.

Brown, Steven R., and Ellithorp, John D. "Emotional Experiences in Political Groups: The Case of the McCarthy Phenomenon." *American Political Science Review* 64, no. 2 (June 1970): 349-366.

Camp, Richard. "The 'Bourgeois' Campaign for Women's Rights in Post-Risorgimento Italy." Paper presented to the Annual Convention of the American Historical Association, December 1975.

Evans, Richard J. Review of Werner Thönnessen, *The Emancipation of Women. Newsletter.* European Labor and Working Class History, no. 8 (November 1975), pp. 43-45.

Gibb, Cecil. "Leadership." In *International Encyclopedia of the Social Sciences,* edited by David L. Sills, 9: 91-99. New York, 1968.

Gosche, Agnes. "Die organisierte Frauenbewegung." *Quellenhefte zum Frauenleben in der Geschichte.* Vols. 1 and 2. Berlin, n.d.

Hackett, Amy. "The German Women's Movement and Suffrage, 1890-1914: A Study of National Feminism." In *Modern European Social History,* edited by Robert J. Bezucha, pp. 354-379. Massachusetts, 1972.

Hobsbawm, E. J. "Labor History and Ideology." *Journal of Social History* 7, no. 4 (Summer 1974): 371-381.

Hoffmann, Walter G. "The Take-Off in Germany." In *The Economic Development of Western Europe: The Late Nineteenth and Early Twentieth Centuries,* edited by Warren C. Scoville and J. Clayburn La Force. Massachusetts, 1969.

Holter, Harriet. "Sex Roles and Social Change." In *Towards a Sociology of Women,* edited by Constantine Safilios-Rothschild, pp. 331-343. Massachusetts, 1972.

Kelly, Aileen. "Revolutionary Women." *New York Review of Books,* 17 July 1975, pp. 20-22.

Lafleur, Ingrun. "Adelheid Popp and the Feminist Education of Austrian Socialists." Paper presented at the Second Berkshire Conference on the History of Women, October 1974.

Lidtke, Vernon L. "Naturalism and Socialism in Germany." *American Historical Review* 79, no. 1 (February 1974): 14-37.

Mannheim, Karl. "The Problem of Generations." In *Essays on the Sociology of Knowledge,* edited by Paul Kecskemeti. 1952. Reprint. London, 1968.

Michels, Robert. "Die deutsche Sozialdemokratie: Parteimitgliederschaft und soziale Zusammensetzung; Die leitenden Persönlichkeiten." *Archiv für Sozialwissenschaft und Sozialpolitik* 23, no. 81 (1906): 471-556.

Moses, Claire Goldberg. "French Feminism: 1848-1900." Paper presented to the Annual Convention of the American Historical Association, December 1975.

Neuman, R. P. "The Sexual Question and Social Democracy in Imperial Germany." *Journal of Social History* 7 (Spring 1974): 278-281.

Otremba, Erich. "Nürnberg: Die alte Reichsstadt in Franken auf dem Wege zur Industriestadt." *Forschungen zur deutschen Landeskunde*. Vol. 48. 1950.

Scott, Joan W., and Tilly, Louise. "Women's Work and the Family in Nineteenth Century Europe." *Comparative Studies in Society and History* 17, no. 1 (January 1973): 36-64.

Shorter, Edward. "Female Emancipation, Birth Control and Fertility in European History." *American Historical Review* 78, no. 3 (June 1973): 605-640.

Soldon, Norbert. "British Women's Trade Unionism, 1874-1931." Paper presented at the Annual Convention of the American Historical Association, December 1977.

Sowerwine, Charles. "Causes and Choices: French Working Women in the Face of Feminism and Socialism, 1899-1914." Paper presented at the December 1975 American Historical Association meeting in Atlanta.

————. "The Organization of French Socialist Women, 1880-1914: A European Perspective for Women's Movements." *Historical Reflections* 3, no. 2 (Winter 1976): 3-23.

Stearns, Peter N. "Adaptation to Industrialization: German Workers as a Test Case." *Central European History* 3, no. 3 (1970): 313-331.

————. "Working-Class Women in Britain, 1890-1914." In *Suffer and Be Still: Women in the Victorian Age*, edited by Martha Vicinus. Bloomington, 1973.

Stearns, Peter N., and Uttrachi, Patricia Branca. "Modernization of Women in the Nineteenth Century." *Forums in History*, 1973.

Stolterfaht, Barbara. Review article of Werner Thönnessen's *Frauenemanzipation. Internationale wissenschaftliche Korrespondenz*, nos. 11-12 (April 1971), pp. 93-94.

Vogelstein, Julie. "Lily Braun: Ein Lebensbild." *Lily Braun: Gesammelte Werke*. Vol. 1. Berlin, n.d.

Weber, Gerda. "Um eine ganze Epoche voraus? 25 Jahre DFD." *Deutschland Archiv: Zeitschrift für Fragen der DDR und der Deutschlandspolitik* 5, no. 4 (April 1972): 410-416.

INDEX

LIBRARY OF CONGRESS CATALOGING IN PUBLICATION DATA

Quataert, Jean H
  Reluctant feminists.

  Bibliography: p.
  Includes index.
    1. Women—Germany—Social conditions.
2. Feminism—Germany—History.   3. Women and
socialism—Germany—History.   4. Women in politics
—Germany—History.   5. Women—Germany—Biography
I. Title.
HQ1627.Q37   301.41'2'0943   79-84011
ISBN 0-691-05276-X